Approaches to Landscape

Approaches to Landscape

Richard Muir

palgrave
macmillan

First published 1999 by
PALGRAVE MACMILLAN
Houndmills, Basingstoke, Hampshire RG21 6XS
and London
Companies and representatives
throughout the world

ISBN-13: 978-0-333-69392-6 hardcover
ISBN-10: 0-333-69392-2 hardcover
ISBN-13: 978-0-333-69393-3 paperback
ISBN-10: 0-333-69393-0 hardcover

A catalogue record for this book is available
from the British Library.

10 9 8 7 6 5 4 3
12 11 10 09 08

Copy-edited and typeset by Povey–Edmondson
Tavistock and Rochdale, England

Printed in China

Contents

List of Illustrations

Introduction

Interest in landscape has grown enormously in recent years. The pattern of this growth has not been of an amalgamating nature, as in a river system, but of a branching character, as in a tree. As different approaches to the understanding of landscape have been developed and refined the divisions between these different branches have widened, so that today there will be few landscape historians indeed who are conversant with the prevailing concepts of landscape iconography, and perhaps fewer post-modernist students of landscape who could interpret a pattern of earthworks at a deserted village site. As the study of landscape has grown, so its branches have grown apart.

The growth in enthusiasm for landscape studies has been sustained for more than two decades, but it is plain that, in the UK particularly, two strong and largely separate strands of interest have been involved. One is represented by a broadly-based upwelling of interest in landscape history among scholars and amateur enthusiasts, and the disciplinary backgrounds of some of the figures associated with the interpretation and popularisation of cultural landscapes underlines the interdisciplinary nature of this field of study: W. G. Hoskins (historian), Christopher Taylor (geographer-turned-archaeologist), Oliver Rackham (botanist), Tom Williamson (archaeologist), Trevor Rowley (geographer/historian), M. W. Beresford (historian), Brian Roberts (geographer), Jack Ravensdale (historian), Mike Aston (geographer-turned-archaeologist) and Della Hooke (geographer). The other strand arises from the development of a new humanistic geography as a reaction to geography's drift into spatial science. Subsequently, this strand has given rise to interest in place, post-modernism, aesthetic approaches to landscape and symbolism in landscapes. Diversity is sometimes a source of strength in landscape studies, a protection against the tyranny of the current fad or an imposed standardisation of thinking. In some ways, however, it is a weakness:

Despite the best efforts of the Landscape Research Group in the UK and the journal *Landscape* in the USA, there is no formalised discipline of landscape studies, with its own methodologies and university departments. In the absence of any organisational or disciplinary unity, landscape studies all too often consist of a great variety of unrelated perspectives, tied only loosely to the environment and its representation. (Mills, 1997 p. 122)

This book is not an attempt to present a new theory of landscape, and neither does it seek to advance one approach or interpretation at the expense of others. Rather, *it aims to identify, introduce and explore the different approaches to landscape.* As with the branches on a tree, some of these approaches are close and share connections, while others are further apart. The aesthetic approach and landscape evaluation are linked by the fact that both concern human tastes in landscape and they have part of their literatures in common. The political realities of life ensure that the studies of power and of symbolism in the landscape will frequently overlap, while the psychological aspects of the human relationship to landscape permeate most fields of enquiry. Within the broad area of landscape study different workers pursue their own specialisms, the nature of which will affect their interpretation of landscape in general and of other specialisms in particular. (My own specialist background is in the field of landscape history.)

The differences between some approaches are quite profound. Landscape historians concerned to discover the evolution of countrysides and towns have traditionally regarded landscape as being like a palimpsest (a document on which the original writing has been erased to make room for other writing but yet is still faintly visible). However, Daniels and Cosgrove, writing from a post-modern perspective, considered that: 'landscape seems less like a palimpset whose "real" or "authentic" meanings can somehow be recovered with the correct techniques, theories or ideologies, than a flickering text displayed on the word-processor screen whose meaning can be created, extended, altered, elaborated and finally obliterated by the merest touch of a button' (1988 p. 8). Underlying this interpretation is a fundamental division in the comprehension of landscape. On the one hand there is the conventional practice of regarding landscape as a material or tangible portion of a natural and cultural environment. On the other there is the treatment of landscape as 'a way of seeing' which is associated with Daniels and Cosgrove and their disciples, who interpret landscape as a painterly way of seeing the world which creates a picturesque view (Duncan, 1995 p. 414).

There is also an implicit difference in outlook between those who might claim to examine cultural landscapes in a scientifically detached manner and those who rejoice in their own engagement with the landscape. Rose explained that:

> Such pleasure in and awe of landscape is often celebrated by geographers, but with hesitation, even treated with suspicion. Pleasure in the landscape was often seen as a threat to the scientific gaze, and it was often argued that the geographer should not allow himself to be seduced by what were described as 'the sirens of *terrae incognitae*' (Wright, 1947, p. 1). (1992 p. 10)

Landscape has many facets and there are many ways in which it can be represented:

> Landscape may be represented by painting, drawing or engraving; by photography, film and theatrical scenery; by writing, speech, and presumably even music and other 'sound images'. Before all these secondary representations, however, landscape is itself a physical and multisensory medium (earth, stone, vegetation, water, sky, sound and silence, light and darkness, etc.) in which cultural meanings and values are encoded, whether they are *put* there by the physical transformation of place in landscape gardening and architecture, or *found* in a place formed, as we say, 'by nature'. . . . Landscape is a medium in the fullest sense of the word. It is a material 'means' (to borrow Aristotle's terminology) like language or paint, embedded in a tradition of cultural significa-tion and communication, a body of symbolic forms capable of being invoked and reshaped to express meaning and values. (Mitchell, 1994 p. 14)

The different interpretations applied to 'landscape' have been explored by Barrell, who considers that the term arose as a painter's word:

> it was introduced from the Dutch in the sixteenth century to describe a pictorial representation of countryside, either as the subject itself of a picture, or as the by-work in a portrait, the background of scenery behind the main subject. Later the word

came to include within its meaning both this sense, of countryside represented in a picture, and another, more loose, of a piece of countryside considered as a visual phenomenon. (1972 p. 1)

He added that:

Both these senses of the word 'landscape' had this in common, that they referred to a tract of land, or its representation in painting, which lay in prospect – that is to say, which could be seen all at one glance, from a fixed point of view; and in this respect both senses referred to particular locations.

Later, in the mid-eighteenth century, however, a more general meaning became associated with the word so that one could speak of 'the landscape' of a place, and this sense goes beyond the spatial confinement which the sense of *a* landscape as a prospect had imposed, and landscape acquired a meaning similar to 'terrain'.

Perhaps the most lucid explanation of the ambiguities surrounding the multiple layers of meaning associated with landscape was provided by Cosgrove (1984). He wrote of the active engagement of the human subject with the material object and the suggestion that 'area' and 'region' might be regarded as the equivalents of 'landscape': 'In other words landscape denotes the external world mediated through subjective human experience in a way that neither region nor area immediately suggest. Landscape is not merely the world we see, it is a construction, a composition of that world. Landscape is a way of seeing the world' (p. 13). The alternative identification of landscape as a passage of scenery which is seen rather than perceived was described by Bryan (1958 p. 1): 'Landscape, the dictionary tells us, is a portion of land or territory which the eye can comprehend at a single view including all the objects it contains.'

The location of landscape study in relation to other academic disciplines has changed with the passing years. Before the Second World War, the study of landscape was widely regarded as being at the very core of geography, and even in 1958, P. W. Bryan, the President of the Geographical Association, felt able to claim that:

the essential core of geography is the relationship between human activity and the physical setting or stage upon which human activity takes place . . . this relationship itself is expressed in the landscape which results from the changes and adaptations of the physical background made by man in his efforts to satisfy his needs . . . with the study and interpretation of this changed landscape as its central feature geography has a distinctiveness of outlook as a whole which marks if off from other subjects. (1958 p. 1)

In the 1950s and 1960s, however, landscape fell from favour in geography. In his *The Nature of Geography* of 1939, Richard Hartshorne, geography's leading guru, had rejected landscape as the central organising concept of geography and argued that the concept of landscape adopted in American cultural geography derived from the German *Landschaft* which had two meanings, one being 'a restricted piece of land' while:

It was, however, also used, as in English, to refer to the 'appearance of a land as we perceive it', e.g. 'the section of the earth surface and sky that lies in our field of vision as seen in perspective from a particular point'. This 'aesthetic' usage of the term enabled users to shift 'from the landscape as sensation to the objects that produce that sensation'. (Olwig, 1996 p. 630)

This, according to Hartshorne, caused confusion, with the same word being used in two different ways: 'Hartshorne's solution to the problem of landscape was essentially to abandon it in favour of geography as a science of region and space' (Olwig, 1996).

The subjective qualities which made landscape unacceptable to geographers in an era of spatial science and quantification would later commend it to geographers who were disorientated and disillusioned by the excesses and failures of the positivist movement. In 1985 Cosgrove wrote that:

Recently, and primarily in North America, geographers have sought to reformulate landscape as a concept whose subjective and artistic resonances are to be actively embraced. They allow for the incorporation of individual, imaginative and creative human experience into studies of the geographical environment, aspects which geographical science is claimed to have devalued at best and at worst ignored. (p. 45)

He continued: 'American humanist geographers have adopted landscape for the very reasons that their predecessors rejected it.

It appears to point towards the experiential, creative and human aspects of our environmental relations, rather than to the objectified, manipulated and mechanical aspects of those relations'. Landscape, though, did not provide a banner under which all factions could unite, and in 1994 Duncan commented: 'There is little question that the new cultural geography is itself fragmenting. For example on the one hand there is a group of scholars who primarily analyse landscapes and, on the other, there are those who concentrate on space and place' (p. 362).

Cosgrove noted that: 'The frequent association in geographical writing of landscape with studies of the impact of human agency in altering the physical environment serves to remind us that landscape is a *social* product' (1984 p. 14). Several writers commented on the importance of landscape in studies of the relationship between humans and their setting, but there was lively discussion concerning the direction which such studies should follow:

> The study of landscape provides for geographers a means of analysing and organizing the surrounding material environment, confirming the major tenet that we look to that material environment for concrete expression of the facts of human experience. Yet despite the well-established position of landscape study within the discipline there remain questions concerning how landscape is defined, and even greater questions concerning the relationship between landscapes and human beings. (Kobayashi, 1989 p. 165)

Kobayashi also writes: 'Geographical definitions of landscape abound, of course, but they are seldom critical, and an attempt to follow through upon upon the logic of these many definitions leads to many loose ends and contradictions.'

Here, I focus on the different approaches to landscape study. A certain amount of subjective judgement has been involved in the identification of these approaches. Were the task to be attempted by a selection of landscape enthusiasts then some approaches would have been recognised by all, while in other respects the choices might be different. Landscape history, landscape evaluation, the perception of landscape, an aesthetic approach, one concerning symbolism or iconography and one concerning the relationship of structure and scenery would probably feature on virtually every list. There is no sign of any halt to the growth in interest in landscape, but whether in years to come there will be a progress to a more coherent discipline of landscape studies or whether, instead, the divisions between the objective and subjective appreciations of landscape will deepen remains to be seen.

Note

I am grateful to my colleague, Dr Heather Norris Nicholson, for her comments on a part of the draft.

References

Barrell, J. *The Idea of Landscape and the Sense of Place 1730–1840* (Cambridge: Cambridge University Press, 1972).

Bryan, P. W. 'Geography and landscape' *Geography* **43** (1958) pp. 1–9.

Cosgrove, D. *Social Formation and Symbolic Landscape* (London: Croom Helm, 1984).

Cosgrove, D. 'Prospect, perspective and the evolution of the landscape idea' *Transactions of the Institute of British Geographers* NS **10** (1985) pp. 45–62.

Daniels, S. and Cosgrove, D. 'Introduction: iconography and landscape' in Cosgrove, D. and Daniels, S. (eds), *The Iconography of Landscape* (Cambridge: Cambridge University Press, 1988).

Duncan, J. S. 'The politics of landscape and nature, 1992–3' *Progress in Human Geography* **18** (1994) pp. 361–70.

Duncan, J. S. 'Landscape geography 1992–3' *Progress in Human Geography* **19** (1995) pp. 41–22.

Hartshorne, R. *The Nature of Geography* (Lancaster, Pennsylvania: Association of American Geographers, 1939).

Kobayashi, A. 'A critique of dialectical landscape' in Kobayashi, A. and Mackenzie, S. (eds), *Remaking Human Geography* (Boston: Unwin Hyman, 1989) pp. 164–83.

Mills, S. F. *The American Landscape* (Edinburgh: Keele University Press, 1997).

Mitchell, W. J. T. 'Imperial landscape' in W. J. T. Mitchell (ed.), *Landscape and Power* (Chicago: University of Chicago Press, 1994) pp. 5–34.

Olwig, K. R. 'Recovering the substantive nature of landscape' *Annals of the Association of American Geographers* **86** (1996) pp. 630–53.

Rose, G. 'Geography as a science of observation: the landscape, the gaze and masculinity' in Driver, F. and Rose, G. (eds), *Nature and Science: Essays in the History of Geographical Knowledge*, Institute of British Geographers Historical Geography Research Series No. 28 (1992) pp. 8–18.

Wright, J. K. '*Terrae incognitae*: the place of the imagination in geography' *Annals of the Association of American Geographers* **37** (1947) pp. 1–15.

1

Landscape History and Landscape Heritage

The spectrum of approaches to the study of landscape is remarkably broad. Some approaches, like geomorphology and the aesthetic approaches to landscape, differ from each other greatly. There are others – such as historical geography and landscape history or landscape history and landscape archaeology – which are only separated by nuances of emphasis and the relative importances accorded to different perspectives and techniques of study. Scholarly interest in landscape origins existed long before the arrival of people who regarded themselves as being landscape historians. This is scarcely surprising, for so long as thoughtful humans have occupied and explored the settings of their existence they must have puzzled over the formation and evolution of countryside and its facets.

As a framework or perspective for organised enquiry, landscape history is still youthful. It can scarcely yet be regarded as a fully-fledged discipline and it does not have a very large theoretical or philosophical literature. Perhaps captivated by the seemingly endless opportunities for investigation which surround them, landscape historians have tended strongly to engage in exploring and solving particular problems of landscape formation rather than in thinking deeply about the nature and parameters of their mission. The challenges seem obvious, the outdoors beckons and the work is its own validation. When the historical geographer investigates the effects of, say, the price of barley on Elizabethan rural society, the results, though scholarly, may be little more than informed speculation, but when the landscape historian explores earthworks, scatters of pottery, air photographs, field names and old documents and *proves* that a village now stands two fields away from where it stood

in Norman times, factual additions have been made to our understanding of that place and of the nature of villages in general. To its
initiates, landscape history offers real discoveries about real places.
This is an important part of its appeal.

Yet as analysis becomes more focused and critical, a rash of
uncertainties emerges: what is landscape? What is the academic
pedigree of landscape history? And what is it that sets landscape
history apart from other branches of study – such as historical
geography, cultural geography or landscape archaeology – which
also exist to explore the evolution of humanity's involvement with
its setting?

Interpretations of 'Landscape'

'Landscape' has several aspects and many nuances of meaning.
Butlin pointed out that: 'One difficulty involving its use and conceptualization derives from an ambiguity of meaning in the German
term "landschaft" from which it derives' (1993 p. 131). He then
quotes Hartshorne (1939 p. 150) to show that *landschaft* can relate
to the perceived appearance of a piece of land – a landscape – but
also 'a restricted piece of land' and, in some German contexts, 'a
region'. Jackson (1986 p. 65) thought that *landskipe* and *landscaef*
had been brought to Britain by Germanic settlers during the Dark
Ages and were related to similar words in German, Dutch, Danish
and Swedish, though these were not always used in the English
sense:

> A German '*landschaft*' can sometimes be a small administrative
> unit. I have the feeling that there is evolving a slight but noticeable
> difference between the way Americans use the word and the way
> the English do. Americans tend to think that landscape can mean
> natural scenery, whereas in England a landscape almost always
> contains a human element. (Jackson 1986)

(This one might dispute, and reference could be made to Linton's
(1963) paper on contrasts in the landscapes of the British Antarctic
Territory and scientific discussions on 'planetary landscapes'.) He
suggested that the word was a combination of 'land', meaning 'a
defined space, a space with boundaries, though not necessarily one
with fences or walls', and 'scape', denoting 'essentially the same as

"shape", except that it once meant a composition of *similar* objects, as when we speak of a fellowship or membership' (p. 67). Thus:

> Taken apart in this manner 'landscape' appears to be an easily understood word: a collection of lands . . . If 'housescape' meant the organisation of the personnel of a house, if 'township' eventually came to mean an administrative unit, then 'landscape' could well have meant something like an organisation, a system of rural farm spaces. At all events it is clear to me that a thousand years ago the word had nothing to do with scenery or the depiction of scenery. (p. 68)

Olwig (1996 p. 631) quoted the axiomatic belief that: 'It is well known that in Europe the concept of landscape and the words for it in both Romance and Germanic languages emerged around the turn of the sixteenth century to denote a painting whose primary subject matter was natural scenery', but he argued that the northern European concept of landscape emerged much earlier than the turn of the sixteenth century and carried, as it still does, a range of meaning that goes far beyond natural scenery: 'When approached in historical and geographical context, it becomes clear that *Landschaft* was much more than "a restricted piece of land." It contained meanings of great importance to the construction of personal, political, and place identity at the time landscape entered the English language' (Olwig 1996).

Schama took a rather different view and regarded the word 'landscape' as a Dutch import to the English language which dated from the end of the sixteenth century:

> And *landschap*, like its German root, *Landschaft*, signified a unit of human occupation, indeed a jurisdiction, as much as anything that might be a pleasing object of depiction. So it was surely not accidental that in the Netherlandish flood-fields, itself the site of formidable human engineering, a community developed the idea of a *landschap*, which in the colloquial English of the time became a landskip. Its Italian equivalents, the pastoral idyll of brooks and wheat-gold hills, were known as *parerga*, and were auxiliary settings for the familiar motifs of classical myth and sacred sculpture. But in the Netherlands the human design and use of the landscape – implied by the fishermen, cattle drovers, and ordinary walkers and riders who dotted the paintings of Esaias

van de Velde, for example – *was* the story, startlingly sufficient unto itself. (1995 p. 10).

A contrasting slant was provided by Yi-Fu Tuan (1979 p. 90), who wrote that:

> Originally, the term 'landscape' referred primarily to the workaday world, to an estate or domain. From the sixteenth century on, particularly in the Netherlands and in England, landscape acquired more and more of an aesthetic meaning: it became a genre of art. Limited to the functional or utilitarian perspective, the concept of 'landscape' is redundant since the more precise terms of estate and region already exist. Limited to the aesthetic perspective, 'landscape' is again redundant since the word 'scenery' offers greater clarity. But we do have the word 'landscape' in addition to the other terms, and it is being used to recognize a special ordering of reality for which a special word is needed.

Tuan also thought that:

> Landscape, from a naive viewpoint, is a sector of reality 'out there.' It is made up of fields and buildings. Yet it is not a bounded entity as a tree or a building is. Nor does landscape mean simply a functional or legal unit such as a farm or a township. Landscape, like culture, is elusive and difficult to describe in a phrase . . . Landscape is . . . a construct of the mind and of feeling'. (1979 p. 89)

A fundamental problem concerning the interpretation of landscape involves the different perspectives adopted by some (but not all) geographers on the one hand and art historians on the other:

> What is landscape? This important question has been answered in many radically different, and possibly mutually exclusive, ways. Is it what's out there, an empirical reality, or a representation, a framed image of some aspect of reality? No two textbooks will agree . . . The two divergent schools of thought generally reflect two rival academic traditions: that of the environmental sciences, particularly geography, and that of the humanities, particularly art history. Only recently have there been explicit attempts to integrate these once traditional approaches, partly influenced by

the recognition that popular views about landscape need to be taken on board, not ignored. (Mills, 1997 pp. 2–3)

Coones regarded landscape as being one of geography's principal traditions, but one that was diverse and problematic:

> The term 'landscape' is itself imprecise, variously implying the generalized or composite visible and visual scene . . . , an actual scenic view . . . and a tract of land owned and inhabited . . . It has been associated with such concepts as environment, region, habitat and 'locale' (an erroneous but well-established English form of the French word *local*). In embodying the qualities of 'place', the interactions of society and nature as expressed on the ground or in the land, and the characteristics of particular environments – especially those altered through human agency and occupance – the idea of landscape is directly tied to several of geography's basic concepts and long-established themes of enquiry. (1992 p. 70)

Lowenthal noted the breadth of the concept: 'Landscape is all-embracing – it includes virtually everything around us – and has manifest significance for everyone' (1986 p. 1). Then he added: 'The sheer multiplicity of interests that impinge on landscape – economic, aesthetic, political – suggest the magnitude of the subject but at the same time seem to preclude the development of any unified perspective'.

The meaning of 'landscape' plainly has changed with the passage of time. In medieval England, according to Mikesell (1968 pp. 575–80), the word denoted a piece of land occupied by a particular group or controlled by a particular lord. By the late nineteenth century, he notes, it was regarded as a portion of territory which the eye could comprehend in a single view. Landscape's visual and scenic connotations developed in the immediate post-medieval period, when the Dutch *landschap* painters were exerting their influence. According to Jackson, 'landscape' and the word 'country' (which he thought derived from the Latin *contra* and signified land lying opposite to or confronting the viewer) both indicate a tract of land which can be seen at a glance and which can be defined as a unit or territory, often the territory of a small rural community. Neither word, he thought, had any legal standing, but both denoted the territory of a poor and illiterate peasant population. As explained below, such 'vernacular' landscapes contrasted with the 'political' landscapes associated with people of position and power:

> In the perception of the crown, the nobility, and the clergy such peasant territories had little importance; clusters of small, temporary, crudely measured spaces which constantly changed hands and even changed in shape and size and use. The land which these fortunate persons possessed – the estate of the nobleman, or of a bishop, the forest of the king, to say nothing of his kingdom – all had a definite, almost sacred origin, with sacrosanct boundaries vouched for in a treaty or charter. (Mikesell, 1968 p. 69)

Not every landscape historian would be happy with this interpretation of 'landscape', and some of us in northern England might decide that 'township' more closely equated with Jackson's 'vernacular landscape'. But townships would not tend to be temporary or to change in shape, size or use; modern thinking would regard them as the ancient life-cells of the countryside with origins which sometimes burrow quite deeply into prehistoric times.

The suggestion that an observer is needed to validate the existence of landscape, which is implicit in Jackson's mention of a tract of land that can be seen at a glance, and which was noted by Meinig (1979), was previously emphasised by the British geographer, R. E. Dickinson: 'What is landscape? Literally it is the scene within range of an observer's vision (Figure 1.1). As many German geographers express it, "It is subjectively experienced by the artist. The geographer tries to describe it objectively and to understand it in its entirety"' (1939 pp. 1–2).

The study of the historic cultural landscape was, according to Coones (1985 p. 5), confused by conflicting interpretations and failed to reflect the unity of its subject matter: 'The term landscape has for long been variously employed to embrace a bewildering diversity of conceptions, definitions, aesthetic visions and academic pursuits.' He did not regard landscape as the creation of a society which was divorced from nature, but rather as an expression of the links between people and their environment and of the operation of social life within particular *milieux*. 'The landscape', he wrote, 'is in truth nothing less than the complex, interrelated and unified material product of the geographical environment, a seamless totality in which the immemorial processes of nature and the much more recent activities of mankind interpenetrate' (Coones, 1985). However, it is

Figure 1.1   To the British geographer, R. E. Dickinson, landscape was 'the scene within the range of an observer's vision', like this scene from the English Lake District. (Richard Muir)

not possible simply to identify landscape as a geographical area which is unified by the interactions between its people and their physical environment. These characteristics are shared with other types of area, not least the geographers' 'regions'. In the early days of academic geography, the definitive feature of geographical expertise was sometimes considered to be the capability to identify and delineate regions. 'Natural' regions were supposed to display a unifying association between physiology, climate, vegetation and so on:

> There were many interpretations, but fundamental to most was the belief that the earth's surface is divided into a mosaic of different regions each of which had a particular character as a consequence of the symbiosis between the physical environment and the society occupying it. Hence they were organic wholes, 'natural regions' which were not to be confused with the artificial regions imposed on the earth's surface by the drawing of political boundaries. (Johnston, 1986 p. 137)

In addition to these natural regions, geographers went on to identify 'formal regions', which were created to serve some practical purpose, like administration, and 'nodal regions', which focused on some particular centre. By the middle of the twentieth century, however, interest in regional geography of the traditional kind was in decline, and in an oft-repeated phrase Kimble suggested that: 'regional geographers may perhaps be trying to put boundaries that do not exist around areas that do not matter'. By this time the aeroplane was turning the world into a neighbourhood and the links between places were more important than any inter-regional breaks, so that: 'Man's region is now the world' (Kimble, 1951).

Early in the twentieth century, France had developed its own regional geography, based on its distinctive countrysides, the *pays*. As propounded by the influential geographer, Paul Vidal de la Blache, the *pays* concept considered that each of these regional countrysides had developed its own distinctive mode of life or *genre de vie*. The unity of the *pays* had not been imposed by physical environmental forces, but had grown from the relationship between the setting and the activities of its occupants. Vidal claimed that there was a law governing the geography of humans, with the environment being capable of grouping and holding together heterogeneous beings in mutual vital relationships: 'Every region is a domain where many dissimilar beings, artificially brought together, have subsequently adapted themselves to a common existence' (1926 p. 10). In emphasising the interaction between a society and its rural setting, the *pays* approach corresponded closely to some interpretations of landscape already mentioned. Coones, in particular, was anxious to underline the human relationship with the physical environment:

> Since the landscape is an expression of the links between people and their environment, and of the operation of societies within particular *milieux*, the study of the cultural landscape separately from the physical geography is highly artificial. In this country the bias of physical geography towards geomorphology has perhaps contributed to this estrangement; in contrast, the traditional Russian conception of a broadly based subject involving not just rocks and landforms but embracing soils, vegetation, hydrology and climate has facilitated the creation of an integrated vision of the geographical environment in which society and nature interact at every turn. (Coones, 1985 pp. 5–6)

However, the *pays* concept was too limited in extent and durability to be regarded as an equivalent to that of landscape. The *pays* had developed in Europe following centuries of close association between peasant communities and their homelands. They were therefore historic features of rural Europe rather than of the world, and would be transformed beyond recognition by modern industrialisation, urbanisation, communications technology and revolutions in land transport. The traditional rural societies which had created the *pays* and similar regions elsewhere in Europe were partly closed societies, consuming locally much of what was produced, and introspective and conservative in their habits. The rural regions were extremely diverse, reflecting the urge to produce crops to supply the needs of local groups. But change, beginning almost everywhere with improvements to the transportation system, ushered in a new era of economic, social and cultural development. To understand these processes of transformation one must regard rural landscapes as systems which are connected to the ebb and flow of energy and matter from different levels in the spatial hierarchy:

> The modernisation of agriculture and the subsequent landscape transformation in Europe cannot be understood by what was going on on the local scene. Rural regions are integrated in bigger

and bigger economies and societies, There are no more buffer structures to exploit them, which at the same time protect them from the broader context. In the national societies that play a growing role in their evolution, transformations are induced by growing economic competition, but also by new attitudes towards land reforms or land consolidation, and by the emergence of new attitudes concerning nature, beauty, local society etc. (Claval, 1988 p. 29)

If landscape and region are not the same, arguments can be made that they are similar or complimentary: 'The study of regions, past and present, not only serves to unite people and place but, by doing so, also penetrates near to the very heart of landscape' (Coones, 1985 p. 10). In recent years, regional geography has experienced a revival of interest although the advocates of a new regional approach have generally been anxious to distance themselves from the old one. This has led to a confusion of areas:

the very term 'region' presently seems to be perceived as so contaminated that concepts like 'place', 'locale', 'locality' and 'territory' are preferred. However, this is often done without specification of the scale of the region we are dealing with and uses of the terminology are often inconsistent and contradictory. In the 'new' regional geography 'place', apparently, can vary in size from a specific location to encompassing large territories. 'Locale' likewise encompasses anything from a room in a house to a nation. (Holmen, 1995 p. 52)

Meanwhile, Cloke, Philo and Sadler recognised 'confusion within the work of particular authors and research groups as they slide from one concept of "locality" to another' (1991 p. 166), and Duncan decided that 'Locality is currently a fashionable term, but it is used in a variety of unclear and sometimes contradictory ways' (1989 p. 246).

Some of the contradictions between 'landscape' and 'region' must derive from changing interpretations of the region:

Analytical thinking is inevitably preoccupied with definitions, classifications, precise measurement and theory. Unable to cope with the region as an ecological expression of human interaction with the land through work, it was dismembered into a variety of types such as nodal, formal, functional and so on and redefined as a species of 'spatial classification'. Thus the region was transmuted from an ecological into a spatial conception, and in the process rendered demonstrably useless for any purpose except the manipulation of administrative data by planners and those who wish to influence them. (Langton, 1988 p. 22)

To avoid further confusion it can be said that landscapes and regions are not the same, although some landscapes might correspond spatially with regions, while landscapes and regions defined as ecological entities have important similarities. The current interest in place (see Chapter 9) is distinguished from the traditional interest in drawing boundaries around 'regions' by the emphasis placed upon the relationship between place and issues of race, ethnicity, gender, class and identity:

This recent work is differentiated from the chorological tradition in geography by the shift away from understanding places in themselves, and towards an appreciation of place as a social and a cultural category. Thus, the ideas of both individual and collective subjects and of self play important roles in these discussions. (Entrikin, 1994 p. 227)

There is uncertainty concerning the relationship between historical geography and landscape history, and between landscape history and cultural geography, while in the English-speaking world these differences are complicated further by different traditional emphases applied on different sides of the Atlantic. The relationship between geography as a whole and landscape history is a complicated one. Taking the UK as an example, several landscape historians are employed in departments of geography and have described themselves as historical geographers, though there are a few geographers (such as the author) who prefer to be regarded as landscape historians. Then there are numerous landscape historians, almost certainly a majority, who do not hold geographical posts (including a few who were disenchanted by the rise of positivism in geography during the 1960s and so preferred to abandon the discipline to develop archaeological careers). Archaeology, particularly landscape archaeology, has proved to be a very fertile source of ideas and data, and it may be the greater attention paid to archaeological information by landscape historians which helps to define the difference between them and most historical geographers. More importantly, it can be argued that historical geographers tend to use study sites within the landscape as means of justifying or refuting particular historical theses while, to the landscape historian, the site is *in its own right* a proper subject for study.

Even so, the traditions interweave and merge like streams in a delta. As Butlin (1993 p. 136) puts it:

> The tradition of historical landscape analysis is . . . universal in the older tradition of historical geography, and its appeal easily understood. It is not a subject confined to geography, and broadens progressively to include a wide range of disciplines and sub-disciplines, including archaeology, industrial archaeology, and urban and planning history.

Echoing the point made earlier in this chapter about the 'get up and go' character of landscape history, he warns that:

> It does, however, pose some difficulties to those who seek a broader, more consciously theoretical engagement with the past, for it does seem to reflect or epitomize a seemingly neutral, objective approach, generally free from explicit theoretical statements and formulations and free from value judgements: the evidence of the landscape is allowed to speak to its skilled interpreters as hard or factual evidence. (Butlin, 1993)

These would be weaknesses if they blinded the interpreter to, say, the institutionalised exploitation and inequality which had helped to produce a medieval fieldscape in England or the calculated slaughter of the bison that removed the animals, and those whose cultures were built around them, from the Great Plains; but there is no valid reason why the story of the evolution of a landscape should be revealed and recounted in a manner which is uninfluenced by ideas and insensitive to human aspirations and suffering. Ultimately, the distinctions between landscape history and historical geography must be blurred, not least because each individual student of the landscape has his or her own perspective.

The Landscape Tradition in North America

In North America, the development of landscape history took place within the broader context of cultural geography, a factor which differentiates the American tradition in landscape studies from that which developed in the European countries. In 1981, Ley wrote that:

If there is one feature distinguishing human geography on each side of the Atlantic then it is surely provided by the enigma of cultural geography. In France it appears that the passing of the subject has been sounded . . . in Britain its popularity has been slender and its survival is uncertain . . . but in North America cultural geography remains a major focus of research and teaching; in 1979 more than one in six members of the Association of American Geographers identified themselves as a cultural geographer. Until the 1970s, the subject remained closely tied to Carl Sauer's Berkeley tradition, perhaps the major research school that has arisen in North American geography. (p. 249)

A tradition of *Landschaftgeographie* had emerged in Germany towards the end of the nineteenth century, with geography being developed as a vehicle for the scientific investigation of regional landscape forms. The appreciation that the shaping of the land had involved human as well as physical agencies paved the way for the development of a cultural geography, which would (at least until recently) enjoy far more popularity in North America than in Europe. Carl O. Sauer (1889–1975), its founder:

contributed more to our interest in landscape than perhaps any other American geographer. Sauer's published writings, as varied and far ranging as they indeed are, examine the role of human activity in altering the natural environment to create the cultural landscape. For Sauer . . . an understanding of the culture that sculptured a landscape was requisite. (Kenzer, 1985 p. 258)

Olwig commented that:

In 1939, when Richard Hartshorne published *The Nature of Geography*, he noted that landscape was 'perhaps the single most important word in the geographic language' of a relatively young American university discipline. This was due in no small measure to Carl Sauer's epoch-making 1925 essay on 'The Morphology of Landscape' (Hartshorne 1939: 149, 155). It was largely through this essay that American geographers were introduced to the many currents of German *Landschaft* geography. 'The Morphol-

ogy''s inspiring encapsulation of the landscape concept's multi-
faceted potentiality can be seen as an outgrowth of the fertile
ideas of German romanticism and natural philosophy. Sauer's
essay motivated a generation of American geographers and laid
the groundwork for Sauer and his colleagues to reevaluate the
concept landscape and to formulate new approaches to it. (1996
pp. 643–4)

Sauer was born in Missouri of German parents and educated for
five years in Germany; he drew upon German concepts about
landscape and ideas about culture deriving from his Berkeley
colleague of the 1920s, the anthropologist, Alfred Kroeber, to
establish a division of geography which had the interaction between
human culture and the physical environment as its focus and which
provided the framework within which most serious North American
work on landscape history took place. This framework was different
from any prevailing in Europe and the whole approach to landscape
was different as a result:

When the history of historical geography in the English-speaking
world comes to be written, the development of the subject in
North America during the middle third of this century will
probably be dominated by one name: Carl Ortwin Sauer. The
history will be different from that of the subject in Britain during
these years. In place of an emphasis on past geographies, albeit
with intervening narratives, there will be an emphasis on the
cultural landscape, a complex amalgam of physically differentiated earth subjected to alteration and adaptation by culturally
differing populations through time, even up to the present. This
sort of geography is often called the Berkeley School of geography. It is linked indissolubly with the name of Sauer, and is
popularly associated with Latin American topics, with animal and
plant domestication and diffusion, and with an emphasis on prehistory. (Williams, 1983 p. 1)

Ley (1981 p. 250), summarising Mikesell (1978), described the traits
of Berkeley geography as including a historical orientation; an
emphasis on man's agency on the physical environment; a preoccupation with material artefacts, a rural and pre-industrial bias, a
heavily empirical field tradition, and a tendency to non-cumulative
unique studies (1981 p. 250).

Kenzer (1985) studied the intellectual landscape of Sauer's formative years and diminished the influence of Berkeley. He believed that the contribution of his boyhood days in Warrenton, Missouri, which epitomised the close neighbourliness of small-town America, and the intellectual consequences of education at Warrenton's prestigious Central Wesleyan College, with its impressive German library, had been greatly underestimated. In any event, when explored from within the context of Sauer's cultural geography, landscape history became culture history and involved its disciples in reconstructing the natural environment and the successive changes wrought upon it by human agency: 'Cultural geography is . . . concerned with those works of man that are inscribed into the earth's surface and give to it characteristic expression' (Sauer, 1931 p. 622). Sauer admired continental geographers, particularly Germans – he had been educated in Germany – and he was influenced by Albrecht Penck's identification of the *chore*, a small region with unity of form and function (Penck, 1928). Sauer seems to have regarded landscape as being synonymous with geography (Kenzer, 1985 p. 258) and saw landscapes as areas made up of a distinct association of forms (or component elements) which were variously physical and cultural. Landscapes resembled Penck's chores; they had their origins in the natural landscape and could be modified and transformed through human occupation to form cultural landscapes. These landscapes therefore existed in both space and time:

> We cannot form an idea of landscape except in terms of its time relations as well as of its space relations. It is in a continuous process of development or of dissolution and replacement . . . historical geography may be considered as the series of changes which the cultural landscape has undergone and therefore involves the reconstruction of past cultural landscapes. (Sauer, 1927 p. 186)

Central to Sauer's cultural geography were concerns with the way that humans transformed the natural environment by domesticating and diffusing forms of plants and animals, exporting farming and other technologies, re-directing water, burning vegetation and so on.

Sauer taught at Berkeley between 1923 and his retirement in 1957, and the Berkeley School was largely composed of his graduate students who shared his interests in the creation of landscape and diffusion of culture. Several, like John Leighly and Marvin Mikesell, developed their own distinguished careers within the Berkeley tradition. One important reason for the difference between the British and the American approaches to landscape study concerned the Berkeley emphasis on the cultural context: 'Carl Sauer believed that understanding in human geography depends on a recognition of historical change. For that reason he never clearly distinguished between cultural and historical geography, adopting one term or the other as a matter of convenience, not logic' (Solot, 1986 p. 508). Sauer was an empiricist who distrusted the use of theory in the social sciences. Quoting from a letter written from Sauer to another distinguished American geographer, Preston James, Williams wrote (1983 p. 9):

> It is clear that Sauer was never happier, and never came to grips more readily with his brand of geography than when he was working in the archive or the field. His methodology was the result of the solving of pragmatic problems. He was very much an empiricist; as he told Preston James in late 1939, 'Curiosity begins with bodies of fact and maintains itself by exploration.'

He rejected an evolutionary approach to culture, one which would analyse its inner workings, and concentrated instead upon culture's material manifestations in the landscape, like settlement forms or field patterns. He did not regard human beings as the direct object of geographical enquiry, and gave priority to the physical expressions of human activity in the landscape.

As a student he was exposed to the extreme environmental determinism propounded by Ellen Semple, but as he matured he rejected the notion that human actions were determined by the nature of the physical environment and the use of preconceived theoretical frameworks in general. Rather than discussing the influence of the environment on human societies, he chose to explore the ways in which human cultures had adapted their environments. Crude determinists, like Semple (1911), had suggested that the non-material aspects of human culture, such as belief, values or 'national character', were imposed upon human societies in the course of occupying a particular environment, but Sauer avoided the issue by ignoring these aspects of culture and focusing on the material effects of culture upon the environment. His intellectual involvement with landscape is explained by Solot (1986 p. 509) as follows:

Each of the major fields of knowledge, Sauer argued, is concerned with a distinct section of reality that is 'naively given'. Just as botany and geology are justified by the existence of plants and rocks respectively, he believed that the existence of places and areas as landscapes provided the rationale for geography. The idea of landscape was critical to Sauer's developing concept of geography because it could easily accommodate his interest in culture. He acknowledged that some of the continental geographers, from whom he drew support for his emphasis on landscape, had been primarily concerned with physical aspects of areas. For Sauer himself, however, culture had geographical significance by virtue of its observable effects on the landscape, and he sought out a tradition within European geography that favored this view. This was the basis for his interest in material culture traits. Cultural forms, as the imprints of humanity upon areas, merited the same kind of geographical interest as natural landscape forms.

A cornerstone of Sauer's cultural geography was the notion of the culture or cultural area: 'The unit of observation must therefore be defined as the area over which a functionally coherent way of life dominates' (Sauer, 1941 p. 11). Though he recognised that there were problems in identifying such an area beyond recognising that it had an intimate interdependence of living, he thought that the key lay in recognising a sufficient accordance of common traits. Sauer did not discover or invent the culture area; the topic of the *Kulturprovinz* had originated in the writings of the enormously influential German political geographer, Friedrich Ratzel (1844–1904). Like other members of the first generation of German academic geographers, Ratzel lived in an era of German self-discovery, when there were political and spiritual urges to identify the characteristics of being German and to define the territory occupied by the German people. When the concept was adopted in North America, the Darwinistic associations with *Lebensraum* were abandoned. Sauer's colleague, A. L. Kroeber, also played an important part in the development of the culture area concept; he had studied the 'culture provinces' of native Americans in the West during the early 1920s, and had characterised the Great Plains as a coherent region defined by the culture of the Plains Indians. (Ratzel had also visited North America, where he had studied communities of German origin and had been struck by the ways in which the European immigrants had imposed themselves upon the native

Americans.) Sometimes, Sauer believed, a gradation in the strength of the defining culture was envisaged, as one moved from the cultural core, through the domain (where other cultural influences appeared) and into realm, where the other influences were stronger. Sauer also discussed cultural hearths. These were areas which served as the cores from which cultural practices and innovations diffused to establish the identity of broader cultural regions. Only a few such hearths had existed, and they were associated with particularly favoured physical environments.

All other work in Sauer's cultural geography focused on the identification and study of cultural landscapes: the landscapes which had been created by the process of interaction between a cultural group and the natural landscape. This interaction and the resultant landscape development could take place over a long period of time, during which the culture of the group concerned would evolve, while ultimately the introduction of a new culture from outside would cause a rejuvenation of the cultural landscape, with a new cultural landscape being superimposed upon the remnants of the old (Sauer, 1925). In developing his ideas about culture areas, Sauer tended to be dismissive of American geographers but an admirer of continental ones, particularly the Germans. (He greatly approved of *The Personality of Britain* by the British archaeologist, Sir Cyril Fox (1932), which demonstrated that some fundamental and enduring aspects of landscape were established in prehistoric time; this book would influence more than one generation of British landscape historians.) But despite his preference for European scholarship, Sauer's culturally-based landscape history was best suited to the parched landscapes of the USA's South-West where Sauer had done so much of his research. These had, within quite recent history, been subjected to the most starkly varied experiences of human colonisation and the impacts of the different cultures were plainly etched into the landscapes. There were, after all, great gulfs of difference between the Pueblo Indians, the Comanche, the Spanish colonists settled around their missions, the ranchers and the homesteaders. In many parts of Europe, the situation was quite different, and continuity and assimilation had led to a blurring of distinctions and a broadening of tradition. In parts of England, for example, open-field farming had existed for a thousand years when the transformation of landscapes and societies by industrialisation began. Apart from a few Scottish incursions and the widely-welcomed arrival of William of Orange, there had been no invasion since the landing of the Normans in 1066, and any cultural differences existing between the provinces were not hard-edged: one might argue all day about whether or not a Suffolk or a Norfolk culture existed, while supposedly 'Celtic' cultural landscape features could prove to be pre-Celtic or non-Celtic.

During the last quarter of this century, the Berkeley approach to landscape studies has encountered criticisms from within the landscape camp. Some of the most important of these concerned Sauer's treatment of culture, which had, as Leighly explained, a central position in his landscape philosophy:

> 'Culture' gave him an organizing principle that runs through most of his scholarship. It provided him immediately with an alternative to unitary 'man,' the term used at Chicago, and to 'ethnic stocks,' which he had used in his Missouri work. Especially when written in the plural 'culture' could embrace the great and small differences among peoples on the earth; it provided a terminology for contrasts and changes that could be handled only awkwardly by 'relations with the environment,' to which Miss Semple's 'influences' had by this time been largely attenuated. (1976, p. 340)

Ley (1980) and Duncan (1980) have criticised the representation of culture in Sauer's work as a conceptual *a priori* rather than something that is actively created by human beings, humanity thus being relegated to a role as the passive carrier of culture. With the development of a new tradition of humanistic geography – largely as a reaction to the sterile economism of spatial analysis – there arose demands for a geography that was more aware of the intricacy of humans, their sensitivity, motivation and behaviour, a geography which could explore the complexity of the perception of places and the nuances of difference that gave each place its identity and significance to people.

Another approach with strong landscape associations that exerted a forceful presence in the American geography of the middle third of the twentieth century was that of 'sequent occupance' developed by Derwent Whittlesey (1929 pp. 162–6). He envisaged a succession of stages in the human occupance of a landscape, which he compared to the colonisation of land by a plant succession, but he considered that the human occupance was far more intricate. If there was a normal evolutionary cycle it was unlikely to be followed because of the probable intervention of unpredictable extraneous forces. There was a genetic aspect to sequent occupance, which was expressed in his notion that: 'Human occupance of area, like other biotic phenomena, carries within itself the seed of its own transformation' (p. 162). Each of the stages was linked to its predecessor or forebear and to its offspring or successor: 'their progression impressed him as being a consequence of internal forces analogous to the multiplication and destruction of living cells' (Mikesell, 1976, p. 151). Thus as farmland is abandoned owing to declining yields, so timber can colonise the land and a new, woodland stage comes into being. Mikesell added that:

> The assumption that landscape evolution could be described in terms of diagnostic stages, that the progression of these stages could be predicted, and that variations from predicted or normal sequences would result from exogenous forces added up to a new generalization about landscape evolution and not merely a re-iteration of what had already been verified. Moreover, since these ideas were evident in physiography and plant ecology, sequent occupance is probably best described as an analogue model – an attempt to transfer concepts from natural science to human geography. (Mikesell, 1976 pp. 152–3)

The concept was well received by American geographers and fuelled an enthusiasm for studies of cultural successions, in which each stage of the human occupance of an area could be treated as plateaus, periods, cross-sections or portraits which were separated by steps corresponding to the replacement of one culture by another; the sum of the plateaus and steps represented the cultural succession. Thus, in a study by Davis, the stages in the sequent occupance of the high plains of Michigan were an 'Indian' period; a period of French fur trading and Jesuit missionary activity; a period of British control; and a period of American forest clearance and pioneering agriculture (1936 pp. 303–41). The stages or plateaus were regarded as periods of relative stability when the human occupance of the area concerned was largely undisturbed and the notion that stages could be studied as cross-sections in time avoided what, at the time, were regarded as problems of confusing geographical and historical objectives.

Following its appearance in 1929, the concept of sequent occupance was enthusiastically adopted and applied by American geographers in the 1930s and 1940s, though in the 1950s interest rapidly diminished. The limitations of sequent occupance had emerged and it was proving to be inherently introspective. According to Whittlesey, the genetics of each stage were established in terms of its predecessor, and human occupance carried within itself the seed of its own transformation. He recognised that extraneous forces were likely to intervene, though Mikesell commented that:

Since cross-sections had doubtful merit in historical research, the methodological value of sequent occupance rested on its one testable hypothesis – the dubious assumption that change results largely from internal forces. But sequent occupance studies in fact usually demonstrated the importance of external forces and diffusion. (1976 p. 162)

Mikesell concluded that: 'since the weaknesses and inherent difficulties of sequent occupance were seldom mentioned, its abandonment in the 1950s may have been prompted by a general but unstated realization that the program, which seemed exciting in the 1930s, had become a routine and redundant exercise a generation later' (p. 165).

In the course of its development, landscape history has benefited enormously from the existence of scholars with exceptional talents for capturing the attention and imagination of an audience far broader than that which exists within the confines of academic life. In the middle of this century, Jacquetta Hawkes and W. G. Hoskins performed this role brilliantly in the UK, while in the USA it was assumed by John Brinckerhoff ('Brinck') Jackson, who launched the magazine, *Landscape,* in 1951, the year in which Hawkes's *A Land* was published in Britain. Jackson was a Harvard graduate in literature and history who was born in Dinard of American parents; he leased a ranch near Santa Fe following his demobilisation at the end of the Second World War. During the war he had served as an intelligence officer, a role which introduced him to maps, aerial photographs and other sources of information about the country ahead of the Allied armies (Meinig, 1979 p. 212). He had studied geography for a year as an invalid following a riding accident, and it was during his recuperation that Jackson decided to launch a magazine focusing on the landscapes of the USA's South-West which would buttress provincial culture and celebrate the humanised landscape. The magazine was launched in 1951; after four issues its scope was broadened, and it became *Landscape: Magazine of Human Geography*. Jackson succeeded in producing a landscape publication which was neither sentimentally folksy nor monopolised by the beauties of the rural scene. Here, the landscape was not to be regarded as scenery to be viewed from afar, but as a setting within which people lived and struggled to earn their livings; cities were not excluded, while human-made intrusions (such as garish ribbon developments and hoardings) gained consideration as items of folk art: 'The sordid little businesses which line our highways represent in many cases a last-ditch stand in the field of individual enterprise: tear them down and we have scored a triumph of deuglification – but at what cost?' (Jackson, 1963–4 p. 2).

In 1986 he confessed that:

> I find the more extreme – and more vocal – forms of American environmentalism to be irresponsible and uncivilised. The best solution I see for this super-aestheticism is a more general recognition of landscape history: less emphasis on the old romantic theme of conflict between man and nature and more emphasis on the political, economic and technological forces which continue to shape our landscapes. I find it encouraging that several American universities now offer courses on the history of our cultural landscape in which such mundane topics as roads and settlement patterns and sports facilities and gardens are discussed, and their evolution touched upon. (p. 80)

Meinig wrote that: 'Jackson never purported to be a research scholar, and he openly assumed the role of the speculative intuitive interpreter reaching beyond the usual realms of science . . . much of his most interesting work remains tentative, contingent upon formal and detailed investigation or experiment' (1979 p. 230).

Jackson did, however, contribute to the conceptual resources of landscape study with his ideas on vernacular landscapes. He suggested that if the individual human being was the fundamental unit within humanity, then the dwelling should be regarded as the elementary unit in the landscape, and he believed that landscape should be treated as a living, *lived-in* world. Full attention should be paid to the day-to-day arenas of ordinary life, the vernacular environments of everyday living: 'I have been chiefly concerned with the commonplace question of what the word [landscape] means in everyday usage, and especially with its meaning in our northwest European and North American history' (Jackson, 1986 p. 65). He distinguished between *political* and *vernacular* landscapes: the latter were the landscapes of the village or rural community and concerned the territories of agricultural subsistence, and the former largely ignored topography in favour of strategic or economic strong points. The political landscape was created from legal decisions, power politics and governmental decisions, but the vernacular landscape was more elusive; its events went largely unrecorded:

we see it as the slow procession of generations of farmers and stockmen and foresters and hunters and migrants, leaving few traces behind of the expansion of fields and villages, the coming of small settlements, their gradual growth and sometimes their disappearance. What survives is less a matter of ruins and half obliterated boundaries than of legends. (1986 p. 70)

Having considered Jackson's ideas about the vernacular landscape, Cosgrove felt that 'Jackson's populist view of landscape is a healthy antidote to the normal focus on elite landscape but it can be pressed too far' (Cosgrove, 1986 p. 77).

Elsewhere Cosgrove commented that:

Jackson has always eschewed disciplinary labels and both in his own writings and through the editorial policy of his journal opened out the concept of landscape in ways which seem to democratise it, liberating both spectator and participant, by writing from the inside and pointing to symbolic meanings which arise from social life in particular geographical settings. Jackson senses that the origins of landscape indicate a new and detached mode of seeing, something more than a shift in artistic and literary taste. (1984 p. 34)

Summarising Meinig (1979 pp. 288–9), he listed the key features of Jackson's landscape idea:

landscape is anchored in *human life*, not something to look at but to live in, and to live in socially. Landscape is a *unity* of people and environment which opposes in its reality the false dichotomy of man and nature which Jackson regards as a Victorian aberration. Landscape is to be judged as a *place for living and working* in terms of those who actually do live and work there. All landscapes are *symbolic*, they express 'a persistent desire to make the earth over in the image of some heaven', and they undergo *change* because they are expressions of society, itself making history through time. (p. 35)

Meinig wrote that: 'Jackson was in close touch with half a dozen fields and fettered to none. He was interacting with some of the best minds in several disciplines and guilds but remained himself the intelligent layman, independent of all the institutional and professional pressures and rigidities' (1979 p. 229).

Landscape History in Europe

Sauer regarded the geographers of continental Europe more highly than those of the English-speaking world. He was influenced by the work of Hettner, Passarge and Krebs, while his fundamental ideas were anticipated by French geographers: Dickinson (1939) quoted the expression of French attitudes by Vallaux (1925), who wrote: 'The transformation of natural regions and the substitution of entirely new or profoundly modified regions is precisely the object of enquiry of human geography.' At the end of the nineteenth century, Otto Schluter produced a concept of the morphology of the cultural landscape; the cultural landscape was said to include both *fixed* and *mobile* forms, the former comprising the effects upon landscape wrought by every period and culture, and the latter including humans, their works and movements; thus, 'The cultural landscape includes, therefore, not only the routes and route patterns, but also the men and goods which move along them' (Dickinson, 1939 p. 2). Schluter regarded the *Landschaft* as a landscape in which the visible natural and human constituents formed a distinct association; he gave priority to the description of landscape and the cataloguing of its contents. Subsequently, the emphasis in geography moved from description to the exploration of relationships between different phenomena

> The study of rural landscapes grew out of the settlement geography of the 1890s and 1900s. Its aim was to describe material features like houses and barns, roads and paths, fields and hedges, pastures and meadows, orchards and vineyards. In Jean Brunhes' *Geographic humaine* [sic] (1909), the study of these elements was clearly imbedded in a positivist conception of science, with an

emphasis on thorough descriptions of reality, on inventories and on regularities. (Claval, 1988 p. 27)

This, however, did not persist, for: 'What happened was the discovery of structural relations between elements which had initially been perceived as isolated from one [an]other' (Claval, 1988).

While clear links can be traced between the work of early human geographers in France and Germany and the development of Sauer's cultural geography, it is not possible to see a strong thread of influence and continuity running through the work of European geographers and into the form of landscape history which is currently flourishing in the UK. Historical geographers made their contributions, but the most influential figures in the shaping of the subject had backgrounds in archaeology and in history. Landmarks or stepping stones in the development of landscape history in Britain were represented in the work of Sir Cyril Fox and O. G. S. Crawford; the publication of *A Land* by Jacquetta Hawkes; the publication of W. G. Hoskins's *The Making of the English Landscape* and the establishment of a form of landscape history which was fieldwork-orientated and firmly rooted in the techniques of archaeology (and local history and geography) by the geographer-turned-archaeologist, Christopher Taylor.

One might scarcely suppose that a book with a somewhat dry and colourless text that was punctuated by a succession of archaeological artefact distribution maps and published by a Welsh museum in 1932 would still exert an influence on the interpretation of British landscapes. When he wrote *The Personality of Britain*, Sir Cyril Fox was Director of the National Museum of Wales. Almost a decade earlier, in his *The Archaeology of the Cambridge Region*, Fox had anticipated the concept which would be demonstrated in his later work: that there is a deeply-rooted cultural distinction between the highland and lowland zones of Britain. The notion of a Britain divided into highland and lowland zones had been expressed by the Oxford geographer, Halford Mackinder, in 1902, though Fox sought 'to express the character of Britain in prehistoric and early historic ages, and to indicate the effect of the environment she afforded on the distribution and fates of her inhabitants and her invaders' (1932 p. 9). The critical pendulum has swung away from the excessive invasionism evident in most pre-1980s accounts of the peopling of Britain but Fox's work, invasion-ridden though it was, was far-sighted and crucially important in that it respected the significance of prehistoric peoples in the making of landscape: a fact to be developed by Taylor, though neglected by Hoskins. The distinction between highland/upland and lowland cultural landscapes has been supported by subsequent research and endures as a fundamental concept in British landscape history (Figures 1.2, 1.3).

Hawkes, an Oxford archaeology graduate from a privileged background in the Cambridge intelligentsia, published *A Land* in 1951; she described her mission in writing the book as a celebration of the creation of Britain and the text in very geographical terms as a 'chronicle of the relationship between men and their land' (p. 183). The most widely-known British geographer of the day, L. Dudley Stamp, recognised the significance of the book immediately:

> It is not often that one can truthfully say of a book that it strikes a new note. Yet this is the case with 'A land.' It is an intensely personal book and Jacquetta Hawkes has the power through her vigorous writing of taking her readers into her confidence and letting them see as she herself sees . . . it is a difficult book to classify, but in essence it is an epitome of the geological and archaeological history of the British Isles, presented in a form attractive to a wide circle of readers who would probably never open a book on geology. (1951 p. 465)

The book was hugely successful and it introduced an enthusiastic public to the idea of landscape evolution; yet in terms of its simple factual content, *A Land* contained nothing that any competent, mainstream archaeologist with an understanding of geology could not have provided. But the style of writing was quite exceptional and was punctuated by passages of pure literary brilliance although these would not ensure *A Land* a special role in the history of landscape thought. What the book did contain was a very early exposition of the sense of place concept and of the relationship between land, lifestyle and social health and development. Hawkes described a workforce that was alienated by the intrusion of machines between hand and material, and she believed that industrialisation severed the essential links between communities and the land, falsifying values so that: 'Production and more production of goods has become an end for which the land may be turned to a wilderness' (p. 190), while she argued that 'the land, *with which* [humanity] *must always continue to live*, shows in its ravaged face that husbandry has been succeeded by exploitation' (p. 177).

This contempt for the modern world was shared by W. G. Hoskins, the most widely celebrated European landscape historian. Better than any other, he captured and conveyed the sense of countrysides that were alive with messages that could be read by initiates into the craft of the landscape historian. Recalling a childhood holiday spent among the scattered farmsteads and high hedgebanks of his native Devon, Hoskins wrote: 'Even then I felt that everything I was looking at was saying something to me if only I could recognize the language. It was a landscape written in a kind of code' (1973, p. 5). Elsewhere, and more famously, he wrote:

> The English landscape itself, to those who know how to read it aright, is the richest landscape record we possess. There are discoveries to be made in it for which no written documents exist, or have ever existed. To write its history requires a combination of documentary research and of fieldwork, of laborious scrambling on foot wherever the trail may lead. The result is a new kind of history which it is hoped will appeal to all those who like to travel intelligently, to get away from the guide-book show pieces now and then, and to unearth the reason behind what they are looking at. (1955 p. 14–15)

Born in 1908, Hoskins came from the lower middle classes of Exeter, where he went to school and to university. His formative years in Devon were to be his making, even if his provincial background and his unfashionable interest in outdoor topics may not always have assisted his academic career as a historian. He taught briefly at Bradford Technical College and became an assistant lecturer in commerce at University College, Leicester, in 1931. During the 1939–45 war he served in the Board of Trade, and in 1947 he founded the Department of English Local History at Leicester; later after an unfulfilling appointment as a reader in economic history at Oxford University from 1951 to 1965 he returned to Leicester, now a chartered university, as Hatton professor. Hoskins, through his *The Making of the English Landscape*, which was published in 1955, demonstrated to a broad readership that the history of places could be a valid and rewarding field of study. He was greatly assisted by his gifts as a writer, and he had an unfailing ability to write at exactly the right level to appeal to his target audience.

However, although Hoskins has been highly acclaimed as a landscape historian – and often wrongly regarded as the founder

Figure 1.2

of the discipline – one may ask whether he really *was* a landscape historian or rather a local historian who loved the countryside? Certainly, he seems to have operated as an experienced and well-qualified historian who had a passionate regard for certain parts of England and certain periods of cultural landscape formation rather

Figure 1.3

Physical settings do not determine the nature of human culture. Here the same religious impulses find similar expressions in megalithic circles on the low, water-girt plains of Orkney island at the Ring of Brodgar (1.2) and on an elevated platform commanding panoramic views of the Lakeland Fells at Castlerigg (1.3). (Richard Muir)

than as one who had acquired expertise in the specialist techniques of landscape archaeology. Surprisingly, given his subject matter, he could neglect geographical factors; in reviewing *The Making of the English Landscape,* E. G. R. Taylor remarked that 'geography is hardly mentioned or considered throughout the book' (1955 p. 511). Then, pointing out that Hoskins had overlooked Dudley Stamp's work on the evolution of scenery, he added:

> There is no doubt that a new pungency would be given to the historian's narrative, stimulating and alive as it already is, were he as constantly aware as is Dr. Stamp of what may be termed regional differentiation. Surface relief and drainage, soil and climate, position and juxtaposition, constitute a totality of conditions which limit and control land use and so lie always behind landscape history. (Taylor, 1955)

Perhaps the fairest appraisal of Hoskins as a landscape historian can be found by combining two assessments by C. C. Taylor. Of Hoskins' most acclaimed work Taylor wrote:

> It is great because it established landscape history as a new and proper branch of historical study. It is great because it is written in a language which is easy to understand and a pleasure to read. It is great because it has inspired two, and perhaps now more, generations of historians, archaeologists, geographers and botanists to follow the master's footsteps and to explore the mysteries of our country's landscape. But its greatest achievement, only matched perhaps by the works of Macaulay and Trevelyan, is that it reached out to, and profoundly affected, hundreds of thousands of ordinary people who would otherwise never have thought about the past. (1988 p. 7)

On the other hand, the report of a day school at Oxford on *W. G. Hoskins and the English Landscape* records:

> Fortunately there was room for some critical reappraisal of Hoskins' contribution. This came more forcefully from Christopher Taylor of the Royal Commission on Historical Monuments. Whilst citing Hoskins' pioneer role in presenting the totality of landscape he suggested that Hoskins was a 'terrible fieldworker'. Noting the 1948 gathering near Leicester which initiated 'lost village' studies, Taylor said that the site chosen by Hoskins for the inauguration shows scant evidence of any such village. He acknowledged, however, that analytical fieldwork as now practised owed its impetus to Hoskins and others of his generation. (Goodey, 1992 p. 2)

Two factors in particular characterised Hoskins's work, and though they may have been essential to the passion of his narratives, they greatly reduced their scope. First, like Hawkes and like Sauer, Hoskins despised the present. Perhaps in a semi-satirical manner, E. G. R. Taylor summarised the closing section of *The Making of the English Landscape* (in which Hoskins lambasted the modern with its profiteering vultures, and then sought solace in the unsullied view from his study window, rather like a school-hating child finding temporary refuge by snuggling up on his mother's lap):

> One has only to lean out of the window to see the ancient church, cold and deserted today save for one weekly hour, while perhaps

fifty or sixty yards away, in a field adjoining the garden, there lies buried the main street of a village wiped out by the Black Death. Tinged with melancholy at this thought, and forgetting the scientists, the vultures and the hyenas, Dr. Hoskins reaches back through the centuries one by one and rediscovers Eden. (1955 p. 413).

Phythian-Adams (1992) believed that Hoskins was engaged in a search for local culture and the home-made civilisation of rural England, and he thought that in his early days at Leicester, Hoskins was strongly influenced by Lewis Mumford and his ideas about the transition from qualitative civilisations, which had perfection as their goal and produced elegant pre-industrial landscapes, and the modern, quantitative civilisations, which were devoted to power. Even so, Hoskins's dislike of the modern was such that he debarred himself from treating a large part of the subject matter of landscape history. At the end of his most celebrated tirade he wrote: 'Barbaric England of the scientist, the military men, and the politicians: let us turn away and contemplate the past before all is lost to the vandals' (1955 p. 299). He regarded the period between the close of the medieval period and the acceleration of the Industrial Revolution as a 'golden age', though he was too intelligent to pretend that iniquity was not as much a part of this past as of the present (Hoskins, 1949 p. 60).

Second, while he taught briefly in Bradford, Hoskins had difficulty relating to the North, and does not appear to have liked it very much. From a reading of *The Making of the English Landscape* a stranger might have imagined that the country to the north of the Trent was a modest appendage of a land whose character was firmly founded upon southern and Midlands landscape motifs. The vast territory formed by the three combined Ridings of Yorkshire rated 20 index entries, Durham none and Cumberland and Northumberland but one each, although little Cornwall had 18 mentions, Hoskins's home county of Devon had 30, Northamptonshire 14, and tiny Rutland, like populous Lancashire, had 8 entries.

Hoskins provided a humane approach to landscape history and succeeded brilliantly in the nigh impossible task of pleasing both the academic world and the general reader. His affinity towards humble rural cultures may have led him to undervalue the part played in landscape evolution by the mighty and by the state, and it may be that he will be best remembered as a great publicist for the cause of landscape history and as a gifted generaliser who could see patterns within the empirical evidence in local history. He did not have an accomplished command of the different fields of technical expertise involved in landscape history; M. W. Beresford, a contemporary of Hoskins's, was a better all-rounder. Beresford produced his *History on the Ground* just two years after the publication of *The Making of the English Landscape*. It was accessible and organised around six journeys or case studies in local history, but though well-written and much admired by students and scholars it failed to capture the national imagination in the manner of Hoskins's more romantic and idiosyncratic style. Beresford, a Midlander who became Professor of Economic History in the University of Leeds, combined with the archaeologist, John Hurst, to instigate and promote the excavation of the deserted medieval village of Wharram Percy in the Yorkshire Wolds, a project which spanned four decades and transformed the understanding of village evolution in England. In his preface to *History on the Ground,* Beresford revealed the breadth of his enquiries, thanking Hurst for introducing him to archaeology and the interpretation of earthworks, the cartographers and archaeological officers of the Ordnance Survey, the air photography unit at Cambridge University, as well as various academics, including Hoskins and the Cambridge geographer, H. C. Darby (1957 p. 13). He also demonstrated the interdisciplinary commitment which established his identity as a true landscape historian by publishing important papers in non-historical journals, with his paper on the lost villages of medieval England being delivered to the Royal Geographical Society and appearing in *The Geographical Journal* (1951 pp. 129–49).

Pathways of influence are difficult to detect or define for the reasons already given. One may argue, however, that the British tradition in landscape history did not begin with Hoskins, and was little influenced by Hawkes or by the formative developments taking place in schools of geography abroad. In Britain, much more than in other European countries, there was a long-standing association between national map-makers and archaeology:

an association personified in General Roy (1726–90) who was not only the effective founder of the Ordnance Survey but may also be regarded as the founder of modern field archaeology. He incorporated in his Map of Scotland his military interest in Agricola's campaigns in that country and his 'Military Antiquities of the Romans in Britain' is a landmark in the history of the subject. (Kirwan, 1953 p. 230)

The link between archaeological plotting and landscape history was renewed by O. G. S. Crawford (1886–1957). He came from Hampshire and was himself influenced by another Hampshire man, H. Sumner, author of *Earthworks of the New Forest* (1917), and by the work of A. H. Allcroft, whose *Earthwork of England* of 1908 may have provided the first written hints of the existence of a subject later to be called 'landscape history'.

Crawford had studied geography at Oxford and had served as a navigator in the Royal Flying Corps. At Oxford, he heard Herbertson lecture on the way in which environment affected human communities and Myres discuss the effects of the geographical setting upon the ancient civilisations of the Mediterranean. He was also influenced by the German concept of *Kulturkreis*, with its concern for the geographical patterns associated with maps showing the distribution of cultural artefacts. Thus, with interests spanning history, geography and archaeology, Crawford was well-positioned to play a leading role in the development of landscape history. Following his release as a prisoner of war he became the first archaeology officer of the Ordnance Survey and proceeded to launch a series of archaeological maps which expressed the high priority that he accorded to the combined study of time and space. In this role he perpetuated the tradition of association between national mapping and archaeology first established by General Roy. The Great War had demonstrated the importance of aerial photography as a source of intelligence, and Crawford recognised that it also had a great archaeological potential. In 1927 he founded *Antiquity*, a serious but readable archaeological journal, which he edited until his death. In 1953 he published an expanded version of lecture notes as *Archaeology in the Field*, a book destined to become a landmark study in the development of landscape archaeology and landscape history.

Though he would be hugely influential in the subsequent development of landscape history, Hoskins was not greatly affected by Crawford's enthusiasm for interdisciplinary approaches, although he did include *Archaeology in the Field* in the bibliography of *The Making of the English Landscape*. A strong thread of influence can be traced from the work of Crawford to that of Christopher Taylor in the present period. The approach to landscape history which Taylor has adopted and developed has directed and motivated numerous followers and dominates modern approaches to landscape history in Britain and beyond. It is based on meticulous fieldwork and high levels of professional competence. These qualities Taylor had acquired during his work as an investigator for the Royal Commission on Historical Monuments, in the course of which he explored extensive areas of Dorset, Cambridge and Northamptonshire, often on a field-by-field basis. The approach was not solely based on painstaking methodologies, for deriving from the high quality/high quantity fieldwork were several crucial concepts. These included a realisation of the enormous contribution that prehistoric societies have made to the evolution of the landscape, and of the fact that the prehistoric population was far more numerous and successful than had generally been allowed. Taylor's work also provided a new understanding of the dynamics of rural settlement, and replaced the characterisation of the village as a stable settlement which exemplified the importance of continuity in the landscape with one which emphasised the responsiveness of settlement to changing local and regional social circumstances. The villages which were revealed by Taylor's fieldwork were frequently structurally complex, leading him to coin the term 'polyfocal' to describe the places which had nucleated around more than one original core. They would sometimes migrate from one site to another or be reorientated in accordance with changes in the patterns of communication. He has also demonstrated the ingenuity of the medieval makers of landscape, one of his most recent investigations being focused on designed medieval landscapes.

A Midlander from Staffordshire, Taylor studied geography at Keele University, but became disenchanted with the subject during its lapse into 'spatial science'. He developed a professional competence in archaeology, but perhaps his greatest asset is an unflagging and insatiable enthusiasm for landscape history which, being unblemished by historical prejudice, allows him to discover as much interest in, say, a nineteenth-century blockhouse or twentieth-century airship hangar as in a twelfth-century moated site. This ability to recognise the fascination in any facet of the human-made scene, 'fashionable' or not, which may reflect the breadth of his former brief as an investigator, combined with a capacity to communicate in language that is simple and direct, has made him a widely-read writer on landscape history:

> Until the middle of the nineteenth century, restaurants as we know them today did not exist. For the upper-class males there were clubs, but most people 'ate out' in the dining rooms of inns. The large railway companies had seen the advantages of providing refreshments at large termini or at major junctions, as in the case

of the famous Great Western refreshment room at Swindon. Even so, restaurants were slow to arrive. The great innovator was one Frederik Gordon, the son of a decorator, who opened a restaurant in the City of London for businessmen in the 1870s; soon after the Holborn Restaurant for middle-class visitors appeared. The project was a success and soon restaurants mushroomed in every large town and city. (Taylor and Muir, 1983 p. 333)

Paralleling the thread linking Allcroft to Taylor, and often entwining or merging with it, was the one representing academic historical geography. For much of this century, historical geography's leading practitioner was H. C. Darby, who regarded it as being at the very core of the larger discipline and as having come into existence as a self-aware field of study in the 1920s and 1930s (Darby, 1983 pp. 421–8). There were historical geographers who took an interest in the continuum of landscape development and there were others who recreated intersections in space and time rather than exploring the evolutionary processes of landscape formation. Darby did both, studying the changing countrysides of England (1951) and also engaging in a major effort to reconstruct the English landscape of the late eleventh century on the basis of information contained in Domesday Book (1952, p. 77). By the last quarter of the present century, historical geography was hardly ever regarded as the most important branch of human geography; some of its adherents had displayed a reluctance to engage in explanation or to participate in the philosophical debates taking place within geography; marginalisation was the price that was paid.

In describing the changing character of historical geography, Baker noted three basic 'styles': the traditional, the modern and the post-modern (Baker, 1988 pp. 5–16). Of the traditional approach he wrote:

Its emphasis has been upon the cultural morphology of landscapes, upon the origins and transformations of distinctive landscape forms and of the personalities of places as expressed in regional assemblages of landscape structures. Such work has been dominantly empirical, thoroughly grounded in appropriate archival and field evidence, and essentially rooted in particular places and periods'. (p. 9)

In outlining what still remains to be achieved by researchers using this frequently adopted style, he wrote: 'we need more syntheses of the puzzling diversity of rural settlements and field systems within individual European countries but we especially lack syntheses of the rural landscapes of Europe as a whole' (p. 10).

Of the studies in the modern style of historical geography Baker thought that:

> The enthusiastic search for spatial order, for models of the evolution of cultural landscapes and for quantitative techniques of analysis which characterises work by 'modernist' contemporary geographers has found scant reflection in papers presented at our Conference [the Permanent European Conference for the Study of the Rural Landscape]. Remarkably few participants have employed either statistical techniques in their analyses or theoretical concepts in their interpretations of European rural landscapes. (1988 p. 11)

He considered that if the modern approaches seemed to place more emphasis on human agency than upon landscape, this tendency was even more marked in the case of the post-modern approaches:

> The roots of 'post-modern' studies in historical geography – those which seek humanistic interpretation rather than scientific explanations – may lie deep in the past of our discipline but it is also clear that more historical geographers have come increasingly to view the study of landscape and place as a concern not only with *patterns* of structures and *processes* of change but also with *symbolic* significance and social meaning. (1988 p. 12)

He added:

> Individual forms within landscapes may be interpreted as social signs which combine into cultural messages of spaces and places which need to be decoded and interpreted as having varied levels of meaning: *ordinary* landscapes deserve and demand *extraordinary* interpretations, because of the individual and collective cultural significance with which they are endowed not only by those who created them but also by successive generations who have experienced them'. (pp. 12–13)

The diversity of approaches existing within historical geography is a part of a wider diversity seen within landscape history and the fields of study with which it interacts. Landscape history has never been the property of a single discipline, and may fortunately have escaped the disadvantages of suffering a conformity imposed in accordance with some currently prevailing dogma concerning what a particular subject should be about. Diversity of approach has always been a characteristic of landscape history, but the divergences have never been so great as to prevent meaningful dialogue between the spokespersons of different perspectives. By drawing its recruits from archaeology, history and geography the subject has been refreshed by the infusion of remarkable talents. It has also been fortunate in its figureheads and public image, for few if any fields of study have been able to produce recruiting officers as eloquent and passionate as Hoskins or as erudite and evocative as Hawkes; while, across the Atlantic, few have been able to inspire and lead such a gifted following of recruits as did Sauer. Differences about the priorities for study or philosophical standpoints have tended largely to pass the subject by. This must in no small part be due to the landscape historian's unshakable confidence in the worth of evolutionary landscape study, for quarrels tend to be most frequent and bitter among the insecure. It may well be that the subject is preoccupied with empirical study and has neglected the development of its theoretical base. Equally, it can be said that within the discipline there are no signs of widespread concern relating to these supposed shortcomings.

Landscape and Heritage

It is clear that landscapes exist as historical texts. The historical aspects of landscape combine with aesthetic and place-related elements to constitute landscape as heritage. Landscape becomes, therefore, a significant component of the overall heritage which endows communities and nations with their identity. Lowenthal considered that: 'Awareness of the past is essential to the maintenance of purpose in life. Without it we would lack all sense of continuity, all apprehension of causality, all knowledge of our own identity' (1979 p. 103), and elsewhere he stated:

The past is everywhere. All around us lie features which, like ourselves and our thoughts, have more or less recognizable antecedents. Relics, histories, memories suffuse human experience. Each particular trace of the past ultimately perishes, but collectively they are immortal. Whether it is celebrated or rejected, attended to or ignored, the past is omnipresent. (1985 p. xv)

Schama, in his study of *Landscape and Memory*, wrote that:

it is clear that inherited landscape myths and memories share two common characteristics: their surprising endurance through the centuries and their power to shape institutions that we still live with. National identity, to take just the most obvious example, would lose much of its ferocious enchantment without the mystique of a particular landscape tradition: its topography mapped, elaborated, and enriched as a homeland. The poetic tradition of *la douce France* – 'sweet France' – describes a geography as much as a history, the sweetness of a classically well-ordered place where rivers, cultivated fields, orchards, vineyards, and woods are all in harmonious balance with each other. (1995 p. 15)

In exploring the convoluted national identity of the English and its relationship to landscape, P. J. Taylor identified an 'upper England', in the Home Counties grouped around London, which dominates the national territory:

What does this upper England look like? What type of landscape do the Anglo-British identify with? Answers to these questions lead us to another paradox of this curious nationalism. The pioneer of industrialization and the most urbanized country in the world is idealized in rural terms: thatched cottages around a village green is the archetypal English scene. Such anti-urban images are themselves quite common in the national landscapes of peoples. The difference for the English is that they are not featured in their own landscape. (1991 p. 151)

He then referred to the German political geographer, Friedrich Ratzel, who claimed that every nation evolved as a symbiotic association of people and land, with the peasant peoples of Europe being shaped by the interactions with their land. Taylor added:

In the USA, nationhood was similarly built upon a non-urban terrain, first the frontier and then 'small town' America, the site of integrity and honesty in contrast to 'big city corruption'.

Although all such national images promote a rural bias in representing the overall nature of a people, they do reflect an aspect of that reality. (p. 153)

The English identification with a rural icon was echoed by Short:

The countryside became, and still is, the most important landscape in the national environmental ideology. It still holds pride of place. In England the two meanings of country, as countryside and nation, are collapsed into one another; the essence of England is popularly thought to be the green countryside – the enclosed fields, the secluded/excluded parklands of the country houses, and the small villages. The nineteenth-century landed elite may have lost economic power in the twentieth century but their symbolic power is still evident in this view, which is widely believed at home and increasingly marketed abroad. The countryside has become the 'real' England, the 'unchanging' England. It has become the land of retreat from an increasingly urban and overwhelmingly industrial society, the place to escape modernity. (1991 p. 75)

In a contrasting earlier appreciation of the relationship between the English and their setting, Lowenthal and Prince had written:

To summarize the relationships between the English people and their landscape, the word 'amenity' offers a key . . . 'Amenity' serves to denote almost every kind of interest in a place and any inherent value that transcends purely economic considerations. It is attached to whatever seems to need protection. In one town 'amenities' are historic buildings and the flavor of the past, in another open spaces, in a third views and vistas, elsewhere facilities for recreation or access to nearby points of scenic interest. The portmanteau quality of the term gives the public a sense of common cause against those to whom land is merely a marketable commodity . . . Not everything done for amenity's sake is well done or unanimously liked, but it is all thought to be well meant. (1964 p. 344)

In nineteenth-century America the popular attitudes towards heritage matters were quite different, and Lowenthal noted that:

The paucity of human history in the landscape had saddened, even appalled, early Colonial settlers and travelers accustomed to the relic features of the Old World. The passage of time, however, habituated American eyes to their *tabula rasa*. And with the Revolution came a new spirit: newness was not only tolerated but positively worshiped, and the lack of historical remains became a matter for self-congratulation. (1976 p. 91)

Elsewhere he noted that: 'Raw, unfinished America dismayed sensitive souls who shared Mme de Stael's view that "the most beautiful landscapes in the world, if they evoke no memory, if they bear no trace of any notable event, are uninteresting compared to historic landscapes"' (1985, p. 114).

In breaking the bonds of empire, the American nationalists believed that they were shedding the imperial country and its long-established traditions as well:

Americans who thus turned their backs on human history renounced not only romantic nostalgia but also a useful adjunct to national identity. Some warned that neglect of the past might vitiate American patriotism. Others, however, found surrogates for historical heritage among such elements as nature, American Indians and classical prototypes. (Lowenthal, 1985 p. 101)

Many Americans found that the magnificence of their natural landscapes amply compensated for the country's missing historical associations, with the worship of nature assuming a high profile during the early decades of the Republic. Lowenthal explained that: 'The historical landscapes of Europe had such a multiplicity of features that they tended to be diffuse and heterogenous. By contrast, American natural landscapes were unified, integrated and coherent. And they suggested a high order of creativity' (p. 103); and further: 'In deifying nature, Americans rejected the proximate for the more remote past, viewing antiquity as eternity rather than as change. They dismissed history to embrace prehistory; the primeval quality of American nature was invoked again and again . . . the historical past was degenerate, whereas primitive nature was strong, savage, pure, and free' (pp. 103–4). As soon as the native Americans ceased to pose a threat they were accepted as symbols of the ancient uniqueness of the unrecorded past of America, while the classical forms and heroes of ancient Greece and Rome were revered in non-historical terms and regarded as prototypes of American virtues. Only after the Civil War and the Centennial, when industrialisation and mass immigration from eastern and southern Europe also fuelled a dissatisfaction with the present, did Americans begin to crave and romanticise the past.

Lowenthal points out that:

> Today's past is an accumulation of mankind's memories, seen through our own generation's perspective. What we know of history differs from what actually happened not merely because evidence of past events has been lost or tampered with, or because the task of sifting through it is unending, but also because the changing pattern continually requires new interpretations of what has taken place. (1979 p. 103)

The past revealed by artefacts, history and memory is not exactly to be equated with what actually happened in former times; rather, it is to a considerable extent a manufactured past which human forgetfulness and imagination have created. Then the plastic past, moulded by human history-makers, can become a focus of identity and a refuge from the anxieties of the present and the future. As Shurmer-Smith and Hannam explain:

> Places in the Western world are socially constructed with a considerable intensity of nostalgia as consciously and unconsciously we create and recreate them with a sense of history. History is not just the traces of the past, but is the outcome of a dialogue between the present and the past; the present itself being many-voiced. As we do this there is a tendency to narrate one history as a prior, dominant history around which supposedly lesser histories compete, and it is this dominant version of the past that will be preserved and represented in physical form, in education and text. What survives intact, is refurbished, or re-created in replica, emerges, in particular locations, from the will of human beings of different powers. Different social groups strive for their interpretation of the past to be territorialised in texts of all kinds, including landscapes, 'not for disinterested reasons, but to help them get what they want or keep what they have got', namely access to economic and cultural capital. (1994, p. 45)

Relics and venerable facets of the scene provide windows on the past:

> We perceive the past through artifacts, physical traces, and objects in the landscape that we believe endured from earlier

times, or 'are old.' Things persuade us of their survival in two distinct ways. One is their resemblance to, or congruence with, forms, styles, or species that are historically antique and obsolete – open field traces, vintage automobiles, classical pediments. This mode of perception might be termed antiquarian; it is essentially humanistic, requiring historical knowledge. The other is our awareness of prolonged use or decay – a worn chair, a wrinkled face, a corroded tin, an ivy-covered or mildewed wall. This mode might be termed senescent, bearing on aging: it is essentially naturalistic, requiring awareness of organic change. (Lowenthal, 1979 p. 108)

The association between landscape and history converts landscape into heritage and introduces a new dimension of significance into any debate concerning the uses and function of countryside:

The ideological importance of the countryside has meant that it has become separated from purely agricultural considerations. The countryside is more than just a place for farmers to grow crops, raise animals and make money. It is a place of broader cultural significance and deeper ideological meaning, a place redolent with historical association, perceptions of nationality and intimations of community. It has become a place of wider political significance. The landscape of power has become the power of landscape to evoke feelings, generate emotions, provide causes. Two important causes have been access to the countryside and the look of the countryside. (Short, 1991 p. 77)

However, the historical associations of places are not fixed and: 'Enduring place myths are . . . susceptible to revision. Place meanings are always being radically and subtly reterritorialized through a reworking of their past' (Shurmer-Smith and Hannam, 1994, p. 47). Similarly, Lowenthal remarked that:

Every act of recognition alters survivals from the past. Simply to appreciate or protect a relic, let alone to embellish or imitate it, affects its form or our impressions. Just as selective recall skews memory and subjectivity shapes historical insight, so manipulating antiquities refashions their appearance and meaning. Interaction with a heritage continually alters its nature and context, whether by choice or by chance. (1985 p. 263)

Much effort is directed towards conservation, yet items of heritage, whether they be a coach house or a passage of countryside, are the products of a particular social order in a particular cultural, temporal and spatial context which cannot be recreated and conserved. Mills remarks that:

> it was in eastern areas that Americans developed ways of creating landscapes that were geared to eliminating the native peoples in favour of staple crops and long-distance trade. Just as the origins of the republic lie in eastern experiences, so, too, eastern landscape transformations are at the root of the development of an American landscape experience. And it is back east that Americans now locate 'heritage landscapes'. In attempting to locate the origins of frontier landscapes in the east, however, museums and heritage sites encounter problems inherent in the presentation and representation of such a disputed past within the landscapes of today. The landscapes of the colonial seaboard were geared to imperialism, slavery and environmental exploitation. Did not Thomas Jefferson transform British imperialism into an 'Empire for Freedom', where decadent traditions would find no root? (1997 p. 106)

The conservation of material fragments of heritage is a selective process, items from the past only surviving where they are valued by modern societies. Thus, according to Shurmer-Smith and Hannam (1994 p. 54), we find old urban fabric associated with both the most- and least-valued environments: 'The means whereby the transition is made from low value "old" to high value "history" is through the process of gentrification.'

The conservation or re-creation of landscapes presents particular problems. In the UK, for example, the conservation of 'unspoilt' countryside is widely supported but the landscapes concerned are seldom the creations of a single distinct historical era. Rather, they are assemblages of facets of countryside of different kinds which have endured for different lengths of time for different reasons. The public concern for conservation also tends to be somewhat selective in terms of what is targeted for preservation. Countryside of the type known to landscape historians as 'early enclosure' is heavily favoured. It includes both ancient fieldscapes and land enclosed and 'privatised' as open field systems were dismantled as a result of undertakings between members of the village community. In both cases it is associated with landscapes of small, irregular fields defined by curving hedgerows (or walls). More numerous in the English Midlands in the time of Chaucer, Shakespeare or Defoe were the landscapes of open-field farming. These countrysides must have been characterised by their lack of diversity and fine detail, with ploughland (corrugated by plough ridges grouped in gently curving strips or lands), common, and shared meadowland filling much if not all the space between the horizons. There are no calls for the recreation and conservation of countrysides such as this; it was the creation of a particular social order and of a remarkably intricate system of non-mechanised farming and could never be revived.

As suggested above, with the exceptions of those of a few retreating wilderness areas, landscapes are cultural products so that their preservation and maintenance would concern the conservation of a culture rather than of a countryside. This becomes plain in a region like the Yorkshire Dales, of which I wrote that the preservation of the traditional countrysides:

> can only be achieved by a wholehearted policy of perpetuating the small farm and of subsidising the small farmer to conserve the traditional features of the landscape . . . the small farmer made the Yorkshire Dales and, when he goes, so too do the priceless vistas of meadow, pasture, wall and barn. In a strange way it is not poverty which threatens the region – the Dalesfolk have coped with poverty for centuries – but wealth. The enchanting beauty wrought over the centuries by the poor people of the Dales may be defaced by rich outsiders in the space of just a few decades. (Muir, 1991 p. 218)

Societies endowed with unprecedented levels of nostalgia and conservational concern are confronted by an equally unprecedented technological ability to transform urban and rural landscapes in ways which obliterate all references to the past. People crave roots and landscape provides a focus for personal and national identity, yet those landscapes which are most redolent of the past and of the attachments between community and land are the very landscapes which, through the smallness of their divisions and the fineness of their historical detail, are most threatened by the forces of modernisation in the countryside.

References

Allcroft, A. H. *Earthwork of England* (London: Macmillan, 1908).

Baker, A. R. H. 'Historical geography and the study of the European rural landscape' *Geografisca Annaler* **70B** (1988) pp. 5–16.

Beresford, M. W. 'The lost villages of medieval England' *Geographical Journal* **117** (1951) pp. 129–49.

Beresford, M. W. *History on the Ground* (London: Lutterworth Press, 1957).

Butlin, R. A. *Historical Geography: Through the Gates of Space and Time* (London: Edward Arnold, 1993).

Claval, P. 'European societies and landscape and the challenge of urbanization and industrialization in the nineteenth and twentieth centuries' *Geografisca Annaler* **70** (1988) pp. 27–38.

Cloke, P., Philo, C. and Sadler, D. *Approaching Human Geography* (London: Paul Chapman, 1991).

Coones, P. 'One landscape or many?' *Landscape History* **7** (1985), p. 5.

Coones, P. 'Landscape geography' in Rogers, A., Viles, H. and Goudie, A. (eds), *The Student's Companion to Geography* (Oxford: Blackwell, 1992).

Cosgrove, D. *Social Formation and Symbolic Landscape* (London: Croom Helm, 1984).

Cosgrove, D. 'Critique and queries' in Jackson, J. B. 'The vernacular landscape' in Penning-Rowsell, E. C. and Lowenthal, D. (eds), *Landscape Meaning and Values* (London: Allen & Unwin, 1986).

Crawford, O. G. S. *Archaeology in the Field* (London: Phoenix House, 1953).

Darby, H. C. 'The changing landscape' *Geographical Journal* **117** (1951) pp. 377–98.

Darby, H. C. *The Domesday Geography of England*, 7 vols (Cambridge: Cambridge University Press, 1952–77).

Darby, H. C. 'Historical geography in Britain 1920–80: continuity and change' *Transactions of the Institute of British Geographers* NS **8** (1983) pp. 421–8.

Davis, C. M. 'The High Plains of Michigan' *Michigan Papers in Geography* **6** (1936) pp. 303–41.

Dickinson, R. E. 'Landscape and society' *The Scottish Geographical Magazine* **55** (1939) pp. 1–15.

Duncan, J. 'The superorganic in American cultural geography' *Annals of the American Association of Geographers* **70** (1980) pp. 181–98.

Duncan, S. 'What is locality?' in Peet, R. and Thrift, N. (eds), *New Models in Geography* Vol II (London: Unwin Hyman, 1989).

Entrikin, N. J. 'Place and region' *Progress in Human Geography* **18** (1994) pp. 227–33.

Fox, Sir Cyril F. *The Personality of Britain: Its Influence on Inhabitants and Invaders in Prehistoric and Early Historic Times* (Cardiff: University of Wales, 1932).

Fox, Sir Cyril F. *The Archaeology of the Cambridge Region*, 2nd edn (Cambridge: Cambridge University Press, 1948).

46   *Approaches to Landscape*

Goodey, B. 'The making of the English landscape' *Landscape Research Extra* (Winter 1992) pp. 1–2.
Hartshorne, R. *The Nature of Geography: A Critical Survey of Current Thought in the Light of the Past* (Lancaster, PA: Association of American Geographers, 1939).
Hawkes, J. *A Land* (London: Cresset Press, 1951). Page numbers quoted refer to the Pelican edn of 1959.
Holmen, H. 'What's new and what's regional in the "new" regional geography?' *Geografiska Annaler* **77**B (1995) pp. 47–52.
Hoskins, W. G. *Midland England: A Survey of the Country Between the Chilterns and the Trent*, Face of Britain Series (London, 1949).
Hoskins, W. G. *The Making of the English Landscape* (London: Hodder & Stoughton, 1955).
Hoskins, W. G. *English Landscapes* (London: BBC, 1973).
Jackson, J. B. 'Goodbye to evolution' *Landscape* **13** (1963–4).
Jackson, J. B. 'The vernacular landscape' in Penning-Rowsell, E. C. and Lowenthal, D. (eds), *Landscape Meaning and Values* (London: Allen & Unwin, 1986).
Johnston, R. J. *On Human Geography* (Oxford: Blackwell, 1986).
Kenzer, M. 'Milieu and the "Intellectual Landscape": Carl O. Sauer's undergraduate heritage' *Annals of the Association of American Geographers* **75** (1985) pp. 258–70.
Kimble, G. H. T. in Stamp, L. D. and Wooldridge S. W. (eds), *Essays in Geography* (London: Longman, 1951).
Kirwan, L. P. 'Review: the geographical study of archaeology' *Geographical Journal* **119** (1953) pp. 228–30.
Langton, J. 'The two traditions of geography, historical geography and the study of landscapes' *Geografisca Annaler* **70**B (1988) pp. 17–25.
Leighly, J. 'Carl Ortwin Sauer 1889–1975' *Annals of the American Association of Geographers* **66** (1976) pp. 337–47.
Ley, D. 'Geography without man: a humanistic critique' Research Paper 24 (University of Oxford, Department of Geography, 1980).
Ley, D. 'Progress report: cultural and humanistic geography' *Progress in Human Geography* **5** (1981) pp. 249–57.
Linton, D. L. 'Some contrasts in landscapes in British Antarctic Territory' *Geographical Journal* **129** (1963) pp. 274–82.
Lowenthal, D. 'The place of the past in the American landscape' in Lowenthal, D. and Bowden, M. J. (eds), *Geographies of the Mind* (New York: Oxford University Press, 1976) pp. 89–117.
Lowenthal, D. 'Age and artefact' in Meinig, D. W. (ed.) *The Interpretation of Ordinary Landscapes* (New York: Oxford University Press, 1979) pp. 103–28.
Lowenthal, D. *The Past is a Foreign Country* (Cambridge: Cambridge University Press, 1985).
Lowenthal, D. 'Introduction' in Penning-Rowsell, E. C. and Lowenthal, D. (eds), *Landscape Meaning and Values* (London: Allen & Unwin, 1986).
Lowenthal, D. and Prince, H. C. 'The English landscape' *Geographical Review* **54** (1964) pp. 309–46.

Meinig, D. W. 'Reading the landscape, an appreciation of W. G. Hoskins and J. B. Jackson' in Meinig, D. W. (ed.), *The Interpretation of Ordinary Landscapes* (New York: Oxford University Press, 1979) pp. 195–244.

Mikesell, M. 'Landscape' in Sills, D. L. (ed.), *International Encyclopedia of the Social Sciences* vol. 8 (New York: Crowell, Collier & Macmillan, 1968) pp. 575–80.

Mikesell, M. 'The rise and decline of "sequent occupance": a chapter in the history of American geography' in Lowenthal, D. and Bowden, M. J. (eds), *Essays in Historical Geography in Honour of John Kirkland Wright* (New York: Oxford University Press, 1976) pp. 149–69.

Mikesell, M., 'Tradition and innovation in cultural geography' *Annals of the Association of American Geographers* **68** (1978) pp. 1–16.

Mills, S. F. *The American Landscape* (Edinburgh: Keele University Press, 1997).

Muir, R. *The Dales of Yorkshire* (London: Macmillan, 1991).

Olwig, K. R. 'Recovering the substantive nature of landscape' *Annals of the Association of American Geographers* **86** (1996) pp. 630–53.

Penck, A. *'Neue Geographie' Jubilums-Sonderband der Zeitschrift der Gesellschaft für Erdkunde zu Berlin* (Berlin, 1928) pp. 31–56.

Phythian-Adams, C. 'Hoskins's England: a local historian of genius and the realisation of his theme' *The Local Historian* **22** (1992) pp. 170–83.

Sauer, C. O. 'The morphology of landscape' *University of California Publications in Geography* **2** (1925), reprinted in Leighly, J. (ed.) *Land and Life* (Berkeley, CA: University of California Press, 1974) pp. 315–50.

Sauer, C. O. 'Cultural geography' in Hayes, E. C. (ed.), *Recent Developments in the Social Sciences*, Lippincott Series in Sociology (1927).

Sauer, C. O. 'Geography, cultural' in Seligman, E. and Johnston, A. (eds), *Encyclopedia of the Social Sciences* vol. 6 (New York: Macmillan, 1931) pp. 621–4.

Sauer, C. O. 'Forward to historical geography' *Annals of the Association of American Geographers* **31** (1941) pp. 1–24.

Schama, S. *Landscape and Memory* (London: HarperCollins, 1995).

Shurmer-Smith, P. and Hannam, K. *Worlds of Desire, Realms of Power* (London: Edward Arnold, 1994).

Semple, E. C. *Influences of Geographic Environment* (New York: H. Hold, 1911).

Short, J. R. *Imagined Country* (London: Routledge, 1991)

Solot, M. 'Carl Sauer and cultural evolution' *Annals of the Association of American Geographers* **76** (1986) pp. 508–20.

Stamp, L. D. 'Reviews' *Geographical Journal* **121** (1951) pp. 511–13.

Sumner, H. *Earthworks of the New Forest* (1917).

Taylor, C. C. (ed.) Introduction to Hoskins, W. G. *The Making of the English Landscape* (London: Hodder & Stoughton, 1988).

Taylor, C. C. and Muir, R. *Visions of the Past* (London: J. M. Dent, 1983).

Taylor, E. G. R. 'Review: the English scene' *Geographical Journal* **121** (1955) pp. 511–13.

Taylor, P. J. 'The English and their Englishness: "a curiously mysterious, elusive and little understood people"' *Scottish Geographical Magazine* **107** (1991) pp. 146–61.

48   *Approaches to Landscape*

Tuan, Y.-F. 'Thought and landscape' in Meinig, D. W. (ed.), *The Interpretation of Ordinary Landscapes* (New York: Oxford University Press, 1979) pp. 89–102.

Vallaux, C. *Les sciences geographiques* (1925).

Vidal de la Blache, P. *Principles of Human Geography* (London: Constable, 1926).

Whittlesey, D. 'Sequent occupance' *Annals of the Association of American Geographers* **19** (1929) pp. 162–6.

Williams, M. ' "The apple of my eye": Carl Sauer and cultural geography' *Journal of Historical Geography* **9** (1983) pp. 1–28.

2
The Practice of Landscape History

Landscape study is uniquely appealing. It has its obvious and much-explored aesthetic dimension, but it also offers intellectual challenges of the most testing kind to engage the problem-solving skills of the landscape historian. Although there are various different approaches to the study of landscape, whether landscape is approached from an aesthetic, cultural, psychological or political perspective, it seems hard to justify any approach which does not require of its followers a basic understanding of landscape origins and formation. Just as art historians engage in studies in depth of artists, their personalities and formative influences as well as the topographical, social, economic and political environments of their existences, so it seems reasonable to presume that all serious students of landscape should have a basic understanding of the physical and cultural processes of landscape creation. Because of the immense inequalities between landscape research accomplished in different parts of the world, in this chapter most examples are derived from the UK, which contains the most intensely researched countrysides, while North American material is also introduced, particularly for the purposes of comparison and contrast.

Aesthetically, landscapes may be regarded as amounting to more than the sum of their components, but each landscape that one experiences is a totality composed of an assemblage of constituents whose origins and development can be researched. Equally, it can be argued, every landscape is the unique product of the complex and singular interactions between its various distinctive components. In a European rural landscape or countryside one might expect to find facets or elements such as fields, woods, settlements, routeways, churches, field walls and hedgerows, and perhaps strongholds and recreational spaces. Each of these facets might be studied as a subject in its own right or, alternatively, each could be regarded in terms of its relationship and contribution to the overall scene. Landscape history embraces both possibilities.

Approaches to Landscape Study

To some extent, landscape might be regarded as being composed or *surfaces* or *spaces* which are defined, linked or fragmented by *networks*. This would describe the patterns of a fieldscape in which the field-spaces were bordered by hedgerows and criss-crossed by lanes and trackways quite well, while farmsteads and churches might be incorporated as *nodes*, though facets like villages – regarded as nodes but with both surface and node characteristics – would be less easy to integrate in such an excessively reductionist approach. It is more acceptable to suggest that most rural landscapes will be found to embody the following elements.

1. Land which has sustained the human occupants for many generations, and which bears the imprints, some prominent and some masked, of centuries of human exploitation, development and redevelopment.
2. Boundaries which define the territorial extent of individual and collective ownerships, forming network patterns which variously both delimit the divisions of property and provide visible statements of a (biologically) territorial nature. These boundaries will also include functional rather than territorial boundaries, like the divisions between individual fields on a single farm. Boundaries will include those between adjacent properties and others which delimit the extents of particular jurisdictions (such as the limits of sanctuary offered by a medieval church or the bounds of an American county). Also evident in the landscape may be fossilised political boundaries marking, say, the life-sustaining territory claimed by a prehistoric community, the extent of a feudal jurisdiction or a former international divide. Prominent in some landscapes are current international or intercultural divides.
3. Monuments and constructions created by humans in association with their economic, political, social and spiritual lives. These would include castles, churches and market-places, which can be

related to particular aspects of human life or forms of behaviour, and also multi-functional monuments like the Neolithic cause-wayed enclosures (large spaces, sometimes on hilltops, which were defined by one or more ring of hyphenated banks and ditches and which seem to have spanned several aspects of life by serving as venues for religious-cum-economic-cum-political gatherings). Typically, creations such as these punctuate land-scape and serve as eye-catchers or foci of interest. Early travel-lers in the USA were often impressed by the 'natural' landscapes, but lamented the absence of highlights and reference points, like steeples, castles or ruins:

> It may seem at first sight surprising that visual images of North America should have enjoyed so little popularity in Europe at a time when travel books were so phenomenally successful. But the books themselves provide the reason. Although the American landscape is often praised in general terms it is consistently described as scenery without history or sentiment. (Honour, 1975 p. 197)

4. Settlements where the inhabitants of the landscape reside. These may form dispersed patterns of farmsteads and hamlets or nucleated clusters of concentrated settlement. Such clusters could be the products of a piecemeal accretion of dwellings or might display the traces of planned or 'regulated' development. In addition to the 'living' settlement patterns, the landscape is also likely to display traces of former patterns in the form of deserted village or farmstead sites or abandoned limbs of settle-ment associated with nucleations which have realigned and expanded in new directions while contracting elsewhere.

As a variation upon this arrangement, one might classify landscapes in functional terms into categories such as landscapes of belief and ritual (the serpent mounds in the woods of Ohio where the Hopewell tribal leaders were buried; Chartres cathedral; Rievaulx Abbey, North Yorkshire); landscapes of conflict (Maiden Castle hillfort, Dorset; West Point military academy; the Maginot Line); landscapes of recreation (Parc des Princes racecourse; New York's Central Park; the New Forest royal hunting reserve, Hampshire), as well as the agricultural and industrial landscapes.

Normally, survey work in landscape history will involve an identification and description of relevant features, followed by an analysis of their evolution and their interaction with the broader cultural landscape setting. Some official surveys may have no brief to enquire beyond the descriptive phase, seeking only to compile an inventory of the contents of a designated area, like a distribution map of prehistoric sites such as might be used to guide planning permission decisions relating to development plans. (The levels of theoretical complexity employed vary greatly; in the context of modern cultural geography some ambitious and complicated explorations of landscape development have been attempted. Domosh took the construction of the New York World Building as a topic for landscape interpretation and sought to discover how one could 'determine the links between a particular landscape artifact, its socio-economic and aesthetic contexts, and the actors who directly produced and/or created that artifact' (1989 p. 347). A relationship was established between microlevel explanations of the building as an expression of personal egos and macrolevel explanations of it as an expression of industrial capitalism.)

The description/classification stage need not be uncontroversial; many human-made features of the landscape have been misunderstood in former times and a few are still mysterious. The confusion can concern disputes or uncertainty regarding whether a type of feature is the creation of natural processes or is of a cultural origin, when a feature was created or what it was used for, or why features associated with a recognised sphere of human behaviour were actually produced. Some of these debates can be illustrated by the case of strip lynchets. Given their name by Crawford (1953) who employed a word deriving from the Old English *hlinc*, a ridge, these are cultivation terraces or benches, mostly around 200 m to 400 m in length and around 15 m to 30 m wide, which occur in groups or 'flights' to give the slopes of upland areas a stepped profile. They have been noted in Iberia and in France and are known as *rideaux* in Picardy. In England they are associated with steeply sloping ground within the lowland zone and are, where not destroyed by later cultivation activities, often associated with the scarps and dry valley slopes of chalk downlands, while in the uplands they are common on the sloping sides of the limestone Dales, where they are known as 'raines'. Around 1882 Lucas noted: 'In Wharfedale (Figure 2.1), Coverdale, Wensleydale, and on the slopes of the hills to the east of Nidderdale, the country is covered with little step-like terraces called "reins" (*pr. reeans*).' Strip lynchets are not confined to calcareous soils, and fine flights can be seen at Challacombe on Dartmoor.'

Figure 2.1 Strip lynchets pleating a hillside at Linton in Wharfedale. (Richard Muir)

The first debate about strip lynchets concerned whether or not they were natural features created by the erosion of the chalk along joint lines, by solution or through the differential erosion of interleaved bands of harder and softer rock (Scrope, 1866). In due course it was demonstrated that strip lynchets were the result of cultivation (Curwen, 1939) but arguments about their age and particular mode of formation remained, with debates concerning whether the level treads or terraces could be created by ploughing alone, or whether much more demanding construction work was involved. A fairly general agreement developed around the notion that chalk slopes were covered in a mantle of rotted material, and while some initial work with picks and spades may have been involved to 'notch' the hillsides, most of the process of lynchet creation was achieved deliberately by ploughing along a generalised contour line (P. D. Wood, 1961). Dating was complicated by the established habit of confusing strip lynchets with the so-called 'Celtic' fields of prehistoric date. However, the fact that they cut 'Celtic' fields and hillforts of the Iron Age and have been found to be underlain by Romano-British sherds suggest post-Roman dates, while Wood (1961) states:

> For the thirteenth century . . . there are the well-authenticated increases in England's population and in the prices of agricultural products; and there are conclusive signs of a spread of cultivation to lands previously considered marginal, not only into the marsh and woodland edges but also on to the hillsides. In Wiltshire, for instance, the hillside acre came to be valued at about half the county average and was to this extent regarded as marginal. (pp. 451–2)

In this way, the interpretation of one small facet of the West European landscape came into being: most (but not all) strip lynchets relate to a period of medieval overpopulation in which land-hungry peasant cultivators converted hillside pastures into mixed farming locations, raising arable crops on the artificially created terraces, while tethering livestock on the 'risers'.

Pillow mounds provide another example of continuing attempts to interpret landscape features. They are low, earthen mounds, often with an oblong, pillow-shaped plan or cigar-like outline and are usually about 30 m (around 100 feet) long and no more than 10 m (around 30 feet) broad. Often known locally as 'buries', most pillow mounds are post-medieval in date, though some belong to the late medieval period. These mounds were deliberately constructed to serve as artificial rabbit warrens when the animals were raised commercially, and in some cases, artificial stone-lined tunnels and bore holes were made, some to serve as rabbit burrows and some to improve drainage. Although there were country people living in the first quarter of the present century who could recall pillow mounds still being used to harbour rabbits, their function was generally forgotten and they were variously mistaken for Neolithic long barrows, thought to be related to Iron Age hillforts, which often contained the mounds or had them nearby, or were simply regarded as mysterious. During the 1920s an antiquarian (unfortunately named Hazzledine Warren) persisted in excavating and publishing a pillow mound at High Beech in Epping Forest in the belief that it was an Iron Age funeral pyre, even after various local old gentlemen wandered up and told him that they could remember the warren being built. Gradually, the truth about the mounds dawned in the realms of landscape history; Crawford and Keiller described some in their *Wessex from the Air* of 1928 (p. 18), though even as late as 1979 E. S. Wood wrote cautiously: 'Some may have been used as warrens later, but some apparently were built as such. It is probably safe to take them all as warrens for practical purposes' (p. 230).

In other cases, the origins and date of a class of features may be undisputed, but the nature of the human usage may be mysterious. The late Neolithic earthworks known as henges illustrate this point; they consist of a central circular space which is defined by enclosing banks and ditches. The 'double banana' form is the most characteristic, with the two semi-circular sets of banks and ditches being separated by opposed entrances and with the ditch normally being placed *within* rather than *outside* the bank, to invalidate any interpretation of the henge as a defensive enclosure. Henges range in diameter from about half a kilometre or a third of a mile to as little as about 45 m or 150 feet. Even so, the individual henge might easily be interpreted as a prehistoric temple with a central sacred area upon which rituals were performed, this being separated from the bank on which the congregation gathered by a ditch marking the division between sacred and profane ground. The thus far insoluble problem associated with this interpretation is the fact that, unlike churches, henges, large or small, frequently occur clustered in trios or in more numerous associations, and it is difficult to imagine why any local community would need more that one temple (Taylor and Muir, 1983 p. 25).

Research in landscape history can concern a single class of monument or a restricted site, but it can also involve whole landscapes: the Norfolk Broads is a case in point. In the middle reaches of the valleys of the rivers Bure, Waveney and Yare in Norfolk are more than 30 lakes or broads of irregular shapes which were assumed to be of a natural origin. It was only as the result of a combined research effort involving experts in archaeology, historical geography, geomorphology and botany that it was appreciated that the broads, with their steep, cliff-like margins and horizontal floors were in fact medieval peat diggings, whose plans related closely to the pattern of medieval property boundaries and which had supplied fuel to the town of Norwich (Lambert *et al.*, 1966). Narrow peninsulas or balks between the broads preserved boundaries, reduced flooding and provided places where the turves could be stacked and dried (Smith, 1966 p. 70). In the course of the research, more than 2 000 boreholes were made, revealing that the stratigraphy on the undisturbed land was quite different from that of the water-filled diggings. These had

flooded following the onset of a severe climatic deterioration around
AD 1300, and the wetland landscape of the Norfolk Broads had
largely come into being by the fifteenth century.

While the individual facets or components of a landscape can be
studied in considerable depth, the landscape, as an assemblage of
these components, will have its own personality. Each landscape is
quite unique in terms of its location, physical structure, contents,
climate and cultural development. It may, however, be possible to
recognise broad underlying patterns of unity and difference, making
it possible to classify landscape on a grand scale. Classification can
be a somewhat sterile exercise, but in the case of the English
landscape, the recognition that there exist two essential cultural
landscape types is leading to important new understandings of the
process of countryside formation. Williamson wrote that:

> The field systems and settlement patterns of medieval England
> displayed a bewildering range of local variation. It is, however,
> arguable that within the lowland zone too complex a system of
> localised classification can serve to obscure a more basic and
> important regional dichotomy; a dichotomy which became in-
> creasingly pronounced from the late medieval period. By the late
> sixteenth century, topographers often distinguished between
> 'woodland' and 'champion' areas of England. (1988 p. 5)

In Elizabethan times, commentators like Harrison knew that
some parts of England, the *champion country*, had extensive areas
of communal strip fields and a nucleated settlement pattern of
compact villages, while others, the *woodland country*, had dispersed
farmsteads and hamlets, more individually held fields enclosed by
hedgerows and much less extensive areas of open communal farmland. With the passage of time, this understanding of the dual
character of English countryside seems to have been forgotten. It
was revived by the historian, Homans, in 1941 (pp. 12–14), though
he favoured an unconvincing cultural explanation and attributed the
woodland countrysides to a persisting Celtic influence, while the
champion countrysides were judged to be Germanic in origin
(Figures 2.2, 2.3). Subsequently, Rackham articulated the differences between the two lowland Englands in a more refined analysis:

> On the one hand, as in Essex or Herefordshire, we have the
> England of hamlets, medieval farms in hollows of the hills, lonely

Figure 2.2 Ancient or woodland countryside is exemplified in this air photograph of Luppitt in Devon, with dispersed settlement, small, irregular fields with thick hedgerows and winding lanes. (Cambridge University collection: British Crown Copyright/MOD, reproduced with permission of the Controller of Her Britannic Majesty's Stationery Office

moats and great barns in the clay-lands, pollards and ancient trees, cavernous holloways and many footpaths, fords, irregularly-shaped groves with thick hedges colourful with maple, dogwood, and spindle – an intricate land of mystery and surprise. On the other hand there is the Cambridgeshire type of landscape, the England of big villages, few, busy roads, thin hawthorn hedges, windswept brick farms, and ivied clumps of trees in corners of fields; a predictable land of wide views, sweeping sameness, and straight lines. These I call Ancient Countryside and Planned Countryside. As slight research will show, the one is the product of at least a thousand years of continuity and most of it has altered little since 1700 . . . The other is, in the main, a mass-produced, drawing-board landscape, hurriedly laid out parish by parish under Enclosure Acts in the eighteenth and nineteenth centuries; but occasionally there survive features, notably woods, that the enclosure commissioners failed to destroy. (1986 pp. 4–5)

Figure 2.3   Planned or champion countryside is represented by scenes like this aerial view of Orwell in Cambridgeshire, with enclosed communal ploughlands defined by geometrical boundaries and a general shortage of scenic detail and variety. (Cambridge University collection)

Having dismissed the ethnic explanation for the division of England into champion and woodland countrysides, Williamson turned to the possibility of an environmental explanation based on soil types, but found:

> Dispersed settlements, enclosed fields, and irregular field systems have traditionally been associated with the late assarting of heavy clays or other 'marginal' land, and at a local level, in parts of Northamptonshire for example, there is probably much truth in such arguments. As an explanation of broad regional variations, however, arguments of this kind are much less convincing. In the south-east of England dispersed settlements and irregular field systems were not confined to the heavier clays, but could be found in areas of lighter soils . . . In short, there is no clear reason why, as a region, the south and east should have been underpopulated and under-exploited at any time in the later Saxon period compared with the Midlands and the north-east. (1988 p. 7)

The consensus view – that the division of lowland England between two landscape or countryside types took place around the closing centuries of the Anglo-Saxon era, with the establishment of communal open-field farming and the formation of nucleated villages in the emerging champion regions – was not disputed. However, Williamson believed that factors operating rather earlier were responsible for the contrasts. He tentatively suggested that repeated migrations had weakened the kin networks of the English settlers, whilst those of the Romanised British people remained strong. This weakening was most pronounced in the Midlands and north-east of England, and it may have allowed neighbourhood groups to form and develop communal responses to the problems of population pressure, which were growing as the period advanced. Arable farming expanded at the expense of woodland pasture and other grazings, the reclaimed land being partitioned among neighbours to produce highly intermixed holdings and giving rise to disputes about the relative quality of lands being apportioned, these leading in turn to the establishment of communal open-field farming in the champion countrysides.

Whatever the origins of the two distinct landscape types, their nature was such that they would guide the future development of their countrysides. In the *woodland* or *ancient* countryside areas, the emphasis was, and would be, on continuity and evolutionary processes. These landscapes contained many ancient features at the time when the *champion* countrysides were forming in adjacent areas, and many of these features would be retained. Patterns of small, densely-hedged fields, deeply hollowed and winding lanes, scattered farmsteads and hamlets and numerous small woods can be seen in Devon, the Welsh Marches and Essex today, just as comparable patterns could have been seen there two or three thousand years ago. In the *champion* or *planned* countryside areas, in contrast, the emphasis lay on revolutionary change. Such change produced, probably simultaneously, the nucleation of settlement and the creation of vast communal strip fields surrounding the new villages.

Sometimes around five centuries after these changes, sometimes in less time, but often scarcely at all, the enclosure and privatisation of land by agreement between village neighbours would gradually dismantle the detailed strip patterns of communal farming. Where the outlines of the champion network survived in living systems of farming for around a thousand years, Parliamentary Enclosure would replace one regulated landscape with another, as the commissioners superimposed a geometrical partitioning into private ownership across the areas of late Saxon or Norman communal farming. And so today, driving across parishes – or even between parts of one parish – one can see the contrast between the angular Enclosure patterns of old champion countryside contrasting with the organic, serpentine lines and heavy hedgerows of ancient countryside.

The study of landscape history can be approached in different ways. These could involve:

(a) the investigation of a particular monument or a class of such monuments, like pillow mounds;

(b) the study of a site or group of similar sites where several types of cultural features are associated, like those of deserted villages, with their holloways, house platforms, fishponds and so on, or hamlets, or courtyard farms (where farmstead, barns, rick yard, middens and byres are grouped around a central courtyard);

(c) the study of areas embracing an association of different sites and monuments, like a section of valley floor locality with dwellings, a watermill and watermeadows, or complete landscapes.

Throughout, the emphasis is upon explanation (rather, say, than on appreciation, as in many aesthetic studies). Landscape historians may feel quite passionately about the beauty and character of their areas of study, but today they will seldom wish to compromise their reputations for detached objectivity by admitting to such emotions or by extolling the visual attractions of places in print. While it is a characteristic of the subject that sites are *in themselves* considered suitable subjects for study, landscape history is not wholly rooted in empiricism. Thus, as with the example of woodland and champion countrysides, or with the recognition that regulation or planning was a commonly occurring feature of medieval villages, landscape historians also seek to build valid generalisations from their investigation of the particular.

The Techniques of Landscape History

It is a strongly pronounced characteristic of landscape history that practitioners need to be aware of (or conversant with) a spectrum of different, and sometimes difficult and specialised, investigative techniques. These involve crafts or sciences like air photograph interpretation; the translation of medieval documents; botanical indentification, and topographical survey work. In addition, landscape historians will quite frequently call upon the expertise of scientists trained in specialisms like carbon-14 dating techniques, palynology (the investigation and identification of ancient pollen grains) or dendrochronology (obtaining dates for wooden objects from tree ring counts). The landscape historian cannot be expected to be skilled in all the different areas of expertise from surveying to archaeological excavation, but he or she should be able to take account of their potential contribution to relevant fields of enquiry.

In addition, landscape history involves attributes which are innate or acquired but which cannot be taught: flair, intuition and experience. Flair will often concern an ability to penetrate a forest of information in order to make a decisive connection. Intuition concerns a strong sense that things have happened in a certain way without the ability to convert the hunch into fact. It can exert a powerful influence in landscape history, where facts can be hard to come by, but it has the capacity to entice one further and further from the true course of events. Experience is particularly valuable for the way in which it will enable the landscape historian to recognise the replication of a pattern of events or identifications accomplished on previous occasions. Frequently, the clues embodied in countryside are too subtle to be communicated in words or images, so that prior experiences of similar phenomena as encountered in the field are invaluable.

The most important specialist sources of evidence employed by landscape historians can be outlined as follows.

Air photographs

These represent some of the most widely useful and, frequently, most accessible sources of information.

The earliest examples were taken over Paris by a balloonist in the 1850s, but it was not until the 1914–18 war that the practical applications of air photography were seriously explored, and in this war, the aerial reconnaissance of enemy dispositions and the prevention of such reconnaissance were the primary roles allocated to the opposed air arms. As a result of the improvements in technology and an enormous multiplication in the numbers of trained pilots resulting from the war, private enthusiasts began to explore the peacetime applications of aerial photography, several of them having discovered independently that unsuspected archaeological features were visible from the air. Most notable of the pioneer aerial archaeologists of Britain were Major G. W. G. Allen who compiled an important archive of photographs of the Oxford region and the outstandingly influential archaeologist O. G. S. Crawford who with A. Keiller, published a remarkable collection of archaeological studies in *Wessex from the Air* in 1928. (Muir, 1983 p. 12)

It was around this time that a recognition of the significance of 'cropmarks' advanced the value of air photography. These are patterns produced on photographs by the shadows cast in cultivated areas where certain plants within a crop grow taller or else are more stunted than their neighbours, or are riper or less ripe, with the differences in ripeness being reflected in colour variations. The patterns are largely produced by differences in the soil and subsoil, with plants growing over silted-up ditches being able to develop deeper root runs and so growing taller and ripening more slowly than their neighbours. In contrast, plants growing in the thin, parched soils covering the rubble from tumbled walls will be more stunted and will ripen faster than those in adjacent areas. Such marks are most apparent in grain crops and are scarcely visible in grassland, where they may only be detected during the spring flush of growth. However, when pastures or parks are subjected to unusually long periods of drought, the 'parch-marks' developing in the most desiccated areas will indicate features, like wall footings or road beds, which lie below the surface. Most pronounced in cereals, cropmarks may be poorly developed but evident in root crops. The clarity of all cropmarks will vary from year to year, depending whether the pattern of weather in the growing season has encouraged deep root penetration of the soil in search of moisture or else has favoured shallow, horizontal root speads. Less clearcut patterns are produced by 'soil-marks' in bare, arable land, which may show the dark, humus-rich soil which has developed in ditches, hollows and natural watercourses, though the marks tend to have a 'blurred' or 'smeared' appearance and will vanish after a few seasons of deep ploughing. Cropmarks were identified by land-based observers during the nineteenth century and were recognised at different sites in the Thames

Figure 2.4 Air photography is a technique of immense value to the landscape historian. In this picture of the deserted medieval village of Hamilton, Lincolnshire, and its setting one can see the remains of the village in the centre of the picture, with its main street surviving as a holloway, its property boundaries and house sites and a rectangular homestead moat, while medieval ridge and furrow patterns give the surrounding fields a corduroy-like texture. (Cambridge University collection)

Valley by the antiquarians John Stone and F. Haverfield, while perhaps the first cropmarks to be detected in air photographs were those revealing the Big Rings henge at Dorchester on Thames, which were taken in 1922–3 (Aston and Rowley, 1974 p. 187).

In Britain during the 1930s, air photography came to be regarded as a serious technique for archaeological discovery, while during the 1939–45 war, intelligence requirements resulted in further technological advances in aircraft and equipment. After the war, J.K. St Joseph, one of the leading wartime air reconnaissance analysts, was appointed to a Curatorship in Aerial Photography at Cambridge University, and in 1962 the university acquired an aircraft; in the course of the next two decades an archive of more than a third of a million pictures was compiled and hundreds of new archaeological sites were discovered.

The photographs used in archaeological and historical work are normally in monochrome and come in two types, 'obliques' and 'verticals'. The former will normally have been taken with a 35 mm or medium format camera pointed through the side windows of the cockpit, and they show a perspective view framed both downwards and across the landscape. Such photographs tend to have a strong perspective aspect, similar to that enjoyed when viewing countryside or townscape from the top of a nearby hill. These photographs, often taken at low altitude, may portray antiquities very well, but they are far from being maps and the distortions resulting from perspective make the plotting of data accurately on to a map by conventional methods very difficult. Vertical air photographs are normally obtained using a large format camera mounted on the floor of the aircraft and pointing directly downwards. In visual terms, they tend to flatten relief and produce results which are less aesthetically appealing, but which can be transferred to a map without much difficulty. During survey work with a large format camera the aircraft is normally flown along a prescribed course at a specified height and speed, and photographs are taken at predetermined intervals to obtain a map-like mosaic coverage.

Air photographs have played a crucial role in the recognition of important facts like the ubiquity of prehistoric communities and the frequency of deserted medieval settlements, both being unexpected and difficult to establish without the evidence from aerial cameras. The images are, however, neutral in matters of temporal and functional identification, inviting the observer to judge or misjudge the information presented. Confronted with landscape features revealed in air photographs, the novice must first determine whether they are of a natural or an artificial nature. Having done this, the next task is to identify the features; here the opportunities to fail may be many, and there is no substitute for the experience gained from previous similar determinations. Sometimes, patterns deriving from modern activities, such as pipe-laying, military engineering and mechanical cultivation, can resemble ancient features (Taylor, 1974, p. 20), while some older features, such as pillow mounds and long barrows, may sometimes appear similar.

Where the more extensive settlement sites are concerned, one must remember that occupation may well have persisted through several centuries, so that the air photographs do not map a moment in the prehistory or history of a landscape, but a long sequence of events. During this sequence, houses could have been demolished and rebuilt in slightly different situations, tracks could have cut across abandoned paddocks, and generations will have been born and have died. In this way, a site depicted as containing a cluster of, say, five circular Iron Age dwellings might not be that of an ancient hamlet, but rather a place where a solitary farmstead was established and then rebuilt and slightly repositioned on four separate occasions. In addition, the density of ancient settlement is not directly proportional to the cropmarks discovered: some subsoil and geological types are particularly responsive to the aerial camera, while others reveal little. The terraces of alluvial gravel which flank many English rivers produce exceptionally fine cropmark images (Webster and Hobley, 1964), and these encourage further surveys which lead to a further overemphasis on the relative importance of these areas on distribution maps of ancient settlement and cultivation. Chalk and limestone also tend to yield good results, but in the Yorkshire Dales the apparent disappearance of evidence of ancient human activity as one passes from the thin, alkaline soils of the Carboniferous Limestone to the sour, coarse or silty soils of the Millstone Grit must greatly overstate any preference that may have existed for the limestone localities.

Earthworks

These are undulations of the land surface which are the last surviving forms of features created by humans. They are, in the long term, perishable features, so that while medieval earthwork sites are quite common, those of a prehistoric age are much more rare. If protected by a carpet of turf, a set of earthworks will have a very long life indeed; but if subject to modern deep ploughing, a system will disappear within a few years. Earthworks will often appear in air photographs, when they are revealed as shadow marks, the images seen from the air being particularly decisive when the ridges, trenches and hollows are lit by the dawn or evening sun, producing long shadows which display even the shallowest of topographical variations. Normally, earthwork sites are much more prominent than cropmark sites when viewed from the ground, though they do share some features in common: they pose problems of identification and they need not necessarily represent the product of a brief moment of human construction work.

When confronted by a set of earthworks, the (novice) landscape historian must first deduce whether the pattern is caused by natural or human agency. This should not be difficult, though occasionally confusion may occur, as with the medieval garden terraces at a site in Wensleydale (North Yorkshire) which were regarded until recently as a natural terracing caused by the differential erosion of the limestone strata of the slope. The experienced observer will easily recognise the gently curving corrugations of medieval (or later) ridge and furrow ploughland, the hollowed street – and ditch-bounded house plot patterns of deserted medieval villages and the track-side shelves which served as platforms for houses, which now survive as raised, rectangular outlines. Some features can confuse because of their similarity in form, so that a low, bowl-shaped mound might, if poorly preserved, be a Bronze Age barrow, a small Norman motte or the remains of the later medieval mound which had carried a windmill (Figure 2.5).

Earthworks found in close association need not necessarily represent a particular period or function, and very useful chronological information may be displayed. Here, the geological principle of superimposition may be invoked, so that if a system of field boundary earthworks is found to be superimposed upon a system of hillfort defences, the fields *must* be younger than the ramparts and ditches that they cut across. This principle is not restricted to earthworks and Williamson (1987) demonstrated that fields charted on nineteenth-century maps of Norfolk must have been in existence when they were overlain by a Roman road. The road detached various triangles of land as it ran across the network of rectangular prehistoric fields. Earthworks can provide special insights into the evolution of countrysides: there are various woods which are presumed to be the surviving vestiges of ancient woodland, yet which contain the unmistakable corrugations of ridge and furrow ploughland, while other woods can be found still to be enclosed by the woodbanks which defined their medieval extents. Earthwork

Figure 2.5   The landscape historian must read the clues contained in the landscape. Here the slight hollow winding between the trees was once the High Street of the village of Childerley in Cambridgeshire. (Richard Muir)

evidence should always be sought and considered, for: 'As is so often the case, what appears as a relatively simple picture when viewed from maps or superficially on the ground, inevitably takes on a highly complex appearance, perhaps impossible to interpret, when treated to analytical field survey' (Brown and Taylor, 1993, p. 107).

Old maps

Reasonably accurate maps that were drawn to a large scale and packed with detail were commissioned by the owners of numerous lowland English estates in the Elizabethan period. Where such maps are available one's understanding of the locality is suddenly catapulted from a rather fuzzy and gap-ridden vision of the medieval landscape, which is based on earthworks, fragmentary documentary references and air photographs, to a situation of intimate acquaintanceship, for every house and every chimney, every hedge, pond and

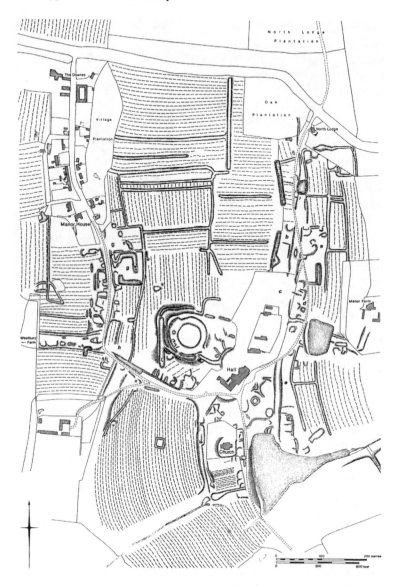

Figure 2.6   The skills of two landscape historians were employed to chart the earthworks of settlement, gardens and plough ridges at Croxton in Cambridgeshire, allowing a reconstruction of the history of the locality. (From A.E. Brown and C.C. Taylor, Cambridgeshire Earthwork Surveys VI, *Proceedings of the Cambridge Antiquarian Society*, vol LXXXII (1993).)

gate may be faithfully represented. Maps such as these are of incalculable value to the landscape historian, but availability is restricted and the range, quality and number of old maps available for study will vary from place to place. Ideally, what the landscape historian seeks is a long sequence of detailed large-scale maps which were produced at regular intervals and which therefore record the successive stages in landscape evolution. What is actually available may be far less, particularly in the more backwoodsy upland areas, where the sequence may begin with a late eighteenth-century commercially produced map at a scale only of around one inch to a mile, followed by the later but more accurate state-sponsored surveys of the nineteenth century.

When dealing with the older maps one must be aware of the shortcomings in technique which formerly existed and aware, too, that measures of artistic licence may have been employed. Thomas Jefferys was a highly-regarded engraver, but when his atlas of Yorkshire was published in 1772 it accorded Ingleborough a height of 5280 feet though the hill is but 2373feet (723 m) high (Raistrick, 1969 p. 51). Also, it is impossible to deduce when he employed a rectangular dot as a convention to represent a specific building, and when it was used in a more generalised way. Large-scale maps could exist as military instruments which provided the artillery with information about ranges and elevations: early cartography had an important political dimension. Improvements in the quality of mapping depended on technological improvements to surveying instruments and on the establishment of a triangulation survey to enable the exact positioning of locations. In Britain, triangulation began with the establishment of a five-mile baseline on Hounslow Heath by General William Roy, which required the use of a special brass scale, 42 inches in length, and the manufacture of theodolites. A triangulation connecting England and France and linking the observatories of Paris and Greenwich was proposed in 1783 and completed in 1787, providing the basis for an accurately surveyed map of Kent at a scale of one inch to one mile, with maps of Sussex and Essex following. The triangulation necessary for a mapping of England and Wales was completed in 1809 and the one inch to one mile survey proceeded during the next three decades. However, in 1824, when Parliament made available funds for the survey of Ireland, the much larger scale of six inches to one mile was adopted. This scale is of far more value to the landscape historian, and the 'six inch' maps of the UK produced in the second half of the nineteenth century are enormously useful.

Britain has the best old map coverage in the world, but the availability of material can vary greatly from locality to locality. Occasionally, large-scale estate maps are available, generally followed in the second half of the eighteenth century by commercially produced maps at scales of one or two inches to the mile by cartographers and engravers such as John Roque and Thomas Jefferys. The Enclosure movement, mainly current in the period 1750–1850, gave rise to some very useful large-scale surveys, with the production of pre-Enclosure maps (commissioned by neighbouring landowners who were keen to obtain an enclosure of lands in their parish by agreement) and the more numerous Enclosure maps, which depicted and determined the patterns of property in a parish following the deliberations of the appointed commissioners. Where there had been no Enclosure Act, a Tithe Award map, dating from the years after 1836, when church tithes in kind were being commuted into money payments, was produced. These maps showed each parcel of land and detail of land use in a parish and they were often produced at the very useful scale of 25 inches to the mile. The maps resulting from the six-inch survey covered England and Wales between 1853 and 1893, and thereafter the changes to the landscape can be traced through the successive editions of the Ordnance Survey maps.

In an 'old' country, such as the UK, the historic maps have tended to depict what was already there but in a 'young' country, such as the USA, the map may serve as a blueprint or template for future development. In North America there were the small-scale surveys produced during the initial exploration of uncharted lands, while surveys at a larger scale were associated not with recording the patterns of human occupance, but in establishing frameworks within which the patterns of occupance and ownership would take place. Sometimes, the surveyor reigned supreme, but sometimes terrain patterns exerted an influence:

> Right-angled planning is eminently suitable for level, uninterrupted land. But it is foiled in hilly areas. In the United States, regional and local differences challenged settlers to adjust ecologically to the survey's design . . . In the Upper Mississippi Hill Country, settled mainly after 1832, the 'forty' [forty-acre tract] was an effective modular unit and a formative influence. Had

smaller parcels been available, attempts to adjust the layout of pioneer farms to the hills and valleys of the region might have been more sophisticated. But the cost of surveying and mapping tracts smaller than forty acres would have been prohibitive. (Johnson, 1978 p. 220)

The adoption of rectilinear property grids at an early stage in the settlement of the USA greatly conditioned the subsequent patterns and determined the existence of straight streets, square blocks and right-angled intersections. It had psychological and emotional repercussions, leading to an enthusiasm for informal, curvilinear forms:

> English landscape gardening attained increasing popularity in America during the nineteenth century, and rejection of rectangularity was associated with the back-to-nature movement, which imparted great momentum to the protective attitude of wilderness lovers during the twentieth century. Ideas of nature and wilderness became linked to the desire for deliverance from the discipline imposed by straight lines. (Johnson, 1978 p. 227)

But familiarity led to the entrenchment of ideas, so that when Canada produced a special stamp designed according to a worldwide settlement theme in 1972 to honour the 22nd International Geographical Conference it showed a grid of 100 squares with the human geography conforming to this net, even though the Old World was full of cultural landscapes which were quite devoid of any grid influences.

Other documents

The documents which record the history of a landscape will be of many different types and ages, and could be in different languages too. In the case of England, where the documentation of landscape has the longest history, the sequence begins around the seventh century with Anglo-Saxon charters which conveyed property from one owner to another. They were generally in Latin and written to a fairly standard formula; sometimes they included a perambulation of the bounds of the estate concerned, which was usually in Old English. The clerks who drafted these charters would have been priests, the only literate members of the population, and may frequently have been attached to minster churches sited on royal estates. The next major source of information is the celebrated Domesday Book of 1086, which was hurriedly compiled to provide William I with a detailed inventory of the taxable assets of his realm. Latin remained the language for legal documents for most of the Middle Ages but, from Tudor times, English became the most important language used in the historical sources although the handwritten forms of English evolve very considerably, with the calligraphy of some periods being easily legible today, whilst that of others is quite difficult.

The perambulations provided in the Saxon charters, with their many mentions of hedges, tracks, pastures and wetlands, can provide useful information about the sort of land uses present in the countrysides of those times. Where such a charter exists it will provide the earliest description of a locality, and give at least a crude impression of whether it was largely cultivated or partly forested, open or enclosed, and how it was partitioned. Taken together, numerous charters relating to regional or provincial units will give broader pictures about the nature of land use and the facets of the landscape. Thus, in terms of England as a whole, Rackham notes that:

> out of 14,342 objects in all English charters, hedges are mentioned (under eight different terms) 378 times; that is, 2.64 per cent of the features are hedges. In North-West Dorset, words for 'hedge' occur 33 times among 526 objects, or 6 per cent; in the Dorset Chalklands, hedges are named six times among 531 objects, or 1 per cent. (1986 p. 12)

Domesday Book must be the world's most celebrated survey. It contains a wealth of valuable historical information, but is frequently misunderstood and mistaken for an attempt to create some sort of archive for the local historians of the future. It is also assumed that the entries record villages and their surroundings, though in fact the fundamental units concerned are estates: the Book does not record communities and their settlements, but the properties of estate owners. When Domesday was being compiled the commissioners sought to discover the answers to a series of questions, such as the number of ploughs that were employed, the value of the estate in the reign of Edward the Confessor (1042–66), and the value in 1086, though the form in which the information was presented varied as the survey proceeded. What was included was remarkable, although the omissions were considerable, including many churches and extensive amounts of common grazing land. In Yorkshire, the gathering of data seems to have been hurried and wayward, and the commissioners may have been rushed to meet their deadline (Palliser, 1993).

Later documents from the medieval centuries can be used to demonstrate the existence and size of communities, so that the records of the poll tax of 1377 show that the doomed North-amptonshire village of Fawsley was then still flourishing, for 90 adults from the locality paid their four pennies (Beresford, 1971, p. 111). The rolls of the manor courts record the local pattern of disputes and misdemeanours, and from the records one can learn a great deal about the nature and evolution of the surrounding countryside, as when villagers are fined for making illegal clearings or 'assarts' in the wood, for damaging the lord's watermill, stealing fish from his artificial fishponds or refusing to work in a sodden meadow.

Landscape archaeology and environmental evidence

Today, the funds for archaeological *excavation* work are in short supply, so little is undertaken except for rescue digs at threatened sites and the emphasis falls heavily on non-invasive methodologies. Landscape historians (sometimes themselves archaeologists) are very keen to learn the results of archaeological excavations, and in earlier times, when attitudes towards invasive techniques in archae-ology were much more relaxed, enthusiasts who were frequently unskilled would attempt excavations. In areas of arable farming, much can be learned from *field-walking*, which does not damage sites and does not demand specialised expertise. The underlying concept involves the notion that most prehistoric, medieval and later communities consumed large amount of pottery, which was widely used for containers in the days when peasant dwellings contained very little carpentry. When pots were broken, the sherds were either trampled into the earthen floor or thrown out on the midden. Some of the broken pottery from the midden would be spread on the land with the manure, to form a thin but widespread distribution. But wherever the field-walker encounters concentrations of sherds, a former settlement site is indicated.

Not only can field-walking indicate the pattern of lost farmsteads, hamlets and villages in a locality, it can also date their appearance and disappearance, for each age has produced its own distinct forms and fabrics of peasant wares, and a site with concentrations of pottery spanning the twelfth to seventeenth centuries can be assumed to have been occupied during that period. Systematic field-walking of an area may reveal not only prehistoric or later sherds, but could produce fragments of gritstone querns used for grinding grain, coins, metal tools and weapons, as well as ancient flint tools and the scatters of flint debris resulting from their manufacture.

Less accessible, but of great value in the reconstruction of former landscapes, is the infomation derived from *pollen analysis.* Pollen grains are very durable, and under favourable circumstances they can survive for many thousands of years; suitable conditions of waterlogging and acidity for pollen survival are provided in peat bogs and lake sediments. Most plants (but not the different grasses) produce pollen of a distinctive form which is identifiable under the microscope, but an estimation of the former vegetational pattern cannot simply be deduced from counting the grains of different species from deposits of a known age. Allowances have to be made for the ways in which the pollen of different species was dispersed, with the wind-pollinated ones tending to produce clouds of grains, while those that relied on insects produced far less. Each plant species has its own pattern of pollen distribution, with the extent of the dispersal and the amount of pollen produced varying considerably. When allowance has been made for all this, the pollen count from a dated site can be used to recreate the landscape of the period concerned, with the detection of cereal pollen and that of weeds associated with disturbed ground indicating the presence of farming, just as an increase in grass pollen in a wooded landscape might denote the creation of clearings in which animals, attracted by the pasture, could be stalked and killed. Caution is used, for changes in vegetational patterns could be due to 'natural' processes, such as climatic change. Normally, pollen diagrams for particular sites are presented in a form which demonstrates the relative rises and falls in the importance of tree species, indicating the effects of climatic change and human interventions.

Where suitable acid wetland and lakebed sites exist, palynology may be the most useful technique available for the reconstruction of the landscapes of the distant past, but in the countries of the western world it is much less useful for work on the medieval or more recent periods; modern interference with many sites and problems of fine-tuning the carbon-14 dating techniques for accuracy in terms of decades rather than centuries are responsible for this. In most cases, the evidence from a pollen site is particular to that place rather than to a broad landscape. Some of the pollen will have been produced locally and some will have drifted in from much further away; the degree to which the evidence from the site is indicative of the botanical patterning of the landscape will diminish with distance from that site: factors such as the direction of the prevailing winds mean that this diminution will not be a simple function of linear distance. Other environmental evidence can be obtained from durable indicators of former conditions, such as the wing cases of beetles or the shells of snails, for particular species were adapted to restricted local conditions – so that the discovery of the shells of snails of a type associated with woodland along just one side of an ancient ditch would probably indicate the existence there of a hedgerow (Powlesland, Haughton and Hanson, 1986).

The Components of Landscape

A humanised or cultural landscape is an assemblage of components which reflect the different uses applied to the natural land surface. These components will be found in different combinations and in different forms, so that the distinctiveness of any landscape will derive from the quantitative and qualitative aspects of the components present. In this way, fields or woodland might be present in particular ratios, be completely dominant or completely absent, while the fields in a fieldscape could be vast or small; open or enclosed; irregular or geometric in plan; organised in local networks or in co-axial systems covering large areas; hedged, ditched, walled or fenced; and if walled, the style of walling could range across a dozen or more different constructional and geological types. Each component in the landscape has its own functional *raison d'être* and its own evolutionary history.

Amongst the *networks*, boundaries play important roles in partitioning territory and in determining future patterns of landscape development. They can be amongst the most important and prominent of landscape features, as with the boundary which formerly marked simultaneously the division between East and West Germany, NATO and the Warsaw Pact and the worlds of capitalism and state socialism, and whose presence was marked in the landscape by depopulated and deforested zones, border observation posts, minefields and barbed wire entanglements. At the other end of the spectrum of importance are the boundaries marked by garden fences or hedgerows. Border landscapes have their own distinctive characteristics, although such landscapes exist in many forms. The scenic qualities associated with a frontier may exist within the current political context, or they may endure as relics of a former political situation. With regard to 'living' border landscapes, Prescott noted that:

> The boundary may be identified in the landscape by two sets of features. First there is the indication of the boundary by means of markers, cut lines, fences and notices. Second there are various constructions designed to allow the smooth application of state functions at or near the boundary. Many travellers will be familiar with customs posts located near barriers across main roads, and stations built on the boundary to allow passengers to be subjected to custom and immigration regulations. (1965 p. 92)

In addition, there are the many features which derive from the existence of the boundary as a division between two different political, economic and cultural worlds. Contrasts in the tariff and subsidy policies employed on different sides of a state boundary can result in different patterns of land use being visible on opposite sides of the boundary, the differences reflecting contrasts in the artificial agricultural environments created by the two governments concerned. The cultural differences encountered in border landscapes are many: for example, the boundary marking a divide between the languages used in street signs, in the architecture displayed in temples or the colours employed to paint street furniture and public transport vehicles. The boundary beween India and Pakistan marks the interface between the brilliant hues of the Hindu cultural arena and the drab costumes favoured in that part of the Muslim world. Finally, the border landscape may either reflect the repulsion of industries which shun strategically vulnerable and invasion-prone and peripheral localities or, conversely, it may exert a special attraction to industries which are enticed to special tariff-free trading areas, cheap immigrant cross-border labour or access to an adjacent market.

Relict or fossilised border landscapes come in many forms. The most celebrated is that of the Great Wall of China, long stretches of which have been restored to a seemingly pristine appearance and

Figure 2.7   Boundaries of many kinds traverse the historic landscapes. Life depended upon land and territories had to be demarcated and defended. The territorial frontierwork of Devil's Dyke is still undated, but it may well belong to the late Roman or early Saxon periods. The effort involved in creating the banks and ditches of such earlier linear earthworks underlines the importance attached to safeguarding land. (Richard Muir)

different sections serve as attractions for domestic and foreign tourists. The wall, which was built to exclude barbarians and restrict the diffusion of agricultural innovations within the Chinese population, lies just a few miles from Beijing and far within the frontiers of the centralised modern state. The relict border landscape which is found in a broad zone on either side of the administrative boundary between England and Scotland reflects the longevity of hostilities in this area, with Hadrian's Wall, built after AD 122, marking a period-ical frontier in the confrontation between the Roman Empire and the proto-Pictish tribes of Scotland, while a number of castles and smaller tower houses, peel towers and bastles commemorate the later antagonisms which ended with the Anglo-Scottish Act of Union of 1707. Frontier landscapes have their own physical characteristics, which may take the form of linear defence works; forts, garrison posts and blockhouses; trading posts; roads and railways which approach the boundary but do not cross it; customs posts; and so on.

P. D. Wood studied the relics of the medieval Anglo-Welsh frontier surviving in Welsh border towns and found that:

> The civilizations which created these towns all expanded from lowland Britain, using urban settlements to hold conquered territory. In contrast, the Welsh contribution to the layout of these towns, apart from the sites of churches dedicated to Dark Age saints, came only in the eighteenth century with the Nonconformist chapels. The cardinal factor in town situation has been the desire by lowlanders to command the routeways into the Celtic west. (1952 p. 54)

He concluded that:

> Considered in general, the pre-industrial Welsh border town was a one-sided affair, a military creation which was really the *English* border town. It has left its mark on the present townscape, but with varying degrees of survival from town to town. Nevertheless the frontier relics . . . are the principal distinguishing features of these towns in the Welsh borderland. The atmosphere evoked by ancient defences, the evidence in masonry and brick and timber of borderland commerce, the efforts of tourist conscious preservation societies are, in combination, sufficient to suggest the regional type. (p. 62)

On medieval England's other frontier, the question of whether frontier location affected settlement or vice versa was investigated by Barrow, who discovered influences in both directions and noted that:

> The pattern of Northumbrian and Cumbrian castles, almost all of them built on the south side of a river crossing, the great bridgehead of Newcastle upon Tyne and the forbidding promontory fortress at Tynemouth serving as the exceptions to prove the rule, cannot be due to accident. They were certainly planned in the knowledge that the Border lay only a short distance to the north and was a mere line which could be crossed at will. A similar pattern may be discerned in Scotland, though it is not so sharply marked. Berwick upon Tweed, Roxburgh, Jedburgh, Peebles, and Hermitage all stood on the north side of the river crossings they

guarded, Roxburgh and Peebles making good use of the angle between two streams. (1996 p. 20)

Frontier landscapes also have their own distinct cultures. The most celebrated of all frontier theories was that published by the American historian, F. J. Turner, in 1893. As an American patriot, Turner was anxious to emphasise the home-grown origin of American institutions, society and national character. Since it was plain that (white) immigrants had imported their European cultures with them, it was necessary to demonstrate the existence of some process of Americanisation which had transformed the European cultural baggage into new sets of outlooks and values. This role, he argued, had been performed by the frontier, where people from a variety of European cultural backgrounds were transformed by the demands imposed by the untamed physical environment. In adapting themselves to meet these challenges, the immigrants shed their old identities and emerged with new, American identities. Turner wrote that:

> For a moment, at the frontier, the bonds of custom are broken and unrestraint is triumphant. There is not *tabula rasa*. The stubborn American environment is there with its imperious summons to accept its conditions; the inherited ways of doing things are also there; and yet, in spite of environment, and in spite of custom, each frontier did indeed furnish a new field of opportunity, a gate of escape from the bondage of the past; and freshness, and confidence, and scorn of older society, impatience of its restraints and its ideas, and indifference to its lessons, have accompanied the frontier. What the Mediterranean Sea was to the Greeks, breaking the bond of custom, offering new experiences, calling out new institutions and activities, that, and more, the ever retreating frontier has been to the United States directly, and to the nations of Europe more remotely. (p. 227)

Turner's ideas received a rapturous reception when first announced, though subsequently they have been widely criticised and are generally regarded as belonging to a romanticised and politically partial interpretation of the frontier (see Berkhofer, 1964). Even so, there is good reason to regard frontier populations as having their own distinctive cultural traits, as represented by the Cossacks of Tsarist Russia or the marcher lords of the frontiers of medieval England.

Frontier zones containing international political boundaries are not found in most landscapes, though the majority of landscapes are criss-crossed by numerous property boundaries. In addition to the current or 'living' boundaries here may also be the visible traces of relict boundaries. In parts of the lowland English countryside these may be marked by long hedgerows pursuing serpentine courses across fieldscapes which are mainly patterned by much shorter hedges:

> But there is one aspect of the estate-boundary, as given in the charter of 976, which is worth dwelling upon for the light it throws on a minor feature of the English landscape. At one point on its eastern boundary, the charter takes us 'along the way to the old ditch'. Walking along this boundary with the help of the 2½-inch Ordnance map, one finds onself dropping down a steep hillside along a cart-track which is shut in on either side by an earthen bank several feet high, i.e., a hollow way. This hollow way – 'the old ditch' – was already 'old' in the tenth century. It can hardly be doubted that it represents the ancient boundary between the estate of Hyple and his ancestors to the west, and that of another (unknown) Celtic landowner to the east. (Hoskins, 1955 p. 31)

Such hedgerows can preserve the courses of ancient estate boundaries which are perhaps a thousand – or even more than two thousand – years old, while Bronze Age boundaries of different kinds have been recognised in several parts of the English uplands. On the Hambleton Hills in Yorkshire, territorial boundaries were marked by alignments of round barrows or Bronze Age burial mounds, which followed the watersheds; later in the Bronze Age, as territorial rivalries increased, these were superseded by 'linear earthworks' composed of banks and ditches, which linked up the barrow landmarks. Similarly, in the Yorkshire Wolds nearby, the building of round barrows ended about 1600BC and great efforts were devoted to building linear boundaries or 'entrenchments' around estates. Features from these ancient partitionings of the countryside can still be traced in the landscape (Spratt, 1981).

Within the boundary network which criss-crosses cultural landscapes there are political boundaries and property boundaries as well as other boundaries which represent a purely functional partitioning of a single property. Sometimes the different levels of boundary are recognisable, as in some English counties like Devon, where single hedgerows mark the ordinary field boundaries, while double hedgerows or double-ditched lanes may mark the very old parish and estate boundaries. Hoskins gave Armourwood Lane in East Devon as an example:

> It originated as a boundary (probably in the seventh century) between the royal estate of Silverton and the Exeter Abbey estate. A double ditch was dug out by slave-labour, and the earth thrown up to form hedgebanks on each side. The 'two-fold ditch' thus becomes a sunken lane running as far as the Saxon boundary required. (Hoskins, 1955 p. 68)

In many different countrysides the most significant patterning of the landscape is provided by the field boundaries. These can be formed by hedgerows, walls, fences or ditches and so on; be organic and curvilinear or planned and geometrical; and be current or living or else relict and existing as earthworks or cropmarks.

In England, archaeological evidence has demonstrated the use of hedgerows in prehistoric times, while the earliest documentary evidence reveals that hedgerows were a common facet of the Anglo-Saxon countryside; we have already noted that 2.64 per cent of landscape features recorded in the charters of this period are hedges (Rackham, 1986 p. 12). Hedgerows vary in their visual qualities, and much of this difference is related to their botanical compositions. It has been suggested (Pollard, Hooper and Moore, 1974) that the botanical composition of a hedgerow indicates its age, which was deducible by applying the formula:

Age of hedge equals ($99 \times$ the number of shrub species) -16

which was frequently applied in the form:

Age of hedge equals number of shrub species per 30 yards $\times$ 100

In fact it has been shown that hedgerow 'dating' of this kind cannot work (Muir, 1996) though in many areas of English countryside one can recognise a difference between the dense, curving old hedgerows, which may be rich in species or be composed of a few highly competitive and invasive species (such as elm or blackthorn), and hedgerows of the eighteenth and nineteenth centuries, which are generally of hawthorn with a few other species which rapidly win footholds (such as wild rose, sycamore, bramble and ash).

Walls tend to be employed as field boundaries in upland areas where stone is abundant and accessible, but where the environmental conditions may be too harsh to favour shrub growth. They tend only to feature in the lowland scene in places where there are exceptional conditions of stone abundance and suitability. It has recently been demonstrated that the ages of walls can sometimes be related to their appearance (Hodges and Wildgoose, 1980). Some of the oldest were built of boulders gathered from the land during the initial agricultural colonisation, while medieval walls sometimes had a bottom course of large, irregular, partially embedded boulders or 'orthostats'. Such walls demonstrate the problems which may be encountered in dating field boundaries, for the technique of building orthostatic walls:

> was widely used in the prehistoric period, for example in the Dartmoor reave [Bronze Age land boundary] walls as well as on the North York Moors . . . In Derbyshire the method was shown to be Romano-British. At Kildale in North Yorkshire the 13th century deer park wall is partly orthostatic. In certain parts of the country it has persisted into modern times, as in the Orkney Islands. (Spratt, 1988 p. 150)

A survey of 'living' orthostatic field walls in the North York Moors suggested dates in the period 1550–1750, with the walls often being built during a process of reclamation on the boundary earthworks of fields colonised in the twelfth century and abandoned in the fourteenth century following the eruption of the Black Death (Spratt, 1988, p. 155). If the walls of 'primitive' construction pose problems, those built during the eighteenth and nineteenth centuries (largely to implement the Parliamentary Enclosure awards) are distinctive not only in terms of the linear geometry that they impose upon the landscapes concerned, but also in terms of their construction. They are built of double courses of stone which decline in size and converge as height increases, until the wall is narrow enough to be spanned by a single course of topstones, while the space between the two walls is packed with stone chips derived from shaping the stones with a hammer. Such walls were built to standards which could be both detailed and exacting.

> Field boundaries are an integral part of the British rural landscape. They are a reflection of the past agricultural history and, as such, are frequently an indicator of changes in agricultural

practices both local and national. Their construction, usually in local materials, often formed the basis of an indigenous craft tradition, with many regional variations in styles and construction methods. (Byrne, 1996 p. 189)

Both field walls and hedgerows can be highly expressive of local cultural traditions. The *clawdd* (plural, *cloddiau*) of Anglesey (Wales) were a regional form of field wall which consisted of earthen banks which were embedded with and faced with stone. Quarried stone was sometimes employed, but usually these walls were built of stones cleared from fields. Originally, gorse may have been planted along the tops of the banks to provide an additional barrier to sheep (Byrne, 1996).

Although temporary 'dead hedges' formed of cut thorny timber were sometimes employed in the medieval period, fences are not an important component of the English countryside, and where post and rail fences are employed they are usually used to patch gaps in neglected hedges. The problem with such boundaries was that until timber preservatives could be employed, the earthfast posts would soon rot and the fence would fall. In parts of North America, by contrast, timber fences are significant components of the cultural landscape and are closely associated with the European colonisation:

> Once the trees were felled crude makeshift fences of tangled branches, rolled logs and piled-up stumps gave place in time to more elaborate and permanent structures. The Virginia fence, also called the worm, snake, or zigzag fence because of its shape, was used everywhere in the East. It consisted of slender logs or split rails laid in a zigzag pattern and intersecting with each other at right angles. There were anything from six to ten rails in each segment and heavy bracing logs were sometimes placed at the intersections. (Williams, 1990 p. 150)

This exemplifies the cultural response to particular environmental conditions, with the response becoming a new component of the landscape environment. Fences of this kind would not have been contemplated in Britain because they were so demanding of the scarce resources of timber and space.

The Virginia fence required great amounts of timber and took up large areas of land. For example, a square field of 160 acres required a ½ mile of fencing on each side (a total of 2 miles) but nearly half as much again if fenced in right-angled zigzags. Therefore a ten-rail, 10 foot length zigzag required at least 15,000 rails. The advantages of the Virginia fence were that it required no post holes, pegs, notches or ties, and it was easy to repair or move to new locations – an important consideration in the incremental enlargement of clearings in the North and the shifting tobacco cultivation in the South. Because no posts were embedded in the ground, it was said to last for 20 to 30 years. More importantly, it was hog-proof. (Williams, 1990)

Post and rail fences were also built in North America, being much less demanding of timber, but requiring the time-consuming digging of postholes and slotting of posts. After colonisation reached the treeless prairies, spiral augurs were employed to drill holes for expensively-imported timbers, while the invention of barbed wire provided a practical method of fencing the range which instituted wholesale cultural changes and was seen to signify the end of the brief era of the free-ranging cowboy. Although the existence of layers of relict cultural features are regarded as an Old World characteristic, such layers may sometimes be recognised in North America. Describing Lyon County in Kansas, where Osage orange trees were used both for hedging and for fence post timber, and where relict hedges can coincide with the alignments of later post and hogwire mesh fences Williams writes: 'Rail, or worm, fences dominated this county in the 1870s when as much as 10 per cent of the county's area was in timber; by 1880, more than 60 miles of hedge fencing was reported here. Barbed wire fencing dominated Kansas after 1885' (1990 p. 173).

Another form of network in the landscape is composed of roads and trackways. With the exception of obviously modern examples, these are notoriously difficult to date, even when excavation techniques are employed, but a distinction can be made between planned networks which are superimposed upon the landscape (such as the Roman and the Parliamentary Enclosure roads of England or the sectionline roads of the USA) and those which have developed in a piecemeal, organic manner, expressing the transport requirements of a community, adjusting to the existing features of the physical and cultural landscapes and also exerting a considerable influence on the subsequent development of the cultural landscape. In England, the Roman roads were built by the military during the pacification of the British chiefdoms to meet strategic needs to move troops rapidly across the country. They were super-imposed unconformably upon fieldscapes (Williamson, 1987) and also across the established networks of unplanned lanes and route-ways (extensive sections of which probably survive within the present network of rural lanes and trackways). The Roman roads formed an essentially radial network focusing upon London and, patched and bypassed in places, this system provided the framework of the transport system until the eighteenth century. The inability of medieval authorities to establish an effective system of road main-tenance was partly responsible for the primacy of waterways and narrow boats in the transport of goods. During the eighteenth and nineteenth centuries, many straight sections of road which super-ficially resembled Roman roads were created as part of the process of Parliamentary Enclosure, but since Enclosure operated on a parish-by-parish basis, these roads often merely traversed a parish from boundary to boundary and went no further. Eventually, an effective strategy for improving regional and inter-regional road transport was discovered with the establishment of turnpike trusts (associations of speculators which invested in road building and improvement works and recouped the outlay by charging tolls). Turnpikes became numerous during the eighteenth century in England and Wales and they were imitated in the USA during the first third of the nineteenth century:

> The legacies of the turnpikes, however, are the highways which follow the old turnpikes such as along the Boston/New York route in New England or the National Road which started west at Cumberland, Maryland, and was completed eventually to Van-dalia, Illinois; later U.S. Highway 40 and its successor, Interstate 70, followed this route. This re-etching of old routes was common throughout the country. (Meyer, 1990 p. 252)

With regard to landscape historical research, less can be deduced from the visual characteristics of roads, lanes and trackways than can be gleaned from a careful scrutiny of, say, field boundaries or settlements. In most West European localities, particularly in the uplands, a network of rambling lanes might as easily have originated in the Iron Age – or even in the Bronze Age – as in the medieval period. Ancient lanes have frequently been worn deeply into the countryside by the passage of shoes, hoofs and wheels, but the degree of hollowing reflects the intensity of traffic and the history of maintenance as well as age, so it is no plain guide to antiquity. The best dating evidence will tend not to come from the road itself, but from its relationship to other landscape elements. It was the relationship of the Roman road, the Pye Lane, to the field pattern across which it ran that allowed Williamson (1987) to demonstrate that the field system predated the Roman era, and similar techniques could be used in reverse to date a road: a road is *younger* than any feature which it cuts or diverts to avoid, but *older* than any feature which is adjusted to its existence. Thus the (Roman section of) the A4 road in Wiltshire diverts around the prehistoric mound of Silbury Hill, showing the road to be younger than the mound, while villages arranged along the road must be younger than it is. Equally, the abandonment of any road must predate any property boundary, building or tree established within its former course.

Moving from networks in the landscape to nodes or foci, much attention has been directed to rural settlement, though it is only relatively recently that effective concepts and frameworks for the interpretation of villages have been established. In the English lowlands and over much of Europe the majority of villages predate the development of large-scale maps, and by the time that such documentary evidence was being created, the basic structural frameworks which constrained the layout of settlements had already been established. In the UK, initial attempts to interpret rural settlement forms tended to be oversimplistic or to be founded on false assumptions, such as the notion that greens were created during the initial establishment of many villages to provide safe havens for the village livestock. During the last couple of decades, Roberts (1987) engaged in a thorough analysis of village layouts and provided a much more comprehensive and intricate system of classification, while Taylor (1983b) used the evidence derived from extensive fieldwork to provide a set of dynamic models of village development. Taylor realised that established approaches, which emphasised continuity and the stability of the village, were flawed, and that the village should be regarded as dynamic and highly responsive to changes existing within the local social and environmental context. Not only were villages shown to shrink and slough off limbs of settlement in response to local or broader adverse circumstances, but they could also, in some cases, be shown to have migrated from one site to another. This might occur in response to commercial concerns, as when a market settlement located astride a little-used track was relocated upon a bustling highway. It was also shown that many villages in England, perhaps a majority, have not grown from the accretion of dwellings around a single nucleus, but from the merging of several settlement clusters, each with its own nucleus. In this way, a seemingly homogenous village might in fact be 'polyfocal', and result from the integration of hitherto free-standing settlements associated with, say, a church, a manor and a priory. Greens could have various origins and need not be original features of the village layout. Some could have attracted settlement because of the medieval shortage of common pasture; some are certainly market-places which were inserted into earlier villages – at the expense of various dwellings – after the local lord had purchased the right to hold a market (Taylor, 1982), while others might have been provided for the village geese and as venues for social functions. Quite often, greens would be encroached upon by houses, and many have disappeared completely.

Perhaps the most important distinction that can be made between villages in terms of their layouts concerns the difference between villages which have developed in a piecemeal and spontaneous manner and those which have been planned or 'regulated'. Although planning is often regarded as a hallmark of the modern era, it can be recognised in the forms of settlements of all medieval centuries. Surprisingly, planning of a village layout can remain detectable around a thousand years after it occurred, even though the actual buildings in the settlement may have been completely rebuilt on twenty or more occasions. At its most obvious, regulation is expressed in straight lines and right-angled intersections, but it can also endure in more subtle forms, as when the frontages of house plots appear to have been defined using a fixed unit of measurement (Sheppard, 1974). Some villages began as regulated settlements and might then gain regulated or unregulated extensions or both, while many unplanned villages acquired planned insertions, as when a section of the settlement was redeveloped to accommodate a medieval market. In general, overall regulation was most likely in cases where the settlement was controlled by a single lord who was able to impose a design without reference to others. The construction of 'closed', regulated villages by local magnates continued after the Middle Ages, first with the construction of new settlements (often to fanciful picturesque designs) to replace old villages obliterated in the course of creating a tract of landscaped parkland around a mansion, and second with the building of dormitory settlements to accommodate the factory workforces associated with accelerating industrialisation. In some cases the designs were severe and functional, while in others, attempts were made to create utopian settlements embodying humanitarian concerns for the well-being of the workers and their families.

Both regulated and organic villages are found in the USA, but there the (European) cultural landscapes are just a few centuries old and information about the spatial ancestry of settlements is usually readily available in maps, documents, deeds, photographs and diaries. Since the formative periods lie well to this side of the medieval period, there is much less dependence on the more specialised techniques of the landscape historian/archaeologist. European traditions relating to nucleated settlement were exported and recreated; different cultural histories found expression in the new villages, but most emphasised the special role of the church as the focus of communal life: 'This was most apparent in Roman Catholic communities where sometimes extraordinarily complex precincts of church, school, convent, parish hall, cemetery, hospital, and even grotto could develop. Often garden shrines to the Virgin Mary abound in such villages' (Conzen, 1990, p. 234). In the Old World, communitarian settlements exist but are normally very rare, and although they are not especially numerous in the USA, they do form a significant part of the village pattern and are associated with distinctive ethnic landscapes. In England, the processes whereby some districts have nucleated settlement and some dispersed seem linked to complex and not fully understood events occurring in the eighth and ninth centuries, as explained in the section entitled 'Approaches to Landscape Study' above. In the USA, nucleated settlement is less abundant and the reasons can readily be related to fairly recent historical factors:

> A combination of the grid survey and the pre-emption and homestead laws encouraged dispersed family settlement across the rural landscape and thereby strongly discouraged nucleated farm villages of the type common in many parts of Europe, in which farmers lived together on village lots and 'commuted' to their farm land. So strong was this reorientation to dispersed living that most American hamlets and villages have developed as commercial crossroads settlements with few or no farm inhabitants. Only in a few circumstances have settlers managed to re-establish nucleated village forms in America. (Conzen, 1990 p. 231)

With the pressures against nucleation being so strong, villages would only tend to form when the cultural traditions were even stronger, as when German settlers established regulated street villages in Missouri. The forces encouraging nucleation were strongest in the cases of certain rigidly organised religious communities, with the Amanda Society creating communitarian settlements in Iowa and the Swedish Janssonist colony being established at Bishop Hill in Illinois. As elements in the landscape, villages have generated an enormous literature. Much of it is of an architectural and a social nature, and much is heavily sentimentalised. Only a tiny fraction relates to the actual genesis and evolution of village landscapes, though the more reliable recent studies contain a wealth of interest.

Having considered nodes and networks, a survey of spaces is needed to complete this brief survey of landscape components. These spaces, occupied by tracts of woodland, expanses of farmland and reservoirs, hill country and parkland, will normally fill most of the visible scene. (In addition to woods, the countryside is also likely to contain plantations, in which spruces, firs or pines are cultivated to yield fast-growing softwood or Christmas trees.) In most parts of Western Europe, woods are misunderstood by those who regard them as the last remaining vestiges of the natural wildwood. England existed as a country of farmland punctuated by islands of woodland in the Bronze Age, and the systematic management of woods to produce timber and wood of different qualities for different purposes began well back in prehistoric time. The visual character of English woodland is determined by three main factors: first, the botanical composition of the wood concerned; second, the system of management traditionally employed there, and third the extent of the abandonment of the old practices of woodmanship.

During the medieval period, almost certainly for centuries before, and for a few centuries afterwards, the great majority of woods were subjected to special systems of management. Coppicing involved cutting timber down to ground level on a felling cycle of between about four and ten years to produce light poles which might be used for wattle, fuel, tool handles or charcoal. It might be imagined that coppicing would prove fatal to the trees, but in fact it had an invigorating effect and some old coppice 'stools' several feet across have probably produced timber for a thousand years or more. Coppiced woodland frequently existed as an understorey growing beneath oaks or elms that grew tall as 'standards' and which were felled on a much longer cycle to produce structural timber, but generally cut down well before they were fully grown:

> It is possible to count the oaks that went into a building. A typical fifteenth century Suffolk farmhouse, rather larger than average, turns out to be made of some 330 trees. Only three trees were as much as 18 inches in diameter, a usual size for a 'mature' oak nowadays; half of them were less than 9 inches in diameter, and one in ten was as small as 6 inches. Such sizes are typical of medieval houses, barns, colleges, and the less grand church roofs. They imply a practice of woodmanship with a rapid turnover of small oaks and no difficulty in replacing them. (Rackham, 1986 p. 87)

Coppiced woodland was useful as a source of light timber and fuel, but was very vulnerable to browsing of the soft new shoots which rose from the stool in the period following coppicing.

Medieval rural communities were deficient in pasture land, but wood pasture offered a system of management which allowed the combination of grazing and the growing of light timber. Instead of being coppiced, trees were beheaded or 'pollarded' at a height which was above the reach of browsing livestock. This system, however, was unstable, and though widespread in late Saxon England, wood pasture declined during the Middle Ages; the closest approach in the landscape of today is provided by landscape 'parkland' where the lawns punctuated by trees mimic the visual aspects of the old land use.

The traditional systems of woodland management have virtually disappeared. Rackham (1986) writes that: 'Until the early nineteenth century woods had outlived many changes in rural society and economics . . . Since 1800 woodland has become linked, to varying degrees, to the boom-and-bust cycles of the modern economy' (p. 92). Countless old deciduous woods have been felled and replanted with a monoculture of alien softwoods, destroying both the ecology and the aesthetic aspects. No less common are the woods which survive, but which display the consequences of the withdrawal of woodmanship, so that with felling withdrawn, the coppice tree appears like an inverted octopus with trunks perhaps a foot thick rather than slender poles arising from the old stool, while pollards carry a top-heavy canopy of heavy boughs. Various relict features may survive to testify to the advance and retreat of woodland. Medieval woods were surrounded by boundary banks; a surprising number of woods still sit within their medieval bounds, while internal woodbanks may endure to mark the division into sections cut according to different rotas. Conversely, the corrugations of ridge and furrow earthworks surviving within a wood will show that woodland advanced across a previously cultivated area.

While the last surviving wildwood remnant might perhaps have been felled in England in the early medieval period, in the USA portions of largely natural woodland survive and evidence of woodland management on an English scale and duration is absent. It would be wrong, however, to imagine that there was normally a simple transition from the natural landscape to one that was almost modern. European settlers are regarded as colonising landscapes clothed in virgin forest, but very frequently they advanced into areas where indigenous people, now demoralised and ravaged by disease and alcohol, had practised systems of hoe cultivation for centuries. When travellers did encounter natural woodland it apparently failed to conform to their picturesque expectations:

> We in England, when we read and speak of the primeval forests of America, are apt to form pictures in our minds of woodland glades, with spreading oaks and green mossy turf beneath – scenes than which nothing that God has given us is more charming. But these forests are not after that fashion: they offer no allurement to the lover, no solace to the melancholy man of thought. The ground is deep in mud, or overflown with water. The soil and the river have no defined margins. Each tree, though full of the forms of life, has all the appearance of death. (Trollope, 1862 p. 82)

In terms of woodland as a facet of landscape, the great differences between the English and American experiences is that in England until quite recent times woodland was not regarded as an impediment to settlement and cultivation, but as a vital resource which, following its reduction to a tolerable minimum acreage in prehistoric times, had to be conserved so far as possible against encroachments by land-hungry farmers and managed as an essential resource. In the USA, while the commercial value of timber was appreciated, the removal of woodland (to clear land, provide materials for house-building, fuel and fencing) formed a brief transitional phase in the history of landscape. Half the original forest cover was removed in the USA and now:

It requires an enormous effort of imagination to see the forests as they once were . . . the end-result of clearing is the elimination of the landscape feature under examination. The result is nothing, or at least, the norm; tamed, domesticated landscape of fields, meadows, intervening patches of woodland and woodlot, of settlements, and suburbs . . . Splash dams, booms, and logging railways are increasingly things of the past and are replaced by highways, trucks, tractors, and chain saws. (Williams, 1990 p. 164)

However, the USA is a big country with climates that are often conducive to tree-growth, so that in the aftermath of felling, regrowth can be an important part of the scene: 'The cutovers are reverting to forest everywhere . . . . Despite the massive destruction of trees by agriculture, logging and fuel gathering, the forest is still a dominant feature of the American visual scene' (Williams, 1990).

Fields derive their personalities from a range of factors: permanent characteristics such as their size, shape and boundaries and transitional ones such as the crop under cultivation and the season. Different types of fields also have their places in the history of cultivation. In parts of England at least, enclosed areas of farmland have existed since the Neolithic period, and the archaeological evidence suggests that phases of cultivation might often be succeeded in phases of abandonment, while the balance between arable and pastoral uses was not fixed but would move with shifts in local climate, ecology and socio-economic changes. In many places, working fieldscapes must have existed for around 6000 years, though episodes of retreat and decay will occasionally have occurred. Working fieldscapes seen in England today are thus the latest in a very long succession of field patterns. In some cases, the legacy of the past is readily apparent to all those who have the most elementary understanding of landscape history, yet even though questions of field systems have lain at the centre of studies in historical geography for more than a century, several fundamental mysteries, such as the origins of open-field farming, remain unresolved.

Many of the questions associated with the fieldscape relate to the larger mystery concerning the division of the working countryside between woodland and champion types (as discussed above). Hall describes the emerging consensus that 'The origin of ridge and furrow seems to be towards the end of the Middle Saxon period c 700–800AD. At this time there was a replanning of the Midland landscape with settlements becoming concentrated in one place and strips laid out' (1994, p. 99). Even so, there is a problem of interpreting the remarkably attenuated 'long strips', which seem to have preceded the establishment of 'conventional' field strips in various places. If unidentified agents were responsible for its imposition, then open-field farming, which endured in places for a thousand years, must be regarded as a form of planned or regulated countryside even though its component forms were devoid of straight lines and grid patterns. When it disappeared, it was frequently superseded by the unmistakable geometrical divisions of Parliamentary Enclosure, though much of the former arrangements will often remain apparent or detectable. Wherever the modern ploughing of old open field ploughland has not taken place, then corrugations and ridges will preserve the patterns of ridge and furrow and also the headlands and joints which formed at the margins of the packages of strips or 'furlongs'.

In the UK the field evidence for the successive nature of fieldscapes is abundant, while both planned and unplanned elements are widespead and they vary in their relative proportions from place to place. In the USA the presence of regulated, rectangular patterns dominate the field and property patterns and the countrysides tell less of extended evolution and more of precipitate changes from natural or native American ecologies, in which indigenous wild species were prominent, to the rather featureless fieldscapes associated with extensive mechanised agriculture. However, such historically uncomplicated 'two-stage' countrysides do not entirely monopolise the scene:

> One observer has detected relict Dutch and French Canadian field systems in the present-day Vermont landscape, and another the Salzburger long-lots of colonial Georgia. When settlement moved into regions surveyed under the national land ordinance, the grid imposed a spatial discipline rarely challenged. Still, some groups from time to time circumvented the system. A small Welsh community in northern Illinois township, for instance, managed to buy contiguous river valley land, dissolve the internal grid boundaries, and then resurvey the land to produce irregularly shaped parcels that ensured each new owner access to the river. (Conzen, 1990 p. 231)

Particularly in the long-settled landscapes of Europe, evidence of the recreational uses of landscape is likely to be present. Bloodsports provided the most popular medieval recreation, and at least 2000 deer parks existed in England:

> The park was a common feature of the medieval landscape and was to be found in substantial numbers in every county in England. It was securely enclosed in order to retain the deer, principally fallow deer and red deer, both for the sport of hunting and as a source of fresh meat throughout the year. The enclosure usually consisted of a combination of a substantial earth bank, topped by a wooden paling fence and with an inside ditch, which together made an impassable barrier. In some districts, the wooden fence might be replaced by a quickset hedge or a stone wall, and where the topography was suitable, for example just below the crest of a steep slope, the paling fence alone might serve. Water seems to have been an effective barrier to the passage of deer and some parks were partly circumscribed by rivers or marshy areas. (Cantor and Hatherly, 1979 p. 71)

Most deer parks passed out of use before the close of the Middle Ages, some being converted into horse or cattle breeding places, but in many places their curving outlines are preserved in hedgerow boundaries and the earthworks constructed to confine the deer frequently survive.

Although small enclosed gardens were associated with the grander medieval houses, it is often assumed that an interest in the aesthetic aspects of landscape and their manipulation was not developed until the seventeenth and eighteenth centuries. In fact, the renowned English landscape park of the era of Lancelot 'Capability' Brown echoed and mimicked the tree-studded lawns of the medieval deer park:

> it might seem that medieval deer parks were very different from later landscape parks; that they were economic and recreational, rather than aesthetic landscapes, and that they were quite distinct from contemporary gardens. Recent research, however, suggests a more complex and subtle picture. Parks were the quintessential symbols of aristocracy. They expressed not only ownership of land, but ownership of land over which the rights of the wider community had usually been extinguished; a notable feature when most of the country was occupied by commons and common fields. (Taigel and Williamson, 1993 p. 33)

The legacy of recreational landscapes tends to be underestimated, though in the British landscape the traces of abandoned gardens are exceptionally common. For reasons that may be hard to fathom, we tend to focus on economic, social and political factors at the expense of others. In England the relics of moats are also extremely common, and these have been interepreted in terms of the defence of the medieval home or the enhancement of the status of the home-owner. However, Taylor (1983a) has shown that a minority of these moats actually surrounded medieval gardens rather than houses and had an aesthetic function. It is also possible for one type of recreational function to be mistaken for another: the hollow that is generally presumed to have been the tiltyard at Bodiam Castle in Sussex had nothing to do with jousting, but was in fact one of a complex of lakes which surrounded the castle and served purely aesthetic functions. Such considerations greatly affected the land-scapes of medieval castles, which cannot be appreciated in purely defensive terms. At Bodiam, whose military pretensions were largely sham, the visitor travelled between sheets of water, saw the reflected castle seeming to rise out of its moat and then passed a cascade as the causeway took him around the unfolding views to an imposing entrance across a moat that was much too wide for defensive needs. At Framlingham Castle in Suffolk, one looked into and across a garden to the lake and deer park beyond. The lake doubtless yielded fish and reeds, but it was also an important landscaping feature. At other great English castles, such as Kenilworth and Leeds, sheets of water were incorporated into large-scale aesthetic arrangements, and special vantage points were provided for the enjoyment of the manufactured scenery.

Recreational landscapes do not exist in isolation, but are closely integrated with the other land-use patterns and social structures. The ritualisation of fox-hunting in the eighteenth century was greatly facilitated by the fact that the leading participants were great landowners who often held adjacent estates, allowing the hunt to gallop across huge expanses of open country; although when Parliamentary Enclosure divided the commons with hedgerows, jumping joined galloping as an important part of the unpleasant ritual. Equally, the development of grouse shooting as an aristo-cratic pastime in northern England was greatly influenced by the enclosures, which brought large swathes of former common land into private ownership and excluded ordinary people from the moors, where the grouse could feed and breed undisturbed.

If the subject matter of landscape history lay only in books then the appeal of the discipline would be far less. In fact the potential to 'read the landscape' is central to the attraction of landscape history and most scenes are an assemblage of living and relict features. This underlies the frequent description of historic landscapes as palimpsests. The comparisons between England and the USA which have been made suggest that, in very general terms, the more stages of cultural evolution that a landscape has passed through then the more facets inherited from the past are likely to be preserved. Landscape study also reveals the contrasts between the planned or regulated and the unplanned or organic modes of change: the former, though often only locally, tending to be revolutionary and the latter, evolutionary. These contrasts are not confined to one facet of the landscape, but are seen again and again, in villages, in property patterns and in fieldscapes, as well as in the contrast between designed landscaped parks and the slowly evolving fieldscapes which may surround them. Landscape history, therefore, involves a study of the evolution of landscapes and their facets, culminating in the ability to explain why the landscapes that we see have their forms and relict features.

References

Aston, M. and Rowley, T. *Landscape Archaeology* (Newton Abbot: David & Charles, 1974).

Barrow, G. 'Frontier and settlement: which influenced which? England and Scotland, 1100–1300' in Bartlett, R. and MacKay, A. (eds), *Medieval Frontier Societies* (Oxford: Clarendon Press, 1996).

Beresford, M. W. *History on the Ground*, 2nd edn (London: Methuen, 1971).

Berkhofer, R. F. Jr, 'Space, time culture and the new frontier' *Agricultural History* **38** (1964) pp. 21–30.

Brooks, R. and Johannes, D. *Phytoarchaeology* (Portland, Oregon: Dioscorides Press, 1990).

Brown, A. E. and Taylor, C. C. 'Cambridgeshire earthwork surveys VI' *Proceedings of the Cambridge Antiquarian Society* **82** (1993) pp. 101–11.

Byrne, R. J. 'Field boundaries in Anglesey, Gwynedd' *Landscape Research* **21** (1996), pp. 189–94.

Cantor, L. M. and Hatherly, J. 'The medieval parks of England' *Geography* **64** (1979) pp. 71–85.

Conzen, M. P. 'Ethnicity on the land' in Conzen, M. P. (ed.), *The Making of the American Landscape* (London: HarperCollins, 1990).

Crawford, O. G. S. *Archaeology in the Field* (London: Phoenix House, 1953).

Crawford, O. G. S. and Keiller, A. *Wessex From the Air* (1928).

Curwen, E. C. 'The plough and the origin of strip lynchets' *Antiquity* **13** (1939), p. 45.

Domosh, M. 'A method for interpreting landscape: a case study of the New York World Building' *Area* **21** (1989) pp. 347–55.

Hall, D. 'Ridge and furrow in the English Midlands' in Foster, S. and Smout, T. C. (eds), *The History of Soils and Field Systems* (Aberdeen: Scottish Cultural Press, 1994) pp. 94–100.

Hodges, R. and Wildgoose, M. 'Roman and native in the White Peak' in Branigan, K. (ed.), *Rome and the Brigantes* (Sheffield: University of Sheffield, 1980) pp. 48–53.

Homans, G. C. *English Villagers of the Thirteenth Century* (New York: Norton 1941).

Honour, H. *The New Golden Land* (New York: Pantheon, 1975).

Hoskins, W. G. *The Making of the English Landscape* (London: Hodder & Stoughton, 1955, page numbers quoted from the Pelican edition of 1978).

Johnson, H. B. *Order Upon the Land: Rectangular Land Survey and the Upper Mississippi County* (New York: Oxford University Press, 1978).

Lambert, J. M., Jennings, J. N., Smith, C. T., Green, C. and Hutchinson, J. N. *The Making of the Broads*, Royal Geographical Society Monograph No. 3 (1966).

Lucas, J. *Studies in Nidderdale* (Pateley Bridge: T. Thorpe, *c.* 1882).

Meyer, D. R. 'The new industrial order' in Conzen M. D. (ed.), *The Making of the American Landscape* (London: HarperCollins, 1990) pp. 249–68.

Muir, R. *History from the Air* (London: Michael Joseph, 1983).

Muir, R. 'Hedgerow dating: a critique' *Naturalist* **121** (1996) pp. 59–64.

Palliser, D. M. 'Domesday Book and the "Harrying of the North"' *Northern History* **29** (1993) pp. 1–23.

Pollard, E., Hooper, M. D. and Moore, N. W. *Hedges* (London: Collins, 1974).

Powlesland, D. with Haughton, C. and Hanson, J. 'Excavations at Heslerton, North Yorkshire 1978–82' *Archaeological Journal* **143** (1986) pp. 53–173.

Prescott, J. R. V. *The Geography of Frontiers and Boundaries* (London: Hutchinson, 1965).

Rackham, O. *The History of the Countryside* (London: J.M. Dent, 1986).

Raistrick, A. *Yorkshire Maps and Map-Makers* (Clapham: Dalesman, 1969).

Roberts, B. K. *The Making of the English Village* (Harlow: Longman, 1987).

Roberts, B. K. *Landscapes of Settlement* (London: Routledge, 1996).

Scrope, G. P. 'The terraces of the chalk downs' *Geological Magazine* **3** (1866) pp. 293–6.

Sheppard, J. A. 'Metrological analysis of regular village plans in Yorkshire' *Agricultural History Review* **22** (1974) pp. 118–35.

Smith, C. T. 'Dutch peat digging and the origin of the Norfolk Broads' *Geographical Journal* **132** (1966) pp. 69–73.

Spratt, D. A. 'Prehistoric boundaries on the North Yorkshire Moors', in Barker, G., (ed) *Prehistoric Communities in Northern England* (Sheffield: 1981) pp. 41–56.

Spratt, D. A. 'Orthostatic field walls on the North York Moors' *The Yorkshire Archaeological Journal* **60** (1988) pp. 149–55.

Taigel, A. and Williamson, T. *Parks and Gardens* (London: Batsford, 1993).

Taylor, C. C. *Fieldwork in Medieval Archaeology* (London: Batsford, 1974).

Taylor, C. C. 'Medieval market grants and village morphology' *Landscape History* **4** (1982) pp. 21–8.

Taylor, C. C. *The Archaeology of Gardens* (Aylesbury: Shire, 1983a).

Taylor, C. C. *Village and Farmstead* (London: George Philip, 1983b).

Taylor, C. C. and Muir, R. *Visions of the Past* (London: J. M. Dent, 1983).

Trollope, A. *North America* (London: Chapman & Hall, 1862) quoted in Miller, C. *Early Travellers in North America* (Dover: Alan Sutton, 1994).

Turner, F. J. 'The significance of the frontier in American history' *Report of the American Historical Association* 1893 pp. 199–227.

Webster, G. and Hobley, B. 'Aerial reconnaissance over the Warwickshire Avon' *Archaeological Journal* **121** (1964) pp. 1–22.

Williams, M. 'Clearing the forests' in Conzen, M. P. (ed.), *The Making of the American Landscape* (London: HarperCollins, 1990) pp. 146–68

Williamson, T. 'Early co-axial field systems on the East Anglian boulder clay' *Proceedings of the Prehistoric Society* **53** (1987) pp. 419–32.

Williamson, T. 'Explaining regional landscapes: woodland and champion in southern and eastern England' *Landscape History* **10** (1988) pp. 5–13.

Wood, E. S. *Collins Field Guide to Archaeology in Britain*, 5th edn (London: Collins, 1979).

Wood, P. D. 'Frontier relics in Welsh border towns' *Geography* **47** (1952) pp. 55–62.

Wood, P. D. 'Strip lynchets reconsidered' *Geographical Journal* **127** (1961) pp. 449–59.

3

The Structure and Scenery Approach

In 1953, a geologist wrote that:

> Knowing about the countryside, that is to say being a naturalist
> or an observer, consists for many people in knowing mainly about
> plants and animals, and their immediate environment. Curiously,
> the shape of the land itself, the naturalist's own environment, as
> well as everyone else's seems passed over by the general interest.
> (Miller, 1953 p. 19)

Most approaches to landscape study concern the interpretation of
the features in the visible landscape, whether this involves the
landscape historian's study of human-made landscape features or
whether landscape is regarded as an accumulation of symbolic
meanings (Figure 3.1). What is described here as the 'structure
and scenery' approach to landscape is as straightforward and as
self-validating as any approach could be. Here, scenery is regarded
as being essentially a product of its geological history, so that the
crested ridge might be interpreted in terms of the origins of its
constituent rocks and the forces of uplift, folding, faulting and
degradation which have raised and sculpted them and produced a
distinctive passage of scenery. The approach has been pursued for
most of this century and in Britain it resulted in the publication of a
succession of books which introduced the structure and scenery
perspective to a non-specialist audience of country-lovers.

The structure and scenery approach, which is closely allied to the
physical geography traditionally taught in schools, is based on the
expertise of geologists and geomorphologists. Before any real

Figure 3.1 Geology can exert a powerful presence in the landscape. A landscape, settlement and economy built on slate in the region of Blaenau Ffestiniog in north Wales. (Richard Muir)

progress could be made in the interpretation of the physical basis of scenery, the science of geology had to be formulated and geomorphological concepts had to be developed to provide interpretations of the finely detailed shaping of the surface of the earth. Leonardo da Vinci (1452–1519) had an appreciation of geology that was far ahead of his time. Departing from conventional thinking, in his notebook of *c*.1506–10, which is known as the *Codex Leicester*, he suggested that the world did not exist as God had made it but had been modified by the elements. He noted that fossils were present in certain rocks and believed that the presence of fossils in mountainous situations could not be explained by the biblical flood, while the intact nature of these fossils argued against their having been transported by violent currents. He was also aware of the stratification of rocks, and realised that this could not be explained in terms of the Great Deluge. These ideas, however, were developed within the context of attempts, essentially medieval in nature, to interpret the human body as a microcosm of the earth: rocks were regarded as the earth's skeleton and Leonardo sought to explain the 'circulation' of the oceans (Figure 3.2).

The progressive aspects of Leonardo's work did not take root and much of the pioneering work in geology was accomplished much later by British scientists. First, it was essential to understand that rocks are not jumbled together in a haphazard fashion but are stratified, and a concept of stratification was pioneered by John Michell (1724–93). James Hutton (1726–97) described the manner in which sediments were deposited on the beds of oceans and rivers in the past just as in the present, and William Smith (1769–1839) associated diagnostic fossils with the different strata and assigned relative ages to the stratigraphical sequences. Though the significance of stratigraphy had been established, during the earlier part of the nineteenth century much attention was devoted to the doctrine of catastrophism and the belief that the geological record could only be interpreted by evoking a series of great natural catastrophes, of which the most recent had been Noah's flood: 'Fossils were once hailed as incontrovertible evidence of the reality of Noah's flood. Since it was soon made clear that they were to be found in different rocks and at different levels there arose the idea of several successive creations each in its turn overwhelmed by a great deluge' (Stamp, 1946 p. 10). Distinguished British geologists, such as Adam Sedgwick (1785–1857) and William Buckland (1784–1856), and the renowned French palaeontologist, Georges Cuvier (1769–1832), all

102

Figure 3.2 Rock type will usually influence the appearance of landscape. This is a glaciated landscape with the smooth slopes and rounded summits characteristic of the Skiddaw Slates in the Lake District. Neighbouring rocks of the Borrowdale Volcanics Series weather into much more craggy and rugged forms. (Richard Muir)

believed that the stratigraphical record was the product of ancient catastrophes, even if they disagreed about the number of floods involved.

William Smith recognised that fossils of the same species could be found in rocks occurring in different parts of the country and realised that fossils could be used to identify strata; in 1815 he published the first geological map of England and Wales. Charles Lyell (1797–1875) published his highly influential *The Principles of Geology* in 1830–3 and provided a more credible geological framework by re-establishing the principle of uniformitarianism, previously presented to the Royal Society of Edinburgh by Hutton in 1785, maintaining that an understanding of the processes affecting the surface of the earth in the past could be gained by studying those processes presently at work. Though this did not produce an instant transformation in geological thinking, it did establish the foundations of geological science. Subsequently, programmes of painstaking geological exploration and mapping established the groundwork upon which interpretations of scenery could be built (Figure 3.3).

For an appreciation of the detailed configuration of the surface of the earth to be gained, a science of landforms was needed. Ideas about the erosion of the land surface and the transportation of eroded materials had existed for many years. Leonardo da Vinci had been aware that rivers could erode their valleys and deposit their loads of eroded materials elsewhere. During the nineteenth century, suspicions that Europe had previously been subjected to an extensive glaciation grew, and a paper on continental glaciation was published by Louis Agassiz (1807–73) in 1840. As the century progressed, better understandings of marine and river erosion were gained, and attempts were made to provide geological explanations for the configuration of the surface of the earth. In 1846, for example, A. C. Ramsay noticed a rough accordance of height in the summits of South Wales and concluded that these summits were the remnants of a former great plain of marine denudation: 'Thus, in Europe, by the close of the last century a sufficient amount of knowledge had accumulated to give rise to a special branch of geology called physiographic geology' (Thornbury, 1954 p. 9).

Thornbury noted that:

We might well refer to the period between 1875 and 1900 as 'the heroic age in American geomorphology,' for during this quarter century there evolved most of the grand concepts in this branch of

104

Figure 3.3 This coastal landscape, on the north Somerset coast at Kilve, owes its personality entirely to the Blue Lias beds which can be seen dipping towards the shore. (Richard Muir)

geology. To a large degree these were the outgrowths directly or indirectly of the work of a group of geologists who were connected with the series of geological surveys of the western United States initiated after the Civil War. (Thornbury, 1954)

Most notable amongst these geologists were C. E. Dutton (1841–1912), G. K. Gilbert (1843–1918) and Major J. W. Powell (1834–1902). They provided the foundations upon which a strong American tradition of geomorphology could be based. During the first half of the twentieth century, the interpretation of the surface of the earth was dominated by the thinking of one American geomorphologist:

The impact on geomorphology of W. M. Davis (1850–1934) was greater than that of any other man. The Davisian school of geomorphology and the American School are practically synonymous terms. Davis was basically a great definer, analyst, and systematizer. Before his time, geomorphic descriptions were largely in empirical terms. Even more important than the many new concepts which he introduced was the fact that he breathed new life into geomorphology through introduction of his genetic method of land form description. He will probably be remembered longest for his concept of the geomorphic cycle . . . which in its simplest analysis is the idea that in the evolution of landscapes there is a systematic sequence of land forms which makes possible the recognition of stages of development, a sequence that he designated as youth, maturity, and old age. His idea that differences in land forms are largely explainable in terms of differences in geologic structure, geomorphic process, and the stage of development has become firmly rooted in the thinking of most students of land forms. (Thornbury, 1954 pp. 10–11)

During his lifetime, Davis encountered criticisms concerning the manner in which slopes are eroded and the likelihood that cycles of erosion would be disrupted by the rejuvenating effects of phases of uplift long before a landscape had passed from youth to old age. Some of his ideas are accessible to the non-specialist and can still provide useful perspectives on the physical landscape. Included here is the notion that landforms can be understood in terms of *structure* (their geological characteristics), *process* (the different processes of erosion which have acted upon them) and *stage* or time – the stage reached in their development. This was summarised by Stamp as follows:

> Briefly, it may be said that land-forms depend first on the nature of the rocks and their disposition (that is, in other words, on lithology and structure), secondly on the climatic conditions, with resulting soil mantle and vegetation cover, under which the sculpturing of the land surface has been and is taking place, and thirdly on the phase or stage within the erosion cycle. (1949 p. 37)

The development of geomorphology provided a basis for the interpretation of the physical landscape:

> It is only within the past few decades that the specialist study of land forms, the science of geomorphology, by developing its own technique, has demonstrated that it is possible to reconstruct a long and often complex history by detailed investigation of the form of the ground and that the details of land relief may bear surprisingly little relationship to the structural geology. (Stamp, 1949)

In the UK, Lord Avebury had produced *The Scenery of England and Wales* in 1888, while the development of the new and better understandings was marked by the publication of books which subjected English scenery to geological and geomorphological interpretations, with *The Scientific Study of Scenery* by J. E. Marr, a pioneering work, having reached its sixth edition by 1920.

A landmark in the establishment of an appreciation of landscape that was rooted in geology arrived in 1938 with the publication of *The Scenery of England and Wales* by A. E. Trueman. The author was an academic geologist who held professorships in the subject successively at the universities of Swansea, Bristol and Glasgow before becoming Deputy Chairman of the University Grants Committee in 1946. Trueman set out to provide an account that would enjoy a broad appeal and would further stimulate the popular interest in the British landscapes and countrysides. In his preface he wrote:

> In this book an attempt is made to describe the scenery of most of England and Wales, and to show how some of the features have

come into being. It has been prepared because I believe that there are many people, motorists and walkers as well as students, who desire this kind of information, and because singularly few works on the subject are available. The recent spate of topographical works of one type or another, many of them of surpassing excellence, is evidence of the great interest taken in the English countryside by increasing numbers of people. And yet the scenic background of the village and church has received little attention. (p. 9)

During the years that followed, other highly successful guides to Britain's structure and scenery would follow, and Trueman helped to explain why such studies would enjoy so much popularity in this country:

In England and Wales we are singularly placed to appreciate the relationship of scenery and structure, for few other parts of the earth's surface show in a similar small area so great a diversity of rock types and of landscape features. 'Britain is a world by itself'; its mountains are not high, nor its rivers long, but within a few hundred miles of travel from east to west an Englishman may see more varieties of scenery than are to be found in many bigger countries. (p. 11)

Trueman did more than to provide an accessible guide to the geological roots of scenery. He demonstrated an appreciation of landscape in the fuller sense, particularly in his descriptions of how the local bedrock would be incorporated in vernacular buildings, buildings which made their own distinctive contributions to the visible scene:

Where so many rocks are available there is naturally a great diversity of building materials. Yet old half-timbered buildings are very abundant, notably in Much Wenlock and Ludlow. In the latter town the red tiles, wearing to a deeper tint than the bricks, give the dominant colour, an indication of its situation on the borders of the red marl country (of the Old Red Sandstone). But Ludlow Castle has the yellow-grey of the Silurian stones. Many villages nearer Church Stretton have also interesting stone houses and in the area of Soudley and Hope Bowdler, and in the Onny valley near Horderley, much use has been made of a local

Ordovician sandstone often showing beautiful purple and yellow-green stripes, quarried in blocks of varied sizes and shapes. (pp. 257–8)

The next stage in the development of a structure and scenery tradition was marked by the publication in 1946 of *Britain's Structure and Scenery* in the popular The New Naturalist series produced by Collins. The author, L. Dudley Stamp, was Professor of Geography at the London School of Economics, a CBE and the only working geographer in Britain who was well known outside the world of academic geography. A prolific author of books on almost every facet of geography, Stamp's approach fell out of fashion in the 1960s when positivism and narrow specialisation were favoured, yet he was a gifted communicator and a highly perceptive observer and reviewer. He began by noting the essential difference between two parts of Britain, pointing out how Sir Halford Mackinder in his now classic book, *Britain and the British Seas*, published in 1902, had made a distinction between two roughly equal halves of the island of Britain:

If one draws a line approximately from the mouth of the Tees to the mouth of the Exe it will be found that all the main hill masses and mountains lie to the north and west, the major stretches of plain and lowland to the south and east. To the north and west lies Highland Britain, to the south and east lies Lowland Britain. (p. 5)

There followed a methodical treatment of the subject matters of geology and physical geography followed by surveys which related physical structure to the scenery of the British regions. The treatment was accessible, and authoritative; but it remained to be demonstrated that a structure and scenery approach could produce results that would be inspirational. Few would have thought it possible.

That demonstration was provided in 1951 with the publication of *A Land* by Jacquetta Hawkes. Andrew Selkirk, the editor of *Current Archaeology*, recalled that:

For the Festival of Britain in 1951, she wrote *A Land*, a poetic invocation of the geology of the land of Britain which, as a teenager, swept me off my feet (I would be interested to know what teenagers of today think of it. Is it still terribly dated, or has it begun to acquire a period patina?) (1996 p. 211)

Although *A Land* covered much of the same ground as his own *Britain's Structure and Scenery*, Stamp realised that Hawkes's book had introduced an originality into the treatment of this subject matter and when reviewing it for *The Geographical Journal* he wished 'this delightful missionary effort every success' (1951 p. 465).

Hawkes's background was in the intelligentsia of Cambridge. Her father, Sir Frederick Gowland Hopkins, was the discoverer of vitamins and her uncle was the poet, Gerard Manley Hopkins. She studied archaeology at Cambridge and married the prominent archaeologist, Christopher Hawkes, though later she left her husband and married the writer, J. B. Priestley. There are few subjects less amenable to prose of a high literary quality than geology and yet *A Land* is a work of exceptional literary merit. It brings a spiritual and sensual perspective to bear on its subject:

I think we are returning to an awareness of our unity with our surroundings, but an awareness of a much more exalted kind than anything that has existed before. The primitive tribesman, to go no further back than the early days of our own species, was still so deeply sunk in nature that he hardly distinguished himself from his environment or from his fellows. This sense of oneness shows itself in totemism and in many forms of magic. In the identification of the name or image with the living person; in summoning rain by spitting water, or in the belief that a man by leaping into the air can make the corn grow tall. In this, just as in the foetal gills, the child repeats the development of the species, he does not distinguish – 'Tis the eye of childhood that fears a painted devil'. (p. 40)

And:

I lie here and feel Earth rustling through space, its rotundity between me and the sun, the shadow above me acting as a searchlight to reveal the stars whose light left them long before there were eyes on this planet to receive it. Now the two little globes of my eyes, unlit in the darkness, look up at their shining globes, and who shall say that we do not gaze at one another, affect one another? (p. 12)

A Land is a most remarkable book. Judged solely as a factual account of the geological foundations of British scenery and the human colonisation of the country it is of little significance and it has far less to say about the configuration of the physical landscape than, say, Stamp's book. It remains fascinating for the manner, teetering on the edge of mysticism but never falling, in which it explores a bonding between the physical landscape and the human spirit:

> Life has grown from the rock and still rests upon it; because men have left it far behind, they are able consciously to turn back to it. We do turn back, for it has kept some hold over us . . . The Church, itself founded on the rock of St Peter, for centuries fought unsuccessfully against the worship of 'sticks and stones'. Such pagan notions have left memories in the circles and monoliths that still jut through the heather on our moorlands or stand naked above the turf of our downs. I believe that they linger, too, however faintly, in our churchyards – for who at the height of its popularity ever willingly used cast-iron for a tombstone? (p. 100)

Like the giants of landscape history, W. G. Hoskins and Carl Sauer, Hawkes despised the modern, and in *A Land* she articulated her belief that the ills of the mid-twentieth-century urban industrial society derived from the alienation of people from the land and rural tradition. She noted the standardisation of life in the modern centralised state and wrote of how men and women had become cut off from the nourishment of the past and, severed from these deep reserves of creative force, they became a sources of ugliness which flooded the lowlands, seeping more slowly among the moors and mountains: 'When underneath all this, culture is no longer sufficiently embodied in each individual, the contrasting delights of locality, the poetry of a people delicately adjusted to varied surroundings, finding their new but always fitting responses, must blur into a grey uniformity' (pp. 215–16).

She contrasted the medieval holy days, which were enjoyed at home amongst neighbours, with the industrial holidays, when every effort was made to escape from the torment and squalor of home:

> So there is a new form of mass migration – no longer for fishing or fowling or the visiting of shrines. Instead a flight from a man-made world too hard, dirty and hideous to allow its inhabitants to

rest, to lie down on the ground or to dance upon it, to turn back to their surroundings for refreshment. Three hundred years ago how impossible it would have seemed that England should be cumbered with towns built as an escape from towns, that half its south and east coasts should be encrusted with red bricks, walled behind concrete, the sea grasped after with iron piers. (p. 209)

This book combined an outline of geological history, a review of vernacular building techniques in stone, a digression on conscious-ness, sketches of prehistoric settlement and English history and a review of regional identities, all presented in sparkling prose and stitched together with Hawkes's ideas about the spiritual bonding between humans, nature and place. Her reasons for writing *A Land* can be debated. Was it inspired by the Festival of Britain? At one point she wrote: 'my intention was no more than to celebrate the creation of Britain and in so doing tacitly to express a love of the result' (p. 214). At another, and more enigmatically, she described scrambling up Castle Hill in Cambridge with her nurse: 'From the top I could see my house a long way off (always an exciting experience, and perhaps in fact the subject of this book)' (p. 192), while in the Preface she wrote: 'If in *A Land* I have often recalled my own childhood, it has not been so much from egotism as from a wish to steal that emotion which uses our own early memories for a realization of the most distant past.' Books on landscape have been written from many perspectives, but none has the same power to set the spine tingling with the magic of their prose and vision.

The structure and scenery approach continued with the publica-tion of *The Living Landscape of Britain* by Walter Shepherd in 1952 and *Geology and Scenery in Britain* by T. G. Miller in 1953. During the second half of the century, however, the gap between the interested amateur naturalist and the trained geologist and geomor-phologist widened. Popular books might offer a general introduc-tion to rock formations and erosion but were, in reality, incapable of providing a competence in the specialised analysis of scenery, while (the inspirational *A Land* apart) they were characterised by a certain sameness. Within geology and geomorphology, specialisation in-creased and the focus shifted away from the interpretation of scenery towards research fields such as the highly technical study of the processes of erosion. Academics like Whittow (1977) and Goudie (1990) have produced authoritative accounts within the broad structure and scenery tradition, yet this tradition has lost the dynamism it enjoyed in the years leading up to the turn of the century.

A basic deficiency of the structure and scenery approach concerns the fact that it is both an *essential* and an *incomplete* approach to the interpretation and understanding of landscape. An appreciation of the underlying geological structures and of the processes of uplift and erosion which have sculpted the land surface are crucial to any analytical investigation, but the story of landscape evolution does not culminate with a comprehension of physical geography. Rather, the geological roots of scenery exist as a stage upon which botanical successions unfold and humans may create a sequence of cultural landscapes. The processes of landscape modification by human agency will frequently be influenced by the character of the underlying terrain but analysis of the relationships between the natural and the human-made worlds must be pursued with caution, for a second deficiency of the structure and scenery approach is that it is prone to being incorporated into attempts at explanation based on environmental determinism. It would be easy, for example, to point to various villages situated on geomorphological landmarks such as spring lines and bridging points on rivers and to offer this as proof that the location of settlements is *determined* by the characteristics of the physical environment. Yet this would be to ignore the multitude of villages which are located at environmentally nondescript places and at sites which are simply poor situations for settlement.

Notions based on environmental determinism can be traced back to Aristotle and Hippocrates. In the eighteenth century, the French philosopher, Baron de Montesquieu (1689–1755), thought that the differences between races and societies could be explained in terms of the influences of environmental factors such as soil and climate. When geography developed as an academic subject in the latter part of the nineteenth century, it took shape within an intellectual climate dominated by Darwinism, an outlook which, by regarding the success of an organism as being governed by the closeness of its adjustment to its setting, accorded to the environment the crucial role in determining the destiny of all species. The most notable geographer of this period was the German, Friedrich Ratzel (1844–1904), who was guided both by Darwinian and Lamarckian perspectives on evolution. Ratzel greatly influenced fellow German geographers and also geographers in the USA, where Ellen C. Semple speculated on the influences of the physical environment in shaping the course of American history and where Ellsworth

Huntington imagined that climate had been a decisive factor in determining the emergence of civilisations. Environmental determinism was an ethically unsatisfactory doctrine since it gave the initiative to the environment and did not allow for human free will or morality as significant factors in any process of decision-making. In the early years of this century a French school of geography identified with the alternative doctrine of possibilism placed the emphasis upon human choice rather than the dictates of the environment. Today we recognise the importance of the natural environment, but we see it operating through a complicated web of social, psychological, economic and political routeways which may operate in ways which variously diminish or intensify the environmental stimuli at different times.

The structure and scenery approach is a halfway-house on the road of landscape interpretation which should be visited by any researchers seeking totally to decipher a particular landscape. Explorations of cultural landscapes will be more securely rooted in place if account is taken of their topographical contexts, and in many cases relationships between terrain and cultural features will be demonstrated. Relationships will frequently be found between settlement form and factors like terrain and altitude; in Nidderdale in Yorkshire, for example, it has been shown that each physical zone of the valley has its own distinctive rural settlement forms (Muir, 1998). Throughout most of the Anglo-Saxon world and Europe published information on geology and geomorphology will be available to facilitate an understanding of the phyical structure and configuration of a particular landscape, though in many less developed parts of the world detailed local surveys are absent and considerable expertise would be required in the construction of any appreciation of structure and scenery.

In Britain during the middle decades of this century, a succession of books introduced a geological approach to scenery to a readership of amateur enthusiasts and country-lovers. To examine these books is to return to a world of bicycle trips, picnic hampers and sensible shoes, and to a time when information about the environment was derived not from television and its celebrity presenters but mainly from books which were generally authored by academics (usually professors). Eventually this vein of writing dried up, partly because of a surfeit of repetition, but in the meantime, *A Land* had been written and landscape had acquired possibly its finest biography.

References

Lord Avebury, *The Scenery of England and Wales* (London, 1888).
Goudie, A. *The Landforms of England and Wales* (Oxford: Blackwell, 1990).
Hawkes, J. *A Land* (London: The Cresset Press, 1951).
Marr, J. E. *The Scientific Study of Scenery*, 6th edn (London: Methuen, 1920)
Miller, T. G. *Geology and Scenery in Britain* (London: Batsford, 1953).
Muir, R. 'The villages of Nidderdale' *Landscape History* **20** (1998).
Selkirk, A. 'Diary' *Current Archaeology* **13** (6) (1996) pp. 209–11.
Shepherd, W. *The Living Landscape of Britain* (London: Faber and Faber, 1952).
Stamp, L. D. Britain's *Structure and Scenery*, 3rd edn (London: Collins, 1949; first published 1946)
Stamp, L. D. 'Reviews: *A Land' The Geographical Journal* **117** (1951) p. 465.
Thornbury, W. D. *Principles of Geology* (New York: John Wiley, 1954).
Trueman, A. E. *The Scenery of England and Wales* (London: Gollancz, 1938) page numbers refer to the Pelican Books edition *Geology and Scenery in England and Wales* of 1949.
Whittow, J. B. *Geology and Scenery in Scotland* (Harmondsworth: Penguin, 1977).

4

Landscapes of the Mind

In experiencing places, we simultaneously encounter two closely related but different landscapes. The one lying beneath our feet and extending to the far horizon is a *real* landscape; it is composed of rock, soil, vegetation and water, is home to an abundance of creatures and has objective past and present existences. The other is the *perceived* landscape, consisting of sensed and remembered accounts and hypotheses about the real landscape. It is, therefore, a selective impression of what the real landscape is like. The impression might be very close to reality, or it might contain some important misconceptions. These might lead, for example, to the neglect of a useful trail, the underestimation of the time needed to scale a peak or a search for birds or plants that prove to be absent in the area. When the one departs, the landscape enduring in the memory to be recalled and recounted will be the one founded on perceptions, not the real landscape.

Yi-Fu Tuan wrote that: 'Landscape . . . is not to be defined by itemizing its parts. The parts are subsidiary clues to an integrated image. Landscape is such an image, a construct of the mind and of feeling' (1979 p. 89). The landscape as perceived by one person is not the same as that perceived by another, for each individual has in his/her mind his/her own cultural and personality filters which select and distort the incoming information. Meinig (Figure 4.1) has described how each member of a small company standing at a vantage point will describe the landscape displayed differently:

It will soon become apparent that even though we gather together and look in the same direction at the same instant, we will not – we cannot – see the same landscape. We may certainly agree that we will see many of the same elements – houses, roads, trees, hills – in terms of such denotations as number, form, dimension, and

Figure 4.1   Meinig wrote that, 'any landscape is composed not only of what lies before our eyes but what lies within our heads'. Some observers looking at this scene might regard the falling water as restful, while others could regard the rugged rocks and swirling currents as elements in a violent landscape. (Richard Muir)

colour, but such facts take on meaning only through association; they must be fitted together according to some coherent body of ideas. Thus we confront the central problem: any landscape is composed not only of what lies before our eyes but what lies within our heads. (1979a pp. 33–4)

Perception studies do not exist merely as an interesting but obscure backwater of the social sciences for:

taking people's perception of places into account as part of our understanding of the pattern of Man's *work* . . . is crucial in that what Man does with his environment . . . arises from how he sees the environment. Perception is not a peripheral matter, for mere academic discussion; it is basic to how men use the world, and hence to very practical issues . . . the use of perception should lie behind the planning and administration of the use of space. This is particularly important where human demands are increasing and spatial resources are getting more scarce. (Wreford Watson, 1975 p. 272)

Ideas about perception have existed since the emergence of sensationalist philosophy in the eighteenth century, but the development of serious frameworks for the investigation and understanding of the nature of perceptions about environments, landscapes and places began in the late 1940s and gathered momentum during the two following decades. Such studies have not only illuminated our understanding of the ways in which humans form decisions about places, but they have also contributed to the historical understanding of processes and phenomena such as colonialism, exploration and colonisation. In each case, it may be found that people were drawn into an area by weakly-founded ideas about its nature and contents, and were subsequently obliged to remodel their ideas and strategies when the high degree of dissonance between the real and the imagined was recognised.

Landscape and the Mind

Wreford Watson noted that: 'Ever since Wright's discussion of mental images as among the *terra incognitae* of geography, geographers have tried to explore the role of perception in the study of place' (1975 p. 271). In 1947, John K. Wright had addressed the Association of American Geographers on: 'Terrae Incognitae: *The Place of the Imagination in Geography*'. He described how:

> although our stone-age ancestors and their descendants down until the dawn of modern times moved back the rim of *terra incognita* bit by bit, their 'known world' was only a pool of light in the midst of a shadow – limitless, for all that was definitely understood and proven. Voyages into this shadow became a favorite theme of poets and story tellers – the theme of the Argonautic myth and the *Odyssey*, of the legends of Sinbad and Saint Brendan. Out of this darkness wild hordes poured forth from time to time to carry fire and sword across Europe – Scyths, Huns, Tartars; it was a mysterious shadow, whence came rumors of strange men and monsters. (1947 p. 1)

Wright thought that geographers were particularly responsive to the challenges of *terrae incognitae*: 'the unknown stimulates the imagination to conjure up mental images of what to look for within it, and the more there is found, the more the imagination suggests to further research' (p. 4). However:

> the imagination might better be compared to a temperamental horse than to an instrument that operates precisely and with objectivity. A highly sensitive function of the mind, it is easily swayed by subjective influences, and for this reason has come in for a share of the disrepute in which subjectivity is often held in scientific circles. (p. 5)

He argued for the creation of professors of a new kind who would raise the standards of literary and artistic expression and direct their scholarship towards the discovery of geographic truth, belief and error in these fields: 'They could do much to keep our eyes open to the Sirens' song and make our voyaging into geographical un- knowns a perenially satisfying venture, for, perhaps, the most fascinating *terrae incognitae* of all are those that lie within the minds and hearts of men' (p. 15). Wright was advocating a 'geosophy', a study of geographies of the mind, the geographical ideas held by people of all kinds; some of these would be close to objective reality, and some further from it (Figures 4.2–4.4, on pp. 120–1).

In 1952, William Kirk, another geographer, provided a more sophisticated and analytical approach to the perception of places, which he expanded in 1963. Kirk had been interested in the German school of Gestalt psychology which had developed around Kurt Koffka, Wolfgang Köhler and Max Wertheimer, who had migrated to the USA in the 1930s. The Gestalt (meaning an organised whole) psychologists regarded the whole as being greater than the sum of its parts and believed that investigations should proceed from above downwards, reversing the normal direction of scientific enquiry. These principles were applied to a range of phenomena, including thinking and perception. Kirk regarded the Gestalt approach as being one that could counter the fractious tendencies splitting geography into human and physical or determinist and possibilist branches or tendencies. He did, incidentally, reject the identification of geography solely as the study of landscape:

> Landscape constitutes one of the most important documents and points of reference in geographical research, but no one could maintain that the study and interpretation of landscape contains all that is geographical. The concept is factually too all-embracing or too restrictive, and in practice tends to break down into the old dichotomy of cultural landscape (for human geographers) and physical landscape (for physical geographers), or, under the influence of the mystic German usage of *landschaft*, dissolves into the concept of area. (1963 p. 361)

Kirk thought that geographers should be concerned with the unified field of the geographical environment, and that within this field the true division of labour concerned the distinction between the real or *phenomenal environment*, consisting of natural phenomena and the physical legacies of human activities, and the perceptual or *behavioural environment*, comprising the ideas about the human setting which have developed in different cultural contexts and according to different socio-economic value systems and the changing human awareness of the environment. He wrote that the concept of the phenomenal environment was an expansion of the normal concept of environment to include not only natural phenomena but environments altered and in some cases almost entirely created by man (p. 364), while 'the facts of the Phenomenal Environment will enter the Behavioural Environment of man, but only in so far as they are perceived by human beings with motives, preferences, modes of thinking, and traditions drawn from their social, cultural context' (p. 366). He added that the same empirical data might arrange itself into different patterns and have different meanings to people of contrasting cultures.

Figure 4.2

Figure 4.3

Figure 4.4

Different landscapes evoke different psychological responses. Here the mist-shrouded view of the mountains around the Old Man of Storr on Skye (4.2) suggests mystery, the scene at Bayham Abbey (4.4) is mystical and the landscape seen from the summit of Carn Brea in Cornwall (4.3) acts like a bridge, combining elements of the mysterious and the mystical. (Richard Muir)

Thus, as Brookfield (1969) observed, decision-makers operating in response to a particular landscape will base their decisions on the environment as they perceive it to be and not as it really is; however, the consequences of the decisions that they make will impact upon the real environment. Cultural factors are likely to condition the perception of a landscape to a considerable degree: a party of Inuit hunters transplanted to the north of Lapland might regard the landscape as hospitable, though most other humans inserted into that setting would consider it strange and threatening. In terms of the colonisation of unfamiliar environments, information has played a vital role, with the growing availability of accurate information tending to narrow the gulf between the phenomenal and behavioural environments and thus reduce the frequency and the severity of the consequences of poorly-informed decisions.

Interest in perception at this time was not confined to psychologists and geographers. In the realms of political science and international relations, Harold and Margaret Sprout studied the influence of environmental factors on international politics, and they identified what they termed 'cognitive behaviourism' as one of the theories concerning the relationship between humans and their environment:

> Cognitive behaviorism is the label that we have selected to designate the simple and familiar principle that a person reacts to his milieu as he apperceives it – that is, as he perceives it and interprets it in the light of past experience. This concept of milieu is variously designated in the special vocabularies of psychological science: 'life-space,' 'psychological field,' 'behavioral environment,' 'psychological environment,' etc. (1957 p. 314)

They added that:

> Cognitive behaviorism simply affirms the elementary first principle that what matters in decision-making is not how the milieu is but how the decision-maker imagines it to be. The next step in linking environmental factors to decisions involves application of some hypothesis as to the decision-maker's environmental knowledge and his mode of using it.

They concluded that:

> With respect to policy-making and the content of political decisions, our position is that what matters is how the policy-maker imagines the milieu to be, not how it actually is. With respect to the operational results of decisions, what matters is how things are, not how the policy maker imagines them to be. In our judgement, a good deal of the confusion which has clouded the discussion of environmental factors in international politics derives from failure to keep this distinction explicit and to observe it rigorously. (p. 328)

In the geographical arena, the ideas of Wright and Kirk on perception combined with those of David Lowenthal (1961) – who

showed that while individuals have personalised behavioural environments, there are also consensus views of the nature of the milieu –
to form the nucleus of a humanistic approach to the subject. This
occurred at a time when mainstream geography was becoming ever
more mired in the dehumanised swamps of spatial analysis. Ultimately, humanistic geography, focusing on real humans in all their
complexities, would vitalise the debilitated discipline, but in the
meantime, a behavioural geography which was concerned with the
processes of perception and decision-making emerged to counteract
the untenable assumptions of the economic models underpinning
spatial analysis. As Walmsley and Lewis (1993 p. 17) explained:

> The initial preoccupation with the relevance of imagination
> (Lowenthal 1975), values and beliefs (Buttimer 1969, 1974), and
> environmental meanings (Tuan 1971) rapidly evolved into a full-
> scale attempt to restore human subjectivity and consciousness to a
> position of prominence within geography (Ley and Samuels
> 1978). This took several directions, including a greater emphasis
> on human values and attitudes (Bowden and Lowenthal 1975;
> Pred 1990), cultural patrimony (Rowntree 1988), the aesthetics of
> landscape and architecture (Cosgrove 1985; Cosgrove and Daniels
> 1988), and the emotional significance of place in human identity
> (Pocock 1981b; Entrikin 1990; Eyles 1985; Eyles and Peace 1990).

They proceeded to quote from Pred (1990 p. 4), who wrote that
what went on in people's minds could not be separated:

> from the construction of unevenly developed built environment,
> from the shaping of landscape and land-use patterns, from the
> appropriation and transformation of nature, from the organiza-
> tion and use of specialized locations for the conduct of economic
> and social practices, from the pattern of movement and inter-
> dependence between such localized activities, from the formation
> of symbolically laden ideology-projecting sites and areas. Human
> consciousness and human geography produce one another.

The expansion of interest in the relationship between the human
mind and the milieu or landscape produced a wealth of research on
the perception of places, some of which was organised into attempts
to construct mental or cognitive maps which would replicate the
subjects' geographical imagination. To select one example from the
many, Shortridge (1984 and 1985) studied popular images of the

American Middle West, earlier described by Meinig as the place alternately praised and damned, yet generally acknowledged to be the cultural core of the nation. 'It is the "heartland," the home of the average or "middle" American. Its Main Street has become a powerful symbolic landscape, evoking images of a "sober, sensible, practical people"' (1979b, p. 167). Shortridge argued that even critics who labeled the place as materialistic and xenophobic never denied its cultural importance (1984 p. 209) and he showed that the term 'Middle West' was first adopted as a regional label in the 1880s as a name which distinguished between the relatively settled central plains and the pioneer zone of the Dakotas in the north-west and the culturally different areas of Texas and the Indian Territory in the south-west. It had Kansas and Nebraska as its core. Just after the turn of the century, writers were including states of the northern plains and old north-west in their perceptions of the Middle West, a practice which had become universal by 1912.

The region was being identified with a pastoral ideal and the qualities of the Mid West matched the widespread American self-image; by this time it was regarded as the cultural core of the nation, a perception which was not seriously challenged until the third decade of the century. In a subsequent study, Shortridge (1985) explored inconsistencies in the popular perceptions about the location and extent of the Mid West. While scholars and journalists shared one view of its location, college students regarded its core as lying in the 'original' setting of Kansas and Nebraska. Natives of Indiana, Michigan and Ohio tended to regard their own states as being part of the Mid West, but outsiders seldom did so. Shortridge considered that regional images explained the differing perceptions of the Mid West; Americans viewed the region in terms of rural, pastoral and small town stereotypes and found it hard to dissociate pastoralism from the perceived regional identity. Thus, when the urban industrial realities changed, as with the development of urbanisation and industrialisation, the public found it easier to shift their perceived Mid West core region westwards rather than to adjust their vision of the region to the new realities. Shortridge wrote that fundamental to his argument was the extremely strong tie that always has existed between pastoralism and the American self-image, with many of the country's most cherished values – including self-reliance, democracy and moral decency – being said to be derived largely from rural, egalitarian society. This system of beliefs was traditionally focused on the 12-state Middle West.

Novels and other forms of creative writing may be extremely influential in the formation of vernacular images of less familiar landscapes. As Pocock has described, the novel was a late arrival on the cultural scene, but when it did arrive, it offered new dimensions to the relationship between people and settings:

> when the novel replaced the epic and drama as the main literary form in the early eighteenth century, its chief novelty was to add to the ancient portrayal of 'life by values' that of 'life in time' . . . Medieval stories had traditionally recounted unchanged moral truths in timeless settings, the plots themselves being freely borrowed between different countries and cultures; now, the novel was time-specific and, thus, by implication, *place-specific* also. (1981b p. 337)

At first, the settings of novels were generalised, but by the time of Jane Austen, detailed sketches of the locations had appeared and by the second quarter of the nineteenth century, the English regional novel had emerged. In the USA, the first North American novelist to enjoy great success with books based on American landscape settings was James Fenimore Cooper, whose *The Spy*, a story set in the Revolutionary War, was published in 1821. North America was perceived as a remarkable and fascinating place:

> The most obvious thing that writers in America could invoke to stress their distinction from the mother country was the physical landscape itself. From its initial discovery, exotic and unknown North America had held great imaginative appeal for Europeans, and accounts and travel literature about it had flourished since Columbus's day. (Barden, 1996 p. 58)

Pocock explored the novelist's image of the North of England (1979b). This consistently conformed to the stereotype of a harsh landscape and climate, a place characterised by mines, industry and deprivation and populated by earnest people with hardened leaders:

> Amongst all the characteristics, natural or man-made, smoke is perhaps the most obvious single indicator or symbol of the North. It is ubiquitous, being the first to greet the visitors and the last visible sign on the horizon at departure; it has darkened the landscape and assails the senses. Its role is evident from the earliest of the social novels. (1979b p. 68)

Pocock noted the potency of the literary image in affecting popular perception of places that would otherwise be little known, remarking that:

> The realm of literature is an important source for student images of place, for in environmental description, no less than in character-drawing or drama, the literary artist is distinguished by his quality of observation and insight . . . The widespread and persistent circulation of the 'message' of particular major works may mean that the literary input to the image of place is high, providing a literary frame of reference with which to approach or view a particular environment. Moreover, given the nature of the environment of the mind, the literary influence may well increase with time, and even persist when contrary evidence is available to refute the traditional image. (1979b p. 62)

Other images of landscapes and places are formed in the course of day-to-day journeys, with the relationship between locations being encapsulated in what geographers have labelled a 'mental map'. In the course of sensing, the mind simplifies complex environmental reality into an environmental image:

> Concerned with locational and spatial characteristics, the 'whereness' content, of the total data store, mental maps constitute the skeletal framework of the more rounded phenomenon of the image, some parts of which are clearly aspatial in nature. (Indeed, part of our response to environment may remain not only unmappable but uncommunicable in any medium, as the strivings of artists, and personal experience, confirm.) (Pocock, 1979a p. 279)

The mental map, unlike the atlas page map, is an ever-evolving construction into which new information is frequently incorporated, as demonstrated in a survey by Canter (1977), who studied the developing mental maps of an American visitor to Central London before arriving and on days 1, 9 and 23 of the visit. A criticism of an involvement with mental maps is that the maps tend to be unique, while even the individual may entertain different perceptions of places depending on, say, whether he or she is considering them as places for recreational visits or evaluating them as centres in which to seek work. A common factor, however, is that images of place tend strongly to be biased towards the home culture and experience of the observer concerned, leading to perceptions of outsiders in 'us' and 'them' terms (Goodey, 1974).

Time and place are firmly linked in perception studies. Prince considered that: 'A fresh understanding of how other people in other times have perceived reality enables us to gain a fuller knowledge of the world in which we live' (1971 p. 24). We must also realise that our relationship with the past is complex; at various times we remould history or indulge in attempts to preserve, and thus change, the relics of the past. But we are also partly the products of our pasts, so that when we reshape our perceptions of the past we also reshape ourselves. Lowenthal notes that:

Nothing ever made has been left untouched, nothing ever known remains immutable . . . It is far better to realize the past has always been altered than to pretend it has always been the same . . . Every relic is a testament not only to its initiators but to its inheritors, not only to the spirit of the past but to the perspectives of the present. (1985 p. 412)

Writers such as Prince and Lowenthal have studied imagined worlds of the past, while Dellheim studied past perceptions of people and place in his exploration of Victorian views of the North of England (1987). Noting that a North–South antithesis in England could be traced back to the twelfth-century tension between King John and his barons and that it had gained a peculiar slant with industrialisation, Dellheim thought that the *locus classicus* was Mrs Gaskell's *North and South* (1855), where North and South were states of mind, not merely stretches of land. There, northerners were presented as energetic, innovative and adventurous, but prone to philistinism and selfishness, while southerners emerged as genteel, romantic and conservative, yet snobbish and soft. Dellheim argued that when approaching Victorian views of the North, it was useful to take account of certain premises derived from the study of environmental perception by geographers:

First of all, perceptions of place vary according to the location, approach, and biases of individuals and groups. Secondly, mental maps are coloured by diverse factors. Landscape, climate, dialect, economy, politics, and culture – all these contribute to the sense of place. Thirdly, we are intolerant of conflicting images. We tend to rate cities and regions positively or negatively on all counts. This is especially true of outsiders with only passing knowledge or enduring ignorance about a place. Finally, mental images of places have important social consequences. They affect political and economic decision-making and patterns of population migration. (1987 pp. 217–18)

It was found that the stereotyping of North and South encouraged a neglect of the differences existing *within* each division. The individuality of the northern towns, their strongly developed civic pride and the intense rivalries that existed between them could be overlooked, while:

> If many northern writers accepted the conventional contrast between the rugged, independent northern character and the soft, polished southern character, they did not view the North as a unitary, homogenous region. Their main concern was to delineate the unique features of their own localities. In so doing they created a sense of identity based upon places rather than class. (p. 218)

It is sometimes suggested that the way in which to understand events and practices of the past is to see the world through the eyes of former cultures. However, the nature of culture is such that this goal is difficult or impossible to achieve. Members of a modern, materialistic society can scarcely begin to appreciate the world of prehistoric predecessors in which a categorisation between religion, economics and the social realm may not have been recognised, and in which gods inhabited trees, rocks and soil. To quote again from Prince, 'For the followers of many religions, reality on earth is only to be experienced through imitations of heavenly archetypes' (1971 p. 24). He notes that Benedetto Croce had attempted to recapture the history of neolithic Liguria or Sicily by inviting his readers to adopt the role of Stone Age Ligurians or Sicilians yet: 'Unless we possess some expression of their abstract thoughts we have no means of knowing whether they would have regarded themselves as neolithic or Ligurian or Sicilian, let alone how they viewed their surroundings' (p. 29). Domesday Book embodied a Norman itemisation of salient facts about eleventh-century England, yet we still do not understand how the Normans perceived the country and the mental images that thoughts of 'England' would evoke in them.

Perceptions of landscape and landscape type will evolve through time. In the eighteenth century, the beach was often regarded as a hostile and dangerous place which lay at the margins of two worlds. During the late eighteenth and early nineteenth centuries, excursions to seaside locations became fashionable in England, and gradually the beach began to be perceived as a place for healthy stimulation and excitement, while during the first half of the nineteenth century, the seaside was used as a venue for risqué relationships in several novels by writers such as Jane Austen and Thackeray (Foden, 1996). Subsequently, the beach became variously a mysterious place for contemplation; a venue for the earnest exploration of geology, sea shells, fossils and evolution; a symbolic borderland between different elements and cultures or betwixt life and death; and finally, with the establishment of cheap holidays with pay in the middle third of the twentieth century, a crowded, overpopulated place of tacky resorts and raucous fun.

People and cultures evolve, and with them evolve perceptions of landscape, just as Cosgrove's studies of Venice show that the history and meaning of the city and its landscape were repeatedly reinterpreted in the light of perceptions and preoccupations of very different societies (Cosgrove, 1982 pp. 162–3). New developments in technology can also affect these perceptions, with the present century witnessing a great acceleration in the pace of change. David Harvey (1990 p. 426) has quoted the poet, Heine, who saw that changes in transport would transform the appreciation of places: 'Even the elementary concepts of time and space have begun to vacillate. Space is killed by the railways. I feel as if the mountains and forests of all countries were advancing on Paris. Even now, I can smell the German linden trees; the North Sea's breakers are rolling against my door.'

While evolution in culture and in the circumstances in the external world which create culture result in changes in the perception of landscape, the simple process of growing up can result in marked changes in landscape perception within a few years of the life of an individual. The youngster's poorly-developed perception of landscape is portrayed by the historian, Barrell, in terms of Hardy's character, Tess of the D'Urbervilles:

Tess, it seems, had not at sixteen progressed far beyond a child's sense of place, as we might put it 'what had been mystery to her then was not much less than mystery to her now'. She knows only a small proportion of the vale and the hills that surround it she has seen only from below, only from Marlott, so that familiar as their contours are from there, the hills have as it were only two dimensions, they are a flat wall on her world beyond which she knows only what she has learned at school. (Barrell, 1982 pp. 352–3)

Yi-Fu Tuan quoted research carried out by the Estvans in the 1950s which showed that when first-grade pupils were shown different pictures of a village, a farm, a town centre and a factory, they often failed to recognise a structured entity – a landscape – in the picture, but:

As the children mature they learn to see landscapes in an increasingly complex manner. When they look at a farmstead they are able to discern that it has a regional context, that it has special functions within a regional economy, and that the scene before them was different in the past and will change again in the future. In other words, they learn to perceive more and more with the mind's eye. (1979 p. 91)

Not only is research into the perception of landscape relevant and revealing, it also embodies a reassertion of the humanity and individuality of people who might otherwise be regarded in aggregate or mechanistic forms. Moreover, it brings us as close as we may ever get to that elusive yet wonderful entity, the sense of place, which creates an emotional human relationship with landscape from what might otherwise be reduced to a cataloguing of rock, soil and plant types.

Visions of the West

Studies of the penetration and colonisation of unfamiliar places show how the images of those places, their contents and climate are regularly modified to accord with new information that becomes available. Some perceptions, however, are deeply rooted and stubbornly retained, so that information which undermines the stereotype is excluded and discounted until a point arrives where it becomes irrefutable and the image of the place concerned must be comprehensively redesigned to accommodate the new facts. In all processes of colonising little-known territory there will be a gap between the landscapes of the imagination and expectation on the one hand, and the geographical realities on the other. If this gap is a wide one, settlers will arrive ill-prepared and poorly adjusted in terms of the realities that are in store for them, and they may modify their approaches, retreat or perish. The notion of discord between the behavioural and phenomenal worlds can be exemplified by cases drawn from the colonisation of the interior of North America.

The image of the continent that awaited Europeans in 1492 and the years that followed has been distorted by myth and America is regarded as having been an untouched wilderness. But:

> The pristine view is to a large extent an invention of nineteenth-century romanticist and primitivist writers such as W. H. Hudson, Cooper, Thoreau, Longfellow, and Parkman and painters such as Catlin and Church. The wilderness image has since become part of the American heritage, associated with a heroic pioneer past in need of preservation. (Denevan, 1992 p. 369)

In fact, however:

> By 1492 Indian activity throughout the Americas had modified forest extent and composition, created and expanded grasslands, and rearranged microrelief via countless artificial earthworks. Agricultural fields were common, as were houses and towns and roads and trails. All of these had local impacts on soil, micro-climate, hydrology, and wildlife. (p. 370)

The construction of this false perception or 'pristine myth' took place not so much during the earliest period of European colonisation, but in the period 1750–1850, when the numbers of the native American population had been reduced by 90 per cent and when Europeans were penetrating the more empty interior areas. By this time, many of the native fields, settlements and earthworks were overgrown and inconspicuous, creating an illusion of emptiness which was projected back in time.

As Watson and O'Riordan describe:

> In a new-found environment it is not what people actually see there so much as what they want to see or think they see that influences their reaction . . . The British and other Europeans

who went to America saw it in terms of what they were running away from, and what they were running away to, as well as what they actually came across once they were there. (1976 p. 1)

There were many striking realities about the new land that could not be masked by illusion: Lowenthal (1968) has described how settlers in North America were suprised by the emptiness of the interior and shocked by the violence of the landscape with its harsh extremes of climate. He thought that: 'Weary weeks on the Atlantic, eyes straining between sky and sea, did not habituate travelers to the continental scale of America. They expected monotony from the sea, but not from the land.' The analogy with the sea occurs frequently in the accounts of the early travellers to the West. The author and retired naval officer, Captain Marryat, wrote in his diary in the 1830s:

Look round in every quarter of the compass, and there you are as if on the ocean – not a landmark, not a vestige of anything human but yourself. Instead of sky and water, it is one vast field, bounded only by the horizon, its surface gently undulating like the waves of the ocean; and as the wind (which blows fresh on the prairies) bows down the heads of the high grass, it gives you the idea of a running swell. (1839 p. 86)

Similarly, Dickens soon afterwards described the prairie as being 'like a sea without water'.

In one of the most remarkable instances of territorial expansion, in 1803, the youthful federation had purchased some 909 000 square miles of land from the French for $15 million, thus doubling the size of the USA. It was then necessary to despatch explorers to report on the extent and contents of the new and largely unknown territory. At first, the gap between perception and reality was so wide as to lose the Rockies, so that there was a measure of consensus that the western cordilleras presented no serious barrier to the expansion of American commerce and settlement westwards to the Pacific. The image of the American interior was rooted more in optimism than in fact, and information gleaned in known areas was freely transposed to the unexplored lands. According to Allen (1971), the predominating concept of the West was of a garden blessed with extremely fertile soil and climates that were soft and salubrious. Some accounts maintained that immense plains stretched as far as the southern ocean, but they were not barren, sandy or even partially arid:

> They were verdant, lush, teeming with game and, most important, available for the spread of an agricultural population. The rivers flowed among the most beautiful dales; the Mississippi and other rivers of Louisiana were analogous to Niles which diffused the fertility of Egypt from their banks. The West was full of hope. (p. 152)

Subsequently, this rose-tinted vision of the continental interior would be replaced by a far more pessimistic perception. Bowden has devalued the influence on nineteenth-century minds of the notion of a 'Great American Desert' lying between the Missouri and the Rockies and he wrote that:

> The history of geographical thought is studded with *idées fixes*, true and false. One of these is the recent academic notion that for fifty years (1820–70) the American public believed that a Great American Desert existed east of the Rockies. The same fixed idea of this earlier view was held by many better-educated Americans in the 1880s and 1890s. The fixed idea is false because the desert belief was far from universally held in America in the mid-nineteenth century. It is doubtful whether the primary-school educated in most regions of the United States ever held a desert image of the lands beyond the Missouri River. Not even among the well-educated in New England, among whom the desert belief was strongest, did the view persist for longer than forty years that a vast desert existed east of the Rockies. (Bowden, 1976 pp. 119–20)

The notion of an arid zone had some basis in mid-century exploration, with an extensive area of the Great Plains north of the Canadian border becoming known as 'Palliser's Triangle' following an expedition in the late 1850s led by Captain John Palliser that described a semi-arid triangular zone. According to Lewis, 'The concept of a desert, or near desert, surrounded to the north-east and north-west by a broad fertile zone, would seem to have been an essential component of the perceptions of the northern grasslands during the 1860s' (1976 p. 43). He concluded that British and Canadian characterisations influenced readers of reports like Palliser's to think things to be worse than they really were on the

American Great Plains. Palliser had overstressed the prominence of sage and cactus: 'this was grassland not sagebrush country, *but to the eye of a man who already had a mental image of the Great American Desert*, sage and cactus doubtless sprang to view' (p. 44). He added:

> people look for what they think should be typical and, finding some examples of this, may 'type' an area, all but regardless of what in fact are its truly typical forms. It is in this way that mental images help to shape the geography of the land . . . This immense illusion . . . which . . . was at its height between 1850 and 1860, just as the tide of immigration rolled up to the Great Plains, enormously affected the peopling of America, and thus the geography of the country, by keeping the plains relatively inert while the Pacific coast became the active frontier of the United States. (pp. 44–5)

Mental images seem to have combined with cultural conditioning to encourage settlers to continue westwards beyond the Great Plains:

> For many settlers from the east, treelessness was proof of the soil's inherent infertility. Coming from a wood-based culture, settlers required vast amounts of cheap timber for fuel, building materials, fencing and farm implements. Popular aversion to the plains may, however, say as much about the needs of later generations for certain levels of capital investment and technological improvements (deep ploughs, barbed wire and cheap wind pumps), along with an unprecedented demand for cheap food, than about any bucolic idiocy peculiar to the first settlers. (Mills, 1997 p. 20)

While the semi-arid lands to the west of the Missouri tended to be regarded as an American Eden until they were explored, and were subsequently stigmatised as a 'great desert', the wet prairie of east central Illinois, currently containing some of the most valuable corn and soyabean belt farmland in the USA, was previously derided for its malarial sloughs and swamps, the extent of which were greatly exaggerated. Winsor (1987 p. 393) has shown that: 'Terrain distortion, once established, would be plagiarized by others', and that:

> Wetness was perceived as the overriding property of the area. Imagery focused on wetness because it was a novel, readily

recognizable characteristic. It was seen as 'typical' and the area was 'typed' as wet, regardless of what was actually representative. Erroneous landscape notions were more persuasive than accurate ones. Travellers passing through the tall-grass prairie constantly scanned the horizon in their search for spatial cues to guide their travels, for this was a landscape with few visible landmarks, whose uniformity led to sensory deprivation and navigational confusion. The pervasive wetness, coupled with the spectre of malaria and the inherent isolation prior to the coming of the railroad, stigmatized the region in the minds of many. The region suffered from adverse spatial stereotyping with particular areas dominating the shared spatial memories, the images of which remained long after the particular wet features were drained. It was prophetic that east central Illinois, initially a region which repelled travelers and settlers, with reclamation has become some of the nation's most valuable farmland. (p. 394)

With regard to the negative stereotyping, one agricultural correspondent wrote in 1876:

The symbol of the country should be changed from the American Eagle to the American goose since it is more fitting for an institution run by water; and then if the water covers the land, our goose will be in her right element and paddle her own canoe, while the eagle will present a bedraggled and woe-begone appearance, as he makes a frantic effort to navigate the rolling billows while his screams of distress will be drowned in the rush and roar of the flood. (Barnard, 1876 p. 369)

The perceptions that really mattered were those held by potential immigrants to the interior. These were based on information derived from several sources: from the journals and official reports produced by explorers; from the letters and diaries of other emigrants; from the paintings and illustrations by frontier artists like Frank Buscher, Karl Bodmer and George Catlin; from those who journeyed to and fro, shifting jobs between the frontier and the settled area; and from those, like the agents of the shipping and railway companies, who had vested interests in stimulating migration. Hudson (1976) wrote that: 'Much can be made of the perceived versus real opportunities open to those who moved towards the Great Plains, whether there was deception in the process of luring people to the west (there was), and whether many who joined in should have done so.' He thought, however, that what was most striking was not the lack of information possessed by pioneers wandering into the unfamiliar grasslands of North Dakota, but instead the apparently well-used networks employed in dispersing information about economic opportunities as they arose.

Though we may tend to imagine that false perceptions of the American interior belong to the pioneering phase, which ended a good century ago, and that accurate impressions developed as soon as the Great Plains were settled, in fact the nature of the region was still being debated through the twentieth century. In 1931, Walter Prescott Webb published *The Great Plains*, in which he argued that:

> the lands beyond the 98th meridian were sufficiently arid to create an institutional break unlike anything encountered before or since on the American frontier, and in the pioneers' encounter with this arid and deficient environment a new and distinctive civilization was born . . . The Dust Bowl [of the 1930s] gave strong support to his thesis and convinced many that the Plains were far drier than the lands east of the 98th meridian. (Bowden, 1976 p. 133)

But while Webb characterised the Great Plains as a permanent and periodic desert, James C. Malin (1944) adopted an ecological approach and presented the region as an agriculturally rich grassland ecosystem which could be farmed productively by those who applied the folk knowledge of the early farmers. Whichever interpretation is correct, the public at large is likely to accept the desert hypothesis, for the region only tends to reach the headlines when the periodic droughts return to stress the population, as in the 1930s and 1950s.

Among the varied perceptions of the American West, the strongest and most pervasive is associated with the romantic image of the frontiersman and cowboy, even though the heyday of the cowboy lasted only from the close of the Civil War until the severe winter of 1886. Allen (1992) believes that much of the invented tradition derived from American interpretations of the European Romantic tradition and developed from roots in the painting and literature associated with the fur trade in the Rocky Mountains during the earlier part of the nineteenth century, when the art of George Catlin, Alfred Jacob Miller and Karl Bodmer was very influential. He wrote that:

The Romantic artists and writers who penetrated the American West did not need to seek meaning and truth in visions of an Arcadia of antiquity for the West itself was Arcadia, a land before the Fall, the virginal creation of God, filled with mythic heroes clad in feathered headdresses or buckskin and homespun. (p. 27)

If the romance of the cowboy era was rooted in the earlier era of the Mountain Men, much of the socio-cultural baggage of the Wild West originated in the eastern states:

Mention the frontier and people envisage Montana or Arizona, not the Tidewater or the Shenandoah; mention new western history and even academics think of women along the Oregon Trail rather than settler–native interaction along the 1680s Tidewater or the impact of Ulster settlers around 1750s Winchester. But it was in these eastern areas that there emerged societal organizations geared to moving inland and racial attitudes that would plague the native peoples . . . Understanding representational filters is crucial, for it is in images, rather in scholarly tomes, that those who are not professional scholars are most likley to come into contact with the frontier. (Mills, 1996 pp. 24–5)

Even the material culture of the cowboy was borrowed from elsewhere, with the lariats, chaps and cattle herding skills being learned from the *vaqueros* who worked on Mexican *haciendas* for *hidalgos* or *patrons*. Soon, however, the image of the West would be adopted as the image of all America as the bold and the meek, the city-dweller and suburbanite, the energetic and the idle all sought to share the mantle of the resolute, independent frontiersman: a role still more magnetic and potent than any attempts to civilise the lethal culture of the gun.

In exploring the popular visions of the physical and cultural landscapes of the North American interior, we find layers of environmental perceptions – many at variance with reality and many at variance with each other – stratified one upon the other. Now the different visions of the past underpin the contests between different versions of history while, when migration to the frontier was a dominating feature of American life, these visions provided the information sources upon which a host of decisions were based. Gossip, rumour and misty or twisted versions of reality determined whether settlers sought Wyoming, Texas or California and how they planned to get there, while bad information could, and often did, cost lives. The myths which conditioned life in the West and our understanding of it have fascinated scholars and have given rise to a rich academic literature. There is no reason, however, to suppose that the American interior is in some way exceptional; perhaps the colonisation of Siberia or Patagonia would reveal quite comparable stories of the perception and misinterpretation of physical and cultural landscapes?

All these ideas are encapsulated in words written by Bowman in 1934 and quoted by Watson and O'Riordan:

> the natural environment is always a different thing to different groups. Its potentialities are absolute, but their realization is a relative matter, relative to what the particular man wants and what he can get with the instruments of power and the ideas at his command and the standards of living he demands or strives to attain. (1976 p. 113)

According to Bowden (1992) the main period in which myths about the American environment and its colonists were created was the middle and late nineteenth century, when the entire body of traditions was either invented or refashioned. Some traditions were developed by political and religious leaders, some by the literary and artistic elites, while some were given form and substance by great figures who provided grand metaphors for the nation. He concluded that:

> The grand invented tradition of American nature as a whole is the pristine wilderness, a succession of imagined environments which have been conceived as far more difficult for settlers to conquer than they ever were in reality. The pristine wilderness in the Northeast took the form of a howling desert wilderness in the seventeenth century. In the eastern United States as a whole, the pristine wilderness became the primeval forest of the nineteenth century. The infertile virgin prairie and the Great American Desert came later in time and space. The ignoble savage, non-agricultural and barely human, was invented to justify dispossession of the Indian and to prove that the Indian had no part in transforming America from Wilderness to Garden . . . With the Indians branded as indolent and incapable of learning the arts of

civilization, America was made by Puritan saint, yeoman, pioneer/frontiersman, sodbuster, cowboy, and latter-day saint: superhuman, overachieving, self-glorifying Americans all. (p. 20)

Visions of Villages

Some perceptions of landscape will persist despite mounting evidence of their inaccuracy and redundancy. Countrysides may be imagined to be vibrant with wildlife and birdsong and spangled with wildflowers long after modern industrial farming equipped with pesticides and herbicides have left them sterile and lifeless. In England, the village exists as a potent symbol of qualities of life which, if they ever existed, are lost; lost, yet now craved by the rootless urban industrial societies. The village has developed a mythology which continues to entrance and beguile masses of people, many of whom display uncertainty and confusion in their understanding of where the idyll ends and reality begins. Members of this community may migrate to the countryside and buy into the village myth and, when they fail to find it waiting for them ready made, they set out, with chintz, pine and rambling roses, to manufacture it for themselves. Now, in scores of commuter-colonised villages new landscapes are contrived to 'recreate' village scenery which never previously existed. At the conclusion of a survey of the evolution of the English village, Yates wrote:

> English rural settlement has been subject to great change, reflecting economic development. The changes have been in form and function, social grouping, and in population. The most static element has been our conception of the village . . . Despite the pillaging of William I, the anarchy of Stephen's reign, the gibbets, rack-renting, eviction, and rick burning and riots, the village is still described in idyllic terms. It is the illusion that beckons, not the reality. (1982 p. 201)

The idyllic village may well be illusory, but this is not to say that it is without influence. It is, in fact, a symbol of durability and great power, and many of those who died fighting for England were motivated by visions of wholesome rural communities and cottage huddles: 'The imagined English village is as much part of the English "heritage" as a hedge or a church or a duck or a sunset' (Matless, 1994 p. 9).

If there is such a thing as a typical English village it can be characterised today as a rural settlement wracked and divided by tensions between its declining indigenous rural working-class population and its immigrant population of affluent and influential middle-class commuters, and as a place which is set within countrysides visually and ecologically devalued by hedgerow removal, the

Figure 4.5   In the popular imagination, English villages seem to symbolise timelessness and stability, and this scene, at Lower Slaughter in the Cotswolds, would seem to encapsulate such sentiments. In fact, like so many others, the village has changed considerably over the centuries, with the built-up area expanding across a riverside green. (Richard Muir)

draining of ponds and wetlands and the intensive use of heavy agricultural machinery and agro-chemicals. In the present context, however, it is not what the village *is* that matters, but what it is *perceived* to be. Despite all the contrary evidence crowding in from the tortured countryside, the village is still widely regarded as a place of rose-decked cottages where comradeship and old-fashioned upright values prevail. In this capacity, the village exists not only as a perception or vision, but also as a powerful symbol. Meinig has shown that: 'Every mature nation has its symbolic landscapes. They are part of the iconography of nationhood, part of the shared set of ideas and memories and feelings which bind a people together' (1979b p. 164). In its capacity as a symbol, the English village could look back on around a thousand years of existence. When the function of the village as a symbol was growing in England, the role was adopted by much younger settlements on the other side of the Atlantic, in New England. Bowden writes that:

> The colonial village became both the icon of New England's exceptionalism in America and proof of the special relationship between old and New England, so important to New England writers who worshipped England and the English landscape in the nineteenth century. With senses bombarded by orators, writers and lithographers, New Englanders found it increasingly easy to project what lay around them backwards to the colonial period: the seemingly unchanging villages on the green that dominated the prosperous yeoman landscape of large two-storey houses. (1992, p. 18)

According to Meinig, there are:

> landscape depictions which may be powerfully evocative because they are understood as being a particular kind of place rather than a precise building or locality. Among the most famous in America is the scene of a village embowered in great elms and maples, its location marked by a slender steeple rising gracefully above a white wooden church which faces on a village green around which are arrayed large white clapboard houses which, like the church, show a simple elegance in form and trim. These few phrases are sufficient to conjure an instant mental image of a special kind of place in a very famous region . . . Our interest is not simply in the fact that such a scene 'says' New England, but more especially in

what New England 'says' to us through the medium of its villages. (1979b p. 165)

Wood continued in a similar vein:

The village is the material symbol of a strongly-held American tradition of New England covenanted community, cultural enlightenment, and democratic self-government. Few historical or geographical descriptions of the United States fail to refer to the formative communities served by the village of tree-shaded green surrounded by a tall-steepled church and white-clapboarded shops and dwellings. (1991 p. 32)

But then he points out that the village tradition is *invented*. Many of the early English settlers in New England came from places where rural settlement was dispersed rather than nucleated, and the sense of community which developed did not depend upon the existence of villages; 'village' was then interpreted not in terms of settlement but only in terms of community, which existed as a social web. The establishment and survival of community did not require the clustering of settlement and Colonial New England was not a place of villages, but rather a land of modest, dispersed single-storey farmsteads. Elswhere, Wood explains that: 'The village encountered in New England today, white-painted, black shuttered, classical-revival dwellings, churches, and stores abutting a tree-shaded green, reflects not continuity with New England's colonial past but a most dramatic change' (1982 p. 343). This change took place in the Federal period, spanning the last generation of the eighteenth century and the first generation of the nineteenth. At this time economic activities became regionalised and New Englanders abandoned their traditional culture moulds to establish a landscape of commercial centres where, hitherto, meetinghouses had stood in isolation. It was only when the settlement pattern changed from being dispersed to being nucleated that 'village' took on its present connotation. When villages had come into existence they were then incorporated into a mythological interpretation of New England settlement and society. Members of the nineteenth-century elite, comprising writers, travellers, lithographers, landscape architects, social reformers and social scientists, created a geographical past which never existed:

Villages housing a culturally enlightened populace became symbolic models for a place-seated pastoral community during this
New England Renaissance . . . we create our own geographies,
consciously or not, and . . . geographies in our minds are crude
approximations or inelegant models of those on the ground, and
vice versa. In creating our own geographies, we justify those of the
past and legitimate those of the present. (Wood, 1991 p. 33)

Thus the educated middle-class inventors of tradition created a
New England of the mind which focused on the village landscape, so
that the village, with its green, shaded by trees and flanked by
church and substantial white houses, became part of the historic
tableau on which the Romantic myths could be enacted. Meanwhile,
villages of the mind were being created by some landed interests in
England, often in attempts to evoke a sentimental vision of the
ancient village (real examples of which existed in their thousands).
At Ripley in North Yorkshire in the earlier part of the nineteenth
century, the Ingilby family, the proprietors, demolished a village of
genuine medieval timber-framed homes and replaced it with a
village of mock-Tudor terraced stone cottages, and at Old Warden
in Bedfordshire the whimsy was of a more eccentric variety: cottages
were built in a variety of designs borrowed from European vernacular buildings, while the villagers were expected to appear dressed
up in cloaks. Villages and the local community were manipulated in
order to project just the vision that the landlord chose to create and
convey. Taigel and Williamson noted that while earlier 'model
villages', like Houghton (in Norfolk), had largely been erected for
the practical reasons associated with replacing settlements destroyed
by emparking in the nineteenth century, estate villages were being
employed to bolster an owner's prestige by demonstrating his
concern for the estate community.

But just as it was the landowner's initials which were seen on
estate houses, so it was his hand which was to be seen in front
gardens. The back garden could be devoted to the pig and the
vegetables; the front was visible, and not to be left to the tender
mercies of the uneducated tenant . . . In his picturesque village at
Harlaxton (Lincolnshire), Gregory Gregory went as far as to
specify which climbing plants were to grow up each house wall.
(1993 p. 93)

Figure 4.6

Figure 4.7

This rubble-walled and thatched cottage in Northamptonshire (4.6) epito-mises the romantic vision of 'Village England'. Dwellings such as these, which were built in the vernacular styles of the English regions, inspired the construction of sentimental parodies, like this cottage orné in Bedfordshire (4.7). (Richard Muir)

In 1789, the Blaise Castle estate at Henbury, near Bristol, was bought by the Quaker banker, John Harford. Fifteen years later he had the idea of creating a small village for retired estate workers, and employed John Nash as his architect:

> The result was Blaise Hamlet, an impossibly quaint group of ten cottages on $1\frac{3}{4}$ acres ranged irregularly round a 'village green'. Variously described as 'on the verge of noddyland' and 'responsible for some of the worst sentimentalities of England', the Hamlet is nevertheless a tour de force of Picturesque theory and the Romantic idealization of country living. (Tinniswood, 1995 p. 109)

Each dwelling was different, and each seemed to embody the attempt to cram as many parodies of vernacular architecture as possible into the space available.

The landscapes of the mind must be given a thorough consideration in any account of the interaction between humans and their settings. Perceptions of landscape are not significant solely as somewhat off-target impressions of reality. Sometimes they have a considerable effect in reshaping reality so that it more closely matches the vision, as when villages are modelled on a romantic misconception of what villages were like. Whole histories have been built on false perceptions of what the past involved, whether this was a past in which early settlers founded villages in New England, or one in which imagined hordes of Anglo-Saxon invaders created countrysides of farmland and villages out of a tangled English wildwood. When we enter the realms of landscape perception, we encounter facets of the scene which are 'seen' not because they are really there but because observers expected to see them there; we discover scenes that are sensed and interpreted in as many different ways as there are viewers to view them, and we find that our own recognition of landscape evolves as we grow older.

References

Allen, J. L. 'Geographical knowledge and American images of the Louisiana territory' *Western Historical Quarterly* **2** (1971) pp. 151–70.

Allen, J. L. 'Horizons of the sublime: the invention of the romantic west' *Journal of Historical Geography* **18** (1992) pp. 27–40.

Barden, T. E. 'Folklore and American democratic literature' in Davies, P. J. (ed.), *Representing and Imagining America* (Keele: Keele University Press, 1996).

Barnard, M. 'From Kankakee County' *Prairie Farmer* **47** (1876).

Barrell, J. 'Geographies of Hardy's Wessex' *Journal of Historical Geography* **8** (1982) pp. 347–61.

Bowden, M. J. 'The Great American desert in the American Mind: the historiography of a geographical notion' in Lowenthal, D. and Bowden, M. J. (eds), *Geographies of the Mind* (New York: Oxford University Press, 1976) pp. 119–147.

Bowden, M. J. 'The invention of American tradition' *Journal of Historical Geography* **18** (1992) pp. 3–26.

Bowden, M. J. and Lowenthal, D. (eds), *Geographies of the Mind* (London: Oxford University Press, 1975)

Bowman, T. *Geography in Relation to the Social Sciences* (New York: Scribner, 1934).

Brookfield, H. C. 'On the environment as perceived' *Progress in Geography* **1** (1969) pp. 51–80.

Buttimer, A. 'Social space in interdisciplinary perspective' *Geographical Review* **59** (1969) pp. 417–26.

Buttimer, A. *Values in Geography*, Association of American Geographers Commission on College Geography, Resource Paper No. 24 (Washington, 1974).

Canter, D. *The Psychology of Place* (London: Architectural Press, 1977).

Cosgrove, D. 'The myth and the stones of Venice: an historical geography of a symbolic landscape' *Journal of Historical Geography* **8** (1982) pp. 145–69.

Cosgrove, D. *Social Formation and Symbolic Landscape* (Totowa, NJ: Barnes & Noble, 1985).

Cosgrove, D. and Daniels, S. (eds), *The Iconography of Landscape* (Cambridge: Cambridge University Press, 1988).

Dellheim, C. 'Imagining England: Victorian views of the North' *Northern History* **23** (1987) pp. 216–30.

Denevan, W. A. 'The pristine myth: the landscape of the Americas in 1492' *Annals of the Association of American Geographers* **82** (1992) pp. 369–85.

Dickens, C. *American Notes for General Circulation* (London: Chapman & Hall, 1842).

Entrikin, N. J. *The Betweenness of Place: Towards a Geography of Modernity* (London: Macmillan, 1990).

Eyles, J. *Senses of Place* (Warrington: Silverbrook Press, 1985).

Eyles, J. and Peace, W. 'Signs and symbols in Hamilton: an iconography of a steel town' *Geografiska Annaler* **72B** (1990) pp. 73–88.

Foden, G. 'On the beach' *The Guardian* 28 June 1996, Friday Review pp. 2–3.

Gold, J. R. and Goodey, B. 'Environmental perception: the relationship with age' *Progress in Human Geography* **13** (1989) pp. 99–106.

Goodey, B. *Images of Place* (Birmingham: Centre for Urban and Regional Studies, University of Birmingham, 1974).

Harvey, D. 'Between space and time: reflections on the geographical imagination' *Annals of the Association of American Geographers* **80** (1990) pp. 418–34.

Hudson, J. C. 'Migration to an American frontier' *Annals of the Association of American Geographers* **66** (1976) pp. 242–65.

Kirk, W. 'Historical geography and the concept of the behavioural environment' *Indian Geographical Journal*, Silver Jubilee Volume (1952) pp. 152–60.

Kirk, W. 'Problems of geography', *Geography* **48** (1963) pp. 357–71.

Lewis, M. G. 'First impressions of the Great Plains and Prairies' in Watson, J. W. and O'Riordan, T. (eds), *The American Environment: Perceptions and Policies* (London: John Wiley, 1976) pp. 37–45.

Ley, D. and Samuels, M. S. 'Introduction: contexts of modern humanism in geography' in Ley, D. and Samuels, M. S. (eds), *Humanistic Geography: Prospects and Problems* (Chicago: Maaroufa Press, 1978) pp. 1–17.

Lowenthal, D. 'Geography, experience, and imagination: towards a geographical epistemology' *Annals of the Association of American Geographers* **51** (1961) pp. 241–60.

Lowenthal, D. 'The American scene' *Geographical Review* **58** (1968) pp. 61–88.

Lowenthal, D. 'Past time, present place: landscape and memory' *Geographical Review* **65** (1975) pp. 1–36.

Lowenthal, D. *The Past is a Foreign Country* (Cambridge: Cambridge University Press, 1985).

Malin, J. C. *Winter Wheat in the Golden Belt of Kansas* (Lawrence: University of Kansas Press, 1944).

Marryat, Captain F. *A Diary in America, With Remarks on its Institutions* (Longman, Orme, Green & Longman, 1839) quoted in Miller, C., *Early Travellers in North America* (Stroud: Alan Sutton, 1994).

Matless, D. 'Doing the English village, 1945–90: an essay in imaginative geography' in Cloke, P. *et al.* (eds), *Writing the Rural: Five Cultural Geographies* (London: Paul Chapman, 1994)

Meinig, D. W. 'The beholding eye. Ten versions of the same scene' in Meinig, D. W. (ed.), *The Interpretation of Ordinary Landscapes* (Oxford University Press: New York, 1979a) pp. 33–48.

Meinig, D. W. 'Symbolic landscapes. Some idealizations of American communities' in Meinig, D. W. (ed.), *The Interpretation of Ordinary Landscapes* (Oxford University Press: New York, 1979b) pp. 164–92.

Mills, S. F. 'Imagining the frontier' in Davies, P. J. (ed.), *Representing and Imagining America* (Keele: Keele University Press, 1996) pp. 24–33.

Mills, S. F. *The American Landscape* (Edinburgh: Keele University Press, 1997).

Pocock, D. C. D. 'The contribution of mental maps in perception studies' *Geography* **64** (1979a) pp. 279–87.

Pocock, D. C. D. 'The novelist's image of the North' *Transactions of the Institute of British Geographers* NS **4** (1979b) pp. 62–76.

Pocock, D. C. D. (ed.), *Humanistic Geography and Literature* (London: Croom Helm, 1981a).

Pocock, D. C. D. 'Place and the novelist' *Transactions of the Institute of British Geographers* NS **6** (1981b) pp. 337–47.

Pred, A. *Lost Words and Lost Worlds: Modernity and the Language of Everyday Life in Late Nineteenth Century Stockholm* (Cambridge: Cambridge University Press, 1990).

Prince, H. C. 'Real, imagined and abstract worlds of the past' *Progress in Geography* **3** (1971) pp. 1–86.

Rowntree, L. 'Orthodoxy and new directions: cultural/humanistic geography' *Progress in Human Geography* **12** (1988) pp. 576–86.

Shortridge, J. R. 'The emergence of "Middle West" as an American regional label' *Annals of the Association of American Geographers* **74** (1984) pp. 209–20.

Shortridge, J. R. 'The vernacular Middle West' *Annals of the American Association of Geographers* 75 (1985) pp. 48–57.

Sprout, H. and M. 'Environmental factors in the study of international politics' *Journal of Conflict Resolution* **1** (1957) pp. 309–28.

Taigel, A. and Williamson, T. *Parks and Gardens* (London: Batsford, 1993).

Tinniswood, A. *Life in the English Country Cottage* (London: Weidenfeld & Nicolson, 1995).

Tuan, Y.-F. 'Geography, phenomenology, and the study of human nature' *Canadian Geographer* **15** (1971) pp. 181–92.

Tuan, Y.-F. 'Thought and landscape' in Meinig, D. W. (ed.), *The Interpretation of Ordinary Landscapes* (New York: Oxford University Press, 1979) pp. 89–102.

Walmsley, D. J. and Lewis, G. J. *People and Environment* (Harlow: Longman, 1993).

Watson, J. W. 'Perception and place' *Geographical Journal* **141** (1975) pp. 271–4.

Watson, J. W. and O'Riordan, T. 'Introduction: image and reality in the American scene' in Watson J. W. and O'Riordan, T. (eds), *The American Environment: Perceptions and Policies* (London: John Wiley, 1976).

Webb, W. P. *The Great Plains* (New York: Ginn, 1931).

Winsor, R. A. 'Environmental imagery of the wet prairie of east central Illinois, 1820–1920' *Journal of Historical Geography* **13** (1987) pp. 375–97.

Wood, J. S. 'Village and community in early colonial New England' *Journal of Historical Geography* **8** (1982) pp. 333–46.

Wood, J. S. ' "Build, therefore your own world": the New England village as settlement ideal' *Annals of the Association of American Geographers* **81** (1991) pp. 32–50.

Wright, J. K. '*Terrae incognitae*: the place of the imagination in geography' *Annals of the Association of American Geographers* **37** (1947) pp. 1–15.

Yates, E. M. 'The evolution of the English village' *The Geographical Journal* **148** (1982) pp. 182–206.

5

Landscape, Politics and Power

Whether one adopts a post-structuralist or a landscape history perspective, it is plain that landscapes often exist as commentaries on the political beliefs and class relationships which surrounded their creation. Such ideas spring easily to mind in settings like that of the eighteenth-century landscape park, where every aspect of the scene seems to have been subordinated to the gratification of the wealthy and influential proprietor, but they are also relevant in the workaday countrysides of most states.

Cosgrove (1984) represented landscape not as an object or an image, but as a 'way of seeing' – one that is rooted in ideology and represents the way in which a given class has represented its property and itself: 'The argument here is that the landscape idea represents a way of seeing – a way in which some Europeans have represented to themselves and to others the world about them and their relationships with it, and through which they have commented on social relations' (1984 p. 1). He added that landscape was a way of seeing that had its own history:

> but a history that can be understood only as part of a wider history of economy and society; that has its own assumptions and consequences whose origins and implications extend well beyond the use and perception of land; that has its own techniques of expression, but techniques which it shares with other areas of cultural practice. (Cosgrove, 1984)

Elsewhere, he argued that the association between landscape and politics had existed for a very long time:

landscape was, over much of its history, closely bound up with the practical appropriation of space . . . its connections were with the survey and mapping of newly-acquired, consolidated and 'improved' commercial estates in the hands of an urban bourgeoisie; with the calculation of distance and trajectory for cannon fire and of defensive fortifications against the new weaponry; and with the projection of the globe and its regions onto map graticules by cosmographers and chorographers, those essential set designers for Europe's entry centre-stage of the world's theatre. In painting and garden design landscape achieved visually and ideologically what survey, map making and ordnance charting achieved practically: the control and domination over space as an absolute objective entity, its transformation into the property of individual or state. (1985 p. 46)

There is no single approach to the study of the politics of landscape and no single perspective which can be brought to bear on it. In most settled and exploited parts of the world successive societies have left their political imprints upon the scene, be they in forms as inconspicuous as a letterbox cast with a British royal cipher standing camouflaged by a coat of green paint in some part of Ireland or as prominent as the vast fieldscapes created by the collectivisation of farming imposed by Stalin in the former Soviet Union. Duncan wrote:

There is little question that the new cultural geography is itself fragmenting. For example, on the one hand there is a group of scholars who primarily analyse landscapes and, on the other, there are those who concentrate on space and place. One of the objects of this review is to point out that, contrary to what some of the latter claim, political analysis is central to landscape interpretation. (1994 p. 362)

Landscape and Politics in Nazi Germany

If politics finds expression in the landscape then it might be imagined that the political influence will be most starkly apparent in areas subject to the most authoritarian and totalitarian of regimes. In Nazi Germany, cultural influences originating in the landscape influenced policy-making, while the theoreticians of the Nazi state had their own distinctive ideas about how landscape should be manipulated in accordance with prevailing doctrines. Influential members of society may embellish and transform land-scapes in manners which express the values and aspirations of that elite. The transmission of influences can also occur in the reverse direction, so that it is possible to identify cases where landscape has conditioned social developments.

In this respect, for example, the forest landscapes of Central Europe inspired a mythology which was subsequently developed and exploited by the Nazi state. Schama wrote that:

> Tacitus's observation that their isolated habitat had made the Germans the least mixed of all European peoples would of course become the lethal obsession of the Nazi tyranny. *Germanentum* – the idea of a biologically pure and inviolate race, as 'natural' to its terrain as indigenous species of trees and flowers – featured in much of the archaeological and prehistorical literature both before and after the First World War. (1995 p. 118)

He added that:

> After 1933, forest themes invaded virtually every realm of art and politics . . . Books that attributed German racial and national distinctiveness to its woodland heritage, like Karl Rebel's 1934 *Der wald in der deutschen Kultur* (*The Forest in German Culture*) and Julius Kober's 1935 *Deutscher Wald, Deutches Volk* (*German Forest, German People*), kept the presses busy and filled the bookstores . . . Wherever possible, Hitler, the Reichsforstmeister Göring, and Himmler were photographed in sylvan settings. (Schama, 1995)

Ramblers and members of the Wandervogel youth movement gathered around bonfires on the forested hills, while in the summer of 1925, 50 000 ultranationalists dressed in historical costumes and marched in brigades to a monument in the woods, some carrying the banner of the medieval Teutonic knights. In such ways the image of the Germans as a forest race, preserved and protected by the embracing woodlands was developed; these images and myths were exploited by the propagandists of German racial cleansing.

A strange relationship between nation, landscape and nature was imagined to exist under the Nazi state. Germans were assumed to possess special abilities to commune with nature and to have unique talents for landscape design: 'Once National Socialism had arrived at the position of demonstrating a qualitatively better German environment, it could derive from it typical Aryan, Nordic or German landscapes. These landscapes, according to the National Socialist conception of race, had to be qualitatively better than those other people lived in' (Groening, 1992 p. 109). Under the National Socialist regime, 'landscape attorneys' (*Landschaftsanwälte*) were appointed, most of whom were landscape architects, and they were presumed to be able to represent the 'views' and 'interests' of the landscape. In Germany, the weird geopolitical notion that each human race was intimately associated with a particular landscape setting preceded the Nazi state and was expressed during the Weimar Republic by the prominent and markedly racist geographer, Ewald Banse (1883–1953). According to the crudely environmentalist doctrine that Banse proposed, human behaviour, development and acts of creativity were, in some mystical fashion, determined by the landscape influences of the motherland (1928). After the Nazis came to power, a variety of odd ideas about landscape were institutionalised. Wiepking-Jürgensmann (1891–1973), a professor of landscape architecture, claimed that the more green a village then the more German it was, and his notions were applied to the territories annexed from Poland. In the office of the Reichscommissioner responsible for strengthening German 'Volkishness' (RKF), a special planning authority was created and charged with the task of establishing a feeling for landscape amongst the Germans settled in these territories. The space was to be imbued with a Germanic character so that Germans settling there would feel at home, love the new home territory (*Heimat*) and defend it with their lives (Groening, 1992 p. 110). Supposedly 'primitive' humans could flourish in a variety of different habitats, but Germans were like specialised plants which demanded the refined habitats of home and a manner of living that was close to nature.

Other nations, it was claimed, lacked the Germans' intimate association with nature, and unlike the Germans, they had no sensitivity to landscape. These failings rendered them unfit as holders of land and therefore liable to be supplanted in conquered lands by Germans, who would manage the territories concerned in more ecologically responsible ways. Groening (Figure 5.1) writes that:

> following an authoritarian concept of society, Germans were
> represented as the highest race, the Aryan race, and due to their

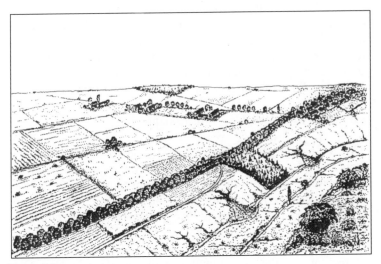

Figure 5.1a

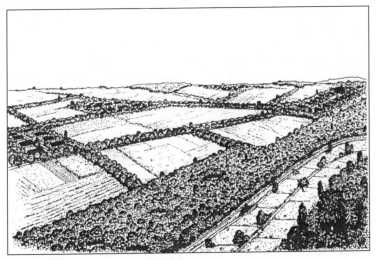

Figure 5.1b

Wiepking's contrasting of 'undesigned cultural landscape' (a) with 'designed German cultural landscape' (b). (From Gert Groening, 'The Feeling for Landscape – a German Example', *Landscape Research* 17 (3) 1992, 108–15 at p. 111)

high 'claims of locality' (*Standortansprüche*), they needed a decidedly distinctive landscape design. Consequently, it was the goal of national socialist landscape design, to elaborate specific characteristics of landscapes as living spaces for German people and tribes in order to create for them 'locality adequate' (*standortferechte*) conditions for living. (p. 112)

He quotes from Wiepking-Jürgensmann:

Time and again the love of plants and landscape breaks forth from our blood and the more seriously we do research and the harder we try to get to the bottom of things, the more we realise, that the feelings for harmonious landscape and the feeling of kinship (*Verwandtschaftsgefühl*) to plants belongs to biological laws within ourselves. (p. 113)

Unfortunately, the preoccupation with landscape in Nazi Germany amounted to far worse than the circulation of a series of distinctly dotty ideas. The myth that only Germans had the mystical sensitivity and kinship with Nature associated with a responsible custodianship of the environment was used not only to fuel national pride but also to legitimise the displacement and removal of 'lower humans' or *Untermenschen*. The unsavoury affair calls to mind the identification in 1942 of Nazi *Geopolitik* by the American geographer and diplomat, Bowman: 'Geopolitics is simple and sure, but, as demonstrated in German writings and policy, it is also illusion, mummery, an apology for theft' (1942 p. 658).

It might be imagined that in an extremely authoritarian state such as that of Nazi Germany, landscape change would be a direct manifestation of the politics and policies of the ruling party. This is not necessarily the case and Rollins (1995) has used the perhaps surprising example of the *Autobahns* of Nazi Germany to demonstrate that party doctrines can be tempered in the form of their impact by external factors. He writes:

Most scholars have identified the National Socialist regime as the essential force behind the *Autobahn*, and have accordingly sought to understand its landscape features as embodiments of the ideology of fascism. Many commentators have also seen the highway as a quintessentially modernist project in which technology triumphed over the environment. Neither interpretation successfully explains one of the *Autobahn's* cardinal features, namely, its unprecedented sensitivity to landscape aesthetics. Both foreign and domestic observers agreed on this point, praising the way in which the *Autobahn's* twin concrete ribbons blended and flowed into the German countryside. This impression of harmony with the landscape was not unfounded: Alwin Seifert and his team of landscape architects tried not only to reconstruct an ecologically sound border alongside the *Autobahn*, but also to use the project as a stepping stone to nationwide environmental reform. (p. 494)

The *Autobahns* had, in fact, complex origins which involved an interplay between Nazi politics, technological modernism and environmental awareness and consideration.

In 1933, Hitler inaugurated work on the first of these routeways, and by the end of 1939 some 3700 km of *Autobahn* had been built, forming a network which symbolised the binding-together of the outposts of the state, creating employment and validating the promise of a car-owning society. Contrary to popular myth, the idea for an *Autobahn* system did not originate with Hitler, but developed in 1926, before the Nazis came to power, among motoring, industrial and municipal interests. Neither was the notion of a modernistic road system unique; landscaped tourist roads, interstate highways and urban freeways were built in the USA at the time of the New Deal, and a private firm built the first Italian *autostrada* in 1924.

An important role in determining the landscape impact and characteristics of the *Autobahns* was played by landscape architects under the leadership of Alwin Seifert, an architect and garden designer from Munich. In 1934 he began to assemble a team of 'landscape attorneys' who influenced the course of the route and the rehabilitation and planting of the landscape in the aftermath of road-building operations. In 1933, Seifert had entered the environmental debate by calling for a natural regimen involving a loose planting of native species at *Autobahn* sites. Sinuous curves were favoured, while travel on the *Autobahn* was:

theorized as the experiencing of successive unified spaces such as a valley, a basin, a forest, or even a field surrounded by hedges. Preserving the connectedness and balance within these individual areas became the planners' rule of thumb. Instead of cutting up the surrounding space, the highway was intended to follow and to emphasize a particular border. (Rollins, 1995 p. 498)

Complex problems of attribution and authorship surround the *Autobahns* of Nazi Germany:

> The simple question *Whose landscape?* yields at least three poten-
> tial authoring groups that worked together to realize the highway
> system. Their cooperation makes it difficult to distinguish the
> landscapers' contribution from those of the Nazi political ma-
> chine which backed the project and the engineers who planned its
> technical aspects. The further fact that the landscapers were
> themselves Nazis, and that engineers learned to apply principles
> gleaned from gardeners, gives these distinctions at times a merely
> heuristic character. (Rollins, 1995 p. 511)

Seifert supported a *Bodenständig* (rooted in the soil or native) aesthetic which would reflect the characteristic uniqueness of a given landscape and this conservative process interacted with the moder-
nising drive to impose technological transformations upon the environment. The synthesis of this dialectic was a particular accom-
modation between transport and environmentalist interests.

The Politics of Landscape in England

The relationships between politics and landscape were well repre-
sented in post-medieval England. Countrysides existing today still preserve characters expressive of the social structures of influence and power which existed two or more centuries ago, while the values of different political doctrines can still be found fossilised in the landscape long after the patterns of party political cleavage in England have been transformed. At different times, in different places and in a variety of ways, landscape can be strongly associated with the state. In post-medieval England, analogies were frequently made between the rural estate and the kingdom, the former being regarded as a microcosm of the latter; the landlord ruled his tenants, the estate was their homeland, self-sufficient in most resources, while the well-managed estate provided a model for the nation. During the troubled years of the Stuart monarchy and Cromwell's rule, the political crises generated much poetic writing and this writing

frequently developed landscape themes. Landscape and statecraft were matched while:

> The writer arrogates to his own persuasion everything natural, harmonious, and unified; the other side is violent, chaotic and therefore against nature . . . Political enemies are placed in gloomy and hideous landscapes to hatch their plots, and in the civil war period these are meticulously contrasted with the good landscapes of orthodox Royalism . . . The art of landscape insists upon continual harmony; it claims to display a model of the blessed land . . . The savage wilderness and the pleasant place are mutually defining opposites; the one is invoked to exorcise the other. (Turner, 1979 pp. 114–15)

Poetry with a political text or subtext was often full of rural landscape analogies. Thus, as Turner describes (p. 105), for Abraham Cowley in *Davideis*, a flooded river became a symbol for the machinations of one's political enemies, a form of extremism that must culminate in civil war:

> a tame stream does wild and dangerous grow
> By unjust force; he now with wanton play
> Kisses the smiling Banks, and glides away,
> But his known Channel stopt, begins to roare,
> And swell with rage, and buffet the dull shore.
> His mutinous waters hurry to the War,
> And Troops of Waves come rolling from afar.
> Then scorns he such weak stops to his free source,
> And overruns the neighbouring fields with violent course.

Attitudes towards social class were also presented in the form of landscape analogies. Fanshawe, in *The Progresse of Learning*, used a landscape metaphor to express his revulsion towards communal forms of ownership and his belief in the necessity for a system of division between the classes:

> Before the Earth was held in severall
> Twas one great feild where all the creatures fedd.
> As in a Common (therefore termd the All)
> Men mixt with beasts together in one shedd
> Upon the ground did take a homely bedd:

Things were not sorted yett, for then there was
No Groves where shady trees were billited,
Nor grass distinguisht from the corne, butt grass
And corne and shady trees were shuffled in one Masse.

In the eighteenth century, the polarisation of politics between
royalists and parliamentarians was gradually superseded by a
political cleavage between Whigs and Tories. This division was
not only reflected in differences of political philosophy and in
attitudes towards society, but also in differences in outlook towards
landscape. The Whigs tended to comprise those groups which had
benefited from the Glorious Revolution of 1688 and the Hanoverian
succession; their membership included the largest of the landowners,
those with important financial interests in the city and wealthy
people engaged in commerce. They were associated with 'progress',
support for a pacific foreign policy and religious toleration. The
Tories, in contrast, had supported the Stuart succession; they were
associated with traditional, conservative values, High Church affiliations, minimal involvement in commerce and paternalistic attitudes towards the lower social classes. The core of their support was
provided by the provincial local gentry and rural squires. These
political differences were given a visual expression; Williamson
noted that in this period, contrasting English political outlooks
had significant repercussions on gardens design. Like houses, landscapes were significant instruments in the political arena:

> They could be used to proclaim the wealth and power, and thus
> by implication the continuing political success, of great land-
> owners: overawing the local population and attracting the un-
> decided to their 'interest'. They could be used to demonstrate a
> governing élite's particular beliefs and ideology and also – as
> advertisements of its taste and knowledge – its fitness to rule.
> (1995 p. 16)

Also, they could be employed by the marginalised and excluded
groups to symbolise their own outlooks and agendas.

Everett described the emergence of a 'national style' of informal
landscape design which emerged after the 1688 settlement. It has
been associated with the rise of constitutional liberty and the greater
security of property, which stimulated the growth of wealth and
attempts to 'improve' the landscape. He wrote:

Figure 5.2   Built for the Duke of Marlborough following his victory over the armies of Louis XIV in 1704, Blenheim Palace is a spectacular expression of power in the landscape. The original gardens and park were formal, but the landscape was remodelled by Brown after 1764. (Cambridge University collection)

Figure 5.3   Wimpole Hall in Cambridgeshire, begun around 1640 and enlarged a century later when the property of the Earl of Hardwick, the Lord Chancellor. (Richard Muir)

Figure 5.4   The park surrounding Wimpole Hall was landscaped by Lancelot Brown in the mid-eighteenth century and remodelled by Humphry Repton in 1801. In the foreground the ridge and furrow patterns from the former villages' fields are plainly visible. (Richard Muir)

The most extensive expression of the informal style was to be found in the parks of what are often described as the great Whig mansions – massive structures apparently designed to fulfill what Adam Smith regarded as the supreme end of improvement, the

Figure 5.5 New Wimpole, the descendant of two villages successively destroyed in the landscaping of Wimpole park. (Richard Muir)

desire to be seen. The normal characteristic of these houses was their setting in vast parks distant from any activity that could be interpreted as their economic base, whether in agriculture, trade or political peculation. Architectural historians sometimes differentiate what may be loosely termed a Whig idea of the placing of the country house from a more traditional pattern in which the mansion was clearly seen as part of a community, with adjacent village and parish church. (1994 p. 38)

He added:

In the Whig idea of the arrangement of landscape it is often difficult to distinguish ideas of taste from the assertive expression of private property and control of territory. The style that had its supreme exponent in 'Capability' Brown (1716–83), characterized by a standard formula of artificial water, clumps and belts of trees, could be stretched over a landscape as far as funds and property would allow, and clearly at a lower cost of planting and

Figure 5.6   Much of the English countryside derives from the exercise of might and influence. Amongst the most influential re-makers of the countryside were members of the Tudor landowning dynasties, like the Knightleys of Fawsley, Northamptonshire, who prospered by destroying villages and repopulating the land with sheep. (Richard Muir)

maintenance than a formal style . . . The principal theoreticians of
Brown's work in his own time were quite deliberate . . . in
equating taste with the heightened display of property and the
appropriation of nature to personal use. (pp. 38–9)

From 1714 to 1742, Robert Walpole's Whig administration
dominated England. His family had its seat at Houghton, in Norfolk, and during the early years of the eighteenth century an intricate
geometric garden was set out around the old hall, which was then
demolished and a new mansion built. The style that was chosen
echoed the political partisanship of the period. As Taigel and
Williamson described it:

From the 1710s, a group of Whig politicians consciously fostered
a style of architecture which claimed to be a more faithful
interpretation of ancient classical buildings than the confused
structures which (with the exceptions of those by Inigo Jones) had
characterized pre-Revolutionary elite residences, or the contemporary Baroque forms favoured by leading Tories. (1993 p. 54)

They added:

It was an appropriate style for the rulers of a nation claiming to be
the true heir to Rome, a style superior to the Baroque of the
decadent French and Spanish. Knowledge of its complex 'natural'
rules (and of Renaissance and classical civilization in general)
marked out the Whig elite as heirs to an ancient tradition, natural
rulers of the nation. (Taigel and Williamson, 1993)

This style was the Palladian, based on ideas systematised in the
sixteenth century by the architect Andrea Palladio, and brought to
prominence in England by Colen Campbell under the patronage of
Earl Burlington. In the second and third decades of the eighteenth
century, Palladianism became closely associated with Whig ideology
and with its claim that English society should be modelled on that of
Republican Rome. In the 1730s, the park at Houghton was redesigned by Charles Bridgeman according to a plan which eliminated
an established network of intersecting avenues and replaced them
with a starker, sparer geometry of parkland and blocks of woodland
so that the expanded park complemented the austere majesty of the
house.

In asserting control over territory, the landowner would sometimes engage in emparking, removing a village located in the vicinity
of a mansion and either evicting its community or relocating the
villagers in a purpose-built settlement, often one set just outside the
park gates to serve as an eye-catching parody of rustic England.
Joseph Damer, first Baron Milton, inherited a fortune made from
money-lending in Ireland and began to transform an estate that he
had acquired in Dorset in 1763. While work was in progress to
design a new mansion to stand beside the medieval Milton Abbey
church during the 1770s, the decision had already been taken to
remove the nearby small town of Milton. Milton disappeared over a
period of twenty years, houses being demolished as their leases
expired. Just a fraction of the families from Milton were resettled in
a new estate village of Milton Abbas, designed, like the mansion, by
Sir William Chambers. Lancelot Brown was employed in landscaping work at Milton in the 1760s, and was also employed at
Nuneham Courtenay in Oxfordshire, where another village was
destroyed, formal elements were removed from the vista and where
the Earl of Harcourt replaced the medieval parish church with a
domed classical structure. Bermingham wrote:

> Throughout the eighteenth century landscape gardens grew more
> extensive. Not only did they absorb village commons within their
> boundaries, but occasionally whole villages that stood in the way
> of a prospect or an improvement were destroyed and rebuilt
> elsewhere. 'Sweet Auburn' in Oliver Goldsmith's 'Deserted Vil-
> lage,' for example, is believed to have been the village of Nune-
> ham Courtenay, destroyed in 1761 to make a garden for Lord
> Harcourt. (1987 p. 11)

In contrast, there was a Tory view of the landscape which stood
apart from the fashionable theories of economics associated with
Adam Smith and the characterisation of humans as self-seeking
individualists. Instead, this view valued tradition, continuity, obligation and sensibility. Ideas about landscape were politicised and
Everett writes that:

> throughout the eighteenth century, and much of the nineteenth,
> arguments about the aesthetics of landscape were almost always
> arguments about politics. Intervention in the landscape was
> understood as making explicit and readable statements about

the political history, the political constitution, the political future of England, and about the relations that should exist between its citizens. In the Tory view, those who abandoned the landscape to the market were also abandoning the order of civil society to fragmentation. (1994 p. 7)

Political conflicts were sometimes symbolised in the construction of the great gardens of the time, particularly in the choice of statuary. At Stowe, in Buckinghamshire, William Kent and Lord Cobham created a tree-girt area known as the 'Elysian Fields' with a slender lake serving as the 'River Styx'. A Temple of Ancient Virtue was provided to accommodate statues of Socrates, Homer, Lycurgus and Epaminondas and close by was a ruined Temple of Modern Virtue containing a headless figure regarded as representing Walpole, while across the water was a Temple of British Worthies, where busts of men selected from the pantheon of Whig heroes were displayed.

It was not just disaffected Whigs who could play this kind of game. Older-style Tories also laid-out politically symbolic gardens. Allen, 1st Earl Bathurst, a close friend of Pope, created a massive geometric landscape in Cirencester Park (Glos) from 1715. He had time on his hands, his public career having been ended by the triumph of the Whigs and the accession of the Hanoverians. In 1741 he erected a statue of Queen Anne (last of the reigning Stuarts) on a tall column, directly in line between his home and the parish church: thus, it is said, symbolizing his support for the Stuarts, and for the closer relationship between church and state which had existed under them. (Williamson, 1995 p. 64)

Such expressions of politics in the landscape, which were quite numerous, were not undertaken in brief flights of self-indulgent whimsy. The garden was a gigantic statement of its owner's affiliations, and gardens were created to impress their owners' political clients and overawe potential supporters.

The Tory perspective on the landscape was influenced by the fact that in Georgian times they were excluded from power by the favouritism accorded to Whigs under Walpole and often belonged to the class of squires and the smaller landlords who were crippled by the high levels of land tax levied to support the expanding

bureaucratic and military machines. The Tories disliked the centralised and corrupt administration and very few of them could afford
the vast geometric gardens being built by the leading Whigs; more
likely to fall within their means in the 1720s and 1730s were
landscapes like those designed by Switzer, with a compact inner
garden whose axes were extended across still-working farmland by
straight rides and avenues. Later, the extensive lawns associated
with parks landscaped by Brown (better known for his landscaping
of the vast spaces controlled by the Whig oligarchs) had much to
commend them, making statements about ownership and status at a
reasonable cost. Taigel and Williamson explained that:

> Unlike extensive areas of geometric gardens, which had to be
> weeded, mowed and clipped, parks were cheap to maintain. The
> open turf had to be grazed, but money could be made from this,
> and also from commercial exploitation of the woods and planta-
> tions within, and around the park. The landowner could, as it
> were, have his cake and eat it. (1993 p. 77)

Thus the landscape park provided the answer to the search for
'affordable magnificence', initiated by Tory writers at the start of the
century.

In another sense, the next generation of parks (designed by
Repton, himself a Tory) were more in sympathy with the Tory
perspective: 'To him, the Brownian park symbolized the exclusivity
of the landed elite, their rejection of a paternalistic involvement in the
life of the local community. This exclusivity, as the French revolution
erupted on the other side of the Channel, he considered increasingly
foolhardy, and dangerous' (Taigel and Williamson, 1993 p. 80).

No political party could arrogate a school of art or design entirely
to itself; Brown designed parks for Whigs and Tories and Repton
created them for arrivistes as well as grandees. Also, the nature of
political philosophy associated with a party may evolve and change.
In Georgian times, the archetypal Tory would have considered that
the resources of his estate should be harnessed to favour the growth
of morality as well as prosperity. Nature, he might argue, existed not
merely to be exploited and incorporated into grandiose displays of
ownership, but should be studied and valued for its harmony. Each
place had its history and traditions and these should be respected
rather than swept away in some blind quest for fashionability. Such
values contrast starkly with those espoused by the Tories of today:

'Perceiving the landscape merely as a setting for an "enterprise culture", modern Conservatism has little room for subtle notions of responsibility, continuity, and balance. A narrow view of the market seems in large part to exclude thought, creativity, and stability, and seeks to conserve nothing but itself' (Everett, 1994 p. 217).

Political affiliations to particular parties found expressions in the landscape, but on the whole these were dwarfed by those many cases where politics found expression in terms of power. Much, perhaps most, of the English countryside is a living monument to the domination of the powerful over the powerless. From the grouse moor to the enclosed and desolate former common and from the hamlet of tenants' cottages to the site of the village abandoned to the flocks of a Tudor lord, landscapes echo the power of property. Williamson and Bellamy wrote that:

By the nineteenth century most of the land of England was firmly under the control of a very small minority of the population. The landscape was no longer a patchwork of smallholdings, its exploitation no longer governed by the long established traditions of local communities. It was now largely enclosed into private fields, and exploited by standardized and efficient agricultural methods. Not only the houses, cottages and country parks, but the whole fabric of the English landscape embodied the tenurial hegemony of the landed élite. It was shaped by their aesthetic preferences, their economic interests and their leisure pursuits. (1987 p. 192)

The most important factor in the creation of this hegemony was Parliamentary Enclosure.

Mitchell writes that: 'The Enclosure movement and the accompanying dispossession of the English peasantry are an internal colonization of the home country, its transformation from what Blake called "a green and pleasant land" into a landscape, an emblem of national and imperial identity' (1994b p. 17). Anyone wishing to see an expression of power in the landscape preserved in its most stark and striking form could do no better than to look across a Parliamentary Enclosure landscape of arrow-straight walls in a location like the Yorkshire Dales, where all the most obvious facets of the human-made landscape – walls, roads and farmsteads – date from the years immediately following the granting of the enclosure award. Parliamentary Enclosure was a means by which areas of communal land (such as commons, some meadows, open field ploughland and even some village greens) could be privatised according to processes which benefited the larger landowners and effectively drove the cottager, small-holder and squatter from the land. The transformations were accomplished on a parish-by-parish basis and would commence when the leading landowners within a parish petitioned Parliament to produce the necessary Act. This accomplished, commissioners would be ratified to preside over the partition of the common land resources. They normally numbered three and were drawn from the privileged local classes to include the landed gentry, clergy and other larger landowners. John Burcham of Coningsby in Lincolnshire served as a commissioner on at least 70 enclosures and John Davis of Bloxham in Oxfordshire had 113 commissions. Such men, along with their collaborators, the surveyors and road, walling and fencing contractors, transformed much of England:

> For the area of land they worked over, the relatively few decades during which most of their work was accomplished, in most parts of England these men were truly some of the most thorough going 'despoilers' of the land, and in some areas the most efficient agents of landscape change ever. (Turner, 1984 p. 160)

The process began with an Act of 1604, affecting Radipole in Dorset, which was largely overlooked, though gradually the momentum of enclosure increased and the majority of enclosures took place within the period 1750–1850. By the time that the last enclosure took place, in 1914, an area equivalent to about one-fifth of England had been transformed. Turner writes that:

> In rounded terms there were about 5,300 acts of enclosure in England in the eighteenth and nineteenth centuries, though with antecedents in the early seventeenth century. These acts include all those passed as private and public local acts and those under the general acts of 1836, 1840, 1845 *et seq*. They account for close on seven million acres, or about 21 per cent of the area of England. (1984 p. 133)

In each parish affected, the commissioners would appoint a surveyor and a valuer to facilitate the redistribution of land into private ownership. It was intended to provide new land allocations which were notionally proportional to the shares previously held in the communal resources. The effect, however was to benefit the wealthy. Stipulations were made for the hedging or walling of the newly allocated holdings, which immediately resulted in a substantial outlay of capital, perhaps £12 per acre, while somewhere around £3 per acre would be levied as a rate to pay for the administrative costs of enclosure. More serious was the loss of access to the vanished open commons, which had provided grazing, bedding and fuel and which had allowed the poorer classes to derive a basic subsistence. In the aftermath of Parliamentary Enclosure there was a slow exodus from the parish as squatters and landless cottagers were followed by the commoners who had sold their new but unviable holdings to neighbours. Others remained to serve as hired labourers for neighbours who had done better from the privatisation of the land.

John Clare, who lived in Helpstone village, was one of numerous members of the intelligentsia who were appalled by the scenic and social consequences of enclosure. In his semi-autobiographical poem *Lubin's Anguish* of 1821 he wrote:

> Inclosure, thou'rt curse upon the land,
> And tasteless was the wretch who thy existence plann'd.
>
> O England! boasted land of liberty,
> With strangers still thou mayst thy title own,
> But they poor slaves the alteration see,
> With many a loss to them the truth is known:
> Like emigrating birds thy freedom's flown;
> While mongrel clowns low as their rooting plough,
> Distain thy laws to put in force their own;
> And every village owns its tyrants now,
> And parish slaves must live as parish-kings allow.

The landscapes created by Parliamentary Enclosure were distinctive and contrasted strongly with neighbouring, unaffected countrysides. They were surveyors' landscapes, created on the maps drawn by the appointed surveyors and then superimposed upon the serpentine lines of the older, organic countrysides. Wherever possible, field boundaries ran arrow-straight, to produce geometrical and angular grids. When complete, they were defined either by walls of freshly quarried and newly hammered stone, all built to a prescribed height and in a standardised manner, or by hedgerows of newly-planted shrubs, all of the same age and usually of uniform species, normally hawthorn.

Marching straight across the rectilinear fieldscape there might be one or more enclosure roads, provided to supersede other roads and tracks made redundant by the changes and built to standardised widths of 30, 40 or 60 feet (Taylor, 1979 p. 173). In the late eighteenth century, improved techniques of road-building became available; there was less need for broad verges which could become the road when the usual track was muddy and rutted, and so most roads were built to widths of less than 45 feet. The new roads would end abruptly at the parish boundary, or link up with an enclosure road previously constructed in a neighbouring parish, or else later be connected with a new enclosure road when the adjacent parish was enclosed. Some landscape features of Parliamentary Enclosure would be added some time after the award, as families which had benefited from the settlement left their homes in the villages or hamlets of the parish and set up new farmsteads located on their compacted holdings, sometimes near the centre of the little domain and sometimes at its margins, by the roadside.

Not only did Parliamentary Enclosure create its own highly distinctive landscapes, it also influenced the spread of other types of landscape. Williamson and Bellamy wrote that: 'The enclosure of the English landscape and the concentration of land in the hands of a small élite were accompanied by a fundamental revolution in attitudes to landed property' (1987 p. 116). In the medieval period there had been no large-scale reorganisation of the landscape for the proclamation of personal status. Holdings of land had been tightly intermeshed and the alteration of countryside on a large scale was difficult: 'It was only with the evolution of private property that the landscape began to be deliberately and extensively shaped for social and aesthetic purposes. For the first time the social élite displayed their power directly in the land' (Williamson and Bellamy, 1987). Most particularly, this display, expressed in assertions of ownership and in the manipulation of scenery, concerned the proliferation of landscape parks, though it was also apparent in the design choices of landowners which were manifest in cottages, churches, other public buildings and farm buildings. Short noted that: 'While transforming the countryside into an ordered mosaic of bounded fields, the same powerful groups were also creating the other major environmental icon, the English landscape garden. One was for profit, the other for delight, but both were an exercise in power' (1991 p. 67).

Parliamentary Enclosure was controversial, and wherever it threatened, lively anti-enclosure meetings were likely to be called in futile attempts to resist the changes. The sentiments of the ordinary villagers were encapsulated in a widely-circulating epigram dating from 1821:

> The fault is great in man or woman
> Who steals a goose from off a common,
> But what can plead that man's excuse
> Who steals a common from a goose?

It would be wrong to regard enclosure as a class conspiracy, but it was the case that at every stage in the process the wealthy and influential were advantaged while the poor were disadvantaged. As Tate pointed out, if the cottager were a freeholder any allotment that he received he would probably have to dispose of to meet the fencing and draining charges, while if his cottage was not a freehold then an allotment to the cottage would pass direct to the landlord. On enclosure the commoner lost his common rights:

> he could no longer turn on the common his scraggy cow, his donkey, his few sheep or his poultry and geese. The minor village officials, the viewers of fields, the letters of cattle, the common shepherd, the hayward, the pinder, lost their occupations, and the pay and petty perquisites which went with them. It is from the social point of view, rather than as a matter of pure economics or economic history, that enclosure (carried out as in fact it was) is to be regarded as a major disaster to the village community. (1967 pp. 174–5)

By the end of the eighteenth century, the gentry and aristocracy owned 70–75 per cent of the land in England, and by the early nineteenth century, well over 5000 Acts of Enclosure had been passed by Parliament. Even supporters of enclosure, like the agricultural reformer, Arthur Young (1804), realised that the consequences for the weaker members of the rural community could be severe, and he expressed his qualms as follows:

> What is it to the poor man to be told that the Houses of Parliament are extremely tender of property, while the father of the family is forced to sell his cow and his land because the one is

not competent to the other; and being deprived of the only motive to industry, squanders the money, contracts bad habits, enlists for a soldier, and leaves the wife and children to the parish? . . . The poor of these parishes may say, and with truth, Parliament may be tender of property; all I know is, I had a cow, and an act of Parliament has taken it from me.

Parliamentary Enclosure had profound effects upon the landscape and it also affected the representation of landscape. Bermingham wrote that:

It is a fact of history that in the eighteenth century, enclosure radically altered the English countryside, suiting it to the needs of the expanding city market. It is a fact of art history that in the eighteenth century, with the 'discovery of Britain,' the English saw their landscape as a cultural and aesthetic object. This coincidence of social transformation of the countryside with the rise of a cultural-aesthetic ideal of the countryside repeats a familiar pattern of actual loss and imaginery recovery. Precisely when the countryside – or at least large portions of it – was becoming unrecognizable, and dramatically marked by historical change, it was offered as the image of the homely, the stable, the ahistorical. (1987 p. 9)

Politics and Landscape Painting

The painting of landscape might seem to some to be a pure, aesthetic act that was divorced from the arenas of politics, class, and social comment. However, Bermingham suggested of painting in Georgian England that: 'there is an ideology of landscape and that in the eighteenth and nineteenth centuries a class view of landscape embodied a set of socially and, finally, economically determined values to which the painted image gave cultural expression' (1987 p. 3). The connections between landscape painting and politics were of several kinds, including, according to Mitchell, a link between artistic output and imperial expansion with, for example, the art in China enjoying its fullest flowering at the height of Chinese imperial power and entering into decline when China began to fall under the influence of English imperialism:

Figure 5.7 The disciplined geometry of Parliamentary Enclosure field walls in Nidderdale. (Richard Muir)

Is it possible that landscape, understood as the historical 'invention' of a new visual/pictorial medium, is integrally connected with imperialism? Certainly the roll call of major 'originating' movements in landscape painting – China, Japan, Rome, seventeenth-century Holland and France, eighteenth- and nineteenth-century Britain – makes the question hard to avoid. (1994b p. 9)

Imperialist influences were also evident in the way that the landscapes and peoples of colonial territory were painted in manners derived from Europe, with antipodean landscapes translated into scenery depicted in the style of Claude Lorrain, or with members of North American indigenous societies removed from their social contexts and represented according to European cultural norms: 'On the whole, the English preferred the Indians who not only devoted themselves to the gentlemanly exercise of hunting but had the manners and reserve of "nature's gentlemen"' (Honour, 1975 p. 228). Short wrote that the early white visitors to Australia produced two artistic responses, the romantic and the neo-classical. Those who responded to the country in a romantic manner imagined noble savages occupying a Garden of Eden.

This was the predominant response in the first thirty years, especially from visiting artists who used the Aborigines as a counterpoint to what they saw as a corrupt, effete western society . . . The longer term settlers saw it differently, they saw the white presence as a mark of progress, with the development of a white, civil society as being a civilizing mission. (1991, p. 198)

The vision that the long-term settlers shared was expressed by John Glover. Glover treated the Australian vegetation with studied accuracy, but:

His treatment of the Aborigines, in contrast, was poor. They are no more than hunched, black dwarves, poorly painted and little understood. They are not the noble savages of Captain Cook. They are at best a touch of romantic interest, at worst wild savages lacking human individuality. These 'native' scenes were for English tastes. They were invented to meet the demands of English buyers of exotica and the romantic. (Short, 1991 p. 199)

While Cosgrove (1984) redefined landscape as a 'way of seeing', Mitchell (1994a) has sought to convert the word from a noun to a verb:

The aim of this book is to change "landscape" from a noun to a verb. It asks that we think of landscape, not as an object to be seen or a text to be read, but as a process by which social and subjective identities are formed. The study of landscape has gone through two major shifts in this century: the first (associated with modernism) attempted to read the history of landscape primarily on the basis of a history of landscape painting, and to narrativize that history as a progressive movement toward purification of the visual field; the second (associated with postmodernism) tended to decenter the role of painting and pure formal visuality in favour of a semiotic and hermeneutic approach [semiotics concern the way in which signs are produced and given meaning and hermeneutics concerns the study of interpretation and meaning] that treated landscape as an allegory of psychological or ideological themes (p. 1).

The aim of the first, contemplative, approach 'is the evacuation of verbal, narrative, or historical elements and the presentation of an image designed for transcendental consciousness . . . The second strategy is interpretative and is exemplified in attempts to decode landscape as a body of determinate signs' (Mitchell, 1994a). The author added that:

It is clear that landscapes can be deciphered as textual systems. Natural features such as trees, stones, water, animals, and dwellings can be read as symbols in religious, psychological, or political allegories; characteristic structures and forms (elevated or closed prospects, times of day, positioning of the spectator, types of human figures) can be linked with generic and narrative typologies such as the pastoral, the georgic, the exotic, the sublime, and the picturesque. (Mitchell, 1994a)

In the collection of essays, *Landscape and Power*, these approaches were absorbed into a model that asked 'not just what landscape "is" or "means" but what it "does", how it works as a cultural practice'. The seven contributors find that landscape production is a political act – whether the result is an English country garden, a Constable, or a photograph. Spatio-temporally specific social relations, constituted through uneven distributions of power, are part of the canvas on which landscapes take place' (Hillis, 1996 p. 243). Ann Jensen Adams (1994) studied identity and seventeenth-century Dutch landscape painting. Art history maintains that naturalistic landscape painting first emerged in Holland at this time: 'Something dramatic happened around 1620 in Haarlem, so the narrative goes, as if scales had suddenly and collectively fallen from the Dutch artists' eyes and they could suddenly see, and faithfully transcribe, the land in which they found themselves' (p. 35). These artists, however, were seldom uncritically and uninterpretively creating transcriptions of the land in which they lived. They would relocate monuments or dramatise their locations. The choice of landscape subjects, their dramatisation and manipulation and their 'naturalisation' appealed to the unique conjunction of political, economic and religious circumstances in a country convulsed by change, the stresses giving new meaning to ordinary and recognisable landscape features. The naturalisation of the land played an important part in the creation of changed communal identities within a nascent nation containing a high level of incomers. In the political arena, the Seven United Provinces had declared their independence from Spain in 1579 and received floods of immigrants attracted by the rising prosperity of Amsterdam and the northern Netherlands. Meanwhile, in the economic sphere, the Provinces exploited an open market economy and engaged in the amassing of capital for investment in great land reclamation projects, while on the religious front Protestantism replaced the Catholic church. The essence of Adams's study was that paintings could influence people to identify with each other or to widen divisions: 'The assumption of this chapter has been that viewing an image (here a landscape) can, through the associations it engenders, create in the viewer a sense of affiliation with or difference from others, an individual identity in relation to a variety of communally held identities' (1994 p. 66).

Paintings of Dutch landscape subjects were extemely well received in Holland and constituted the most popular genre of painting. The people were intimately associated with their territory; the nation was engaged in huge reclamation and drainage projects, and the threat of devastation by flooding was always present. Certain other factors made Holland unique in Europe. A large proportion of the dunes and peat bogs were owned by those who worked on them rather than by feudal lords. Not only were feudal landlords unusually deficient, there were also differences in national leadership. The Dutch insisted in exerting some democratc control over their leaders and so were rejected by the potential monarchs that were approached. As a result they had no king or queen and thus no figure in whom national power, symbolic or otherwise, could be invested. Consequently: 'With no individual in whom to invest the symbols of national identity and when faced with the problem of the creation of a communal identity, the Dutch turned to their land' (Adams, 1994 p. 44). They hung paintings of their landscapes on their walls in places where others might have hung portraits of the monarch.

The scenes that were represented did not necessarily reproduce actual landscapes. Commercial enterprise and farming activity tended to be excluded, while the commercial ships of the Dutch East India Company were ignored. With regard to this apparent masking of commerce, expressed, for example, in a preference for archaic representations of ferryboats on rivers rather than of barges on the new canals, Adams wrote:

> Early in the century commercial enterprises may not have yet had a place among the personal ideals deemed appropriate to express publicly. Although the amassing of property in this world was considered a sign of salvation in the next, at the same time the

professed ideal was the favoring of spiritual matters over involvement in the material world. (1994 p. 58)

However, other factors, might also have been at work, and the images provided the urban dweller with a passport to the countryside. On another level, 'their nostalgic themes could serve to assuage guilt for a past landscape that was rapidly being changed if not destroyed by contemporary commercial enterprise. Finally, they are a visual appropriation and dominance of that countryside, a visual variation on an economic relation that by the seventeenth century was firmly established' (Adams. 1994). This, Adams noted, was a dominance that conveniently overlooked the contemporary economic transformation being accomplished on the land by affluent groups to make it symbolically available to a much wider spectrum of society. The visual preoccupation served a vital role for a population which always lived in the shadow of the catastrophic flood. Dutch painters provided an imaginative control over nature by 'removing' national monuments and relocating them on sites with safer, more elevated terrain. 'Dutch landscape paintings thus could focus communal attention to the taming and control of a potentially threatening enemy' (1994, p. 65).

The dramatisation of the Dutch landscape and its sense of history in paintings played significant political roles. It served to reassure a diverse population which was engaged in creating new political institutions, and 'It visually gave this population a sense of stability through a fabricated communal history in the land. (It may also have made this exceedingly flat and, to many immigrants, foreign land more familiar, more like the lands from which they came' (Adams, 1994). To people of diverse origins, classes and outlooks who were divided by potentially disruptive cultural differences, 'These paintings offered a communal identity on several levels, legitimizing their themes through naturalizing and historicizing them, offering security where none in fact was to be had' (1994, p. 66).

The possession of paintings of the national landscape could buttress claims of belonging to that nation; Elizabeth Helsinger (1994) suggests that the ownership of landscape picture books, such as J. M. W. Turner's *Picturesque Views of England and Wales*, issued in parts between 1826 and 1835, provided the ascendent urban middle class with the means visually to own England and to claim membership of the meaningful national community before the passing of the Reform Act of 1832. She wrote:

By the late eighteenth century, tours of Britain by the British were well established among the upper and, increasingly, the middle classes. The sights to which these tourists traveled belonged to private estates; they included ruins and natural wonders as well as contemporary houses, parks and industries. Their owners were increasingly interested in displaying them to a genteel traveling public. Guides, guidebooks, hours of admission, and all the familiar structures of tourism were already in place. Drawings and paintings of such sights, initially commissioned by owners for their own viewing, developed into a business in its own right. By the early nineteenth century, books reproducing views of England's landscape sights addressed an audience of potential or vicarious tourists . . . The purchaser is offered visual possession of an England whose images have been placed in circulation. For their largely middle-class intended audience, this might be construed as a gesture toward inclusion within the ranks of the landowners, who still retained primary political and social authority in England in the years preceding the enactment of the Reform Bill in 1832. Purchase these books and you too may gain at least visual access to the land. (pp. 104–5)

A subordinate theme in the account concerns the artists' attitudes towards the rural working classes appearing in the pictures: 'Do the rural laborers in Turner's landscapes indicate his support for their eventual enfranchisement, or do his more "carnivalesque" canvasses encapsulate his patrons' fears that increasing social mobility would also mean labor's violation of the "natural" alliance of property and "landed" identity?' (Hillis, 1996 p. 243).

There are many facets to the relationship between landscape and politics. Barrell (1990) has described how, in the second half of the eighteenth century and the early years of the nineteenth century, a correct taste in landscape was regarded as a test and vindication of claims to the right to govern. Expanding on his identification of the relation between the ability to generalise, a correct taste in landscape, and the claim to be capable of exercising political authority, he wrote:

In so far as the representation of panoramic prospects serves as an instantiation of the ability of the man of 'liberal mind' to abstract the general from the particular, it was also understood to be an instantiation of his ability to abstract the true interests of humanity, the public interest, from the labyrinth of private interests which were imagined to be represented by mere unorganised detail. (Barrell, 1990 pp. 32–3)

He added that: 'It was precisely the ability of the liberal mind of the free citizen to do this which constituted his claim to be a citizen, a free man, or, as he was often described (though the phrase has a range of meanings) a "public man" ' (Barrell, 1990 p. 34). Having a commanding view of the scene corresponded to the ownership of an extensive estate and with being of sufficient social stature to peer down on the world. Contrasting with the ability to survey the panoramic plan of the landscape was the occluded view of those 'private' men of narrow experience who were locked in the country-side and unable to take the broad view, and who were therefore disqualifed from the ability to abstract and generalise: 'The char-acteristic imagery of occluded landscapes – a cottage, for example, embosomed in trees which permit the distance to appear only as spots or slices of light, is emblematic of a situation in life from which no wider prospect is visible' (Barrell, 1990 p. 34).

The relationship between politics and landscape can take many forms. The character and configuration of the landscape could suggest certain policies or support certain myths, with the British 'island' and Swiss 'mountain' identities being extreme examples. More significantly, patterns of influence and control existing within societies become manifest in the landscape, where they may be fossilised. First, in the English Midlands, the exercise of the influ-ence of the landed classes produced Parliamentary Enclosure, which had the ancillary effect of imposing a hedgerow network across open countrysides where nobles, yeomen and squires had previously galloped freely in pursuit of the fox. As a result, a form of hunting more orientated towards jumping obstacles developed, but mean-while, the power of the elite gained a new physical expression in the countryside with the planting of woods of 2–20 acres as fox coverts, places where foxes could shelter and gather, in the freshly created fields; thus beginning a new chapter in the story of the impact of power on the landscape. Political influences can also be involved in the representation of landscape, with the choice and the manipula-tion of the subject matter serving to convey a message or reinforce an attitude. Most of these effects result from the fact that we do not live detached from landscape but within it; it is our milieu and we are a part of the scene. In July 1997 the supporters of bloodsports organised a mass demonstration in London to protest against a forthcoming parliamentary debate on the banning of hunting with hounds. The demonstrators were presented as representatives of the English and Welsh countryside; this guise was accepted with very little questioning by the media, which failed to recognise that the countryside contains millions who despise hunting with hounds. By clothing their (unpopular) cause in the wholesome mantle of countryside/landscape the bloodsports enthusiasts sought to sway public opinion and thus exercise power.

References

Adams A. J. 'Competing communities in the "Great Bog of Europe", identity and seventeenth-century Dutch landscape painting' in Mitchell, W. J. T., (ed.), *Landscape and Power* (Chicago: University of Chicago Press, 1994) pp. 35–76.

Banse, E. *Landschaft und Seele* (Munich, 1928).

Barrell, J. 'The public prospect and the private view: the politics of taste in eighteenth-century Britain' in Pugh, S. (ed.), *Reading Landscape: Country-City-Capital* (Manchester: Manchester University Press, 1990) pp. 19–40.

Bermingham, A. *Landscape and Ideology: The English Rustic Tradition, 1740–1860* (Berkeley, Calif., 1987).

Bowman, I. 'Geography *vs* geopolitics' *Geographical Review* **32** (1942).

Cosgrove, D. *Social Formation and Symbolic Landscape* (London: Croom Helm, 1984).

Cosgrove, D. 'Prospect, perspective and the evolution of the landscape idea' *Transactions of the Institute of British Geographers* NS **10** (1985) pp. 45–62.

Duncan J. 'The politics of landscape and nature, 1992–93' *Progress in Human Geography* **18** (1994) pp. 361–70.

Duncan, J. and Duncan, N. '(Re)reading the landscape' *Environment and Planning D: Society and Space* **6** (1988) pp. 117–26.

Everett, N. *The Tory View of Landscape* (New Haven, Conn.: Yale University Press, 1994).

Groening, G. 'The feeling for landscape – a German example' *Landscape Research* **17** (1992) pp. 108–15.

Helsinger, E. 'Turner and the representation of England' in Mitchell, W. J. T. (ed.), *Landscape and Power* (Chicago: Chicago University Press, 1994).

Hillis, K. 'Reviews: *Landscape and Power*' *Journal of Historical Geography* **22** (1996) pp. 243–4

Honour, H. *The New Golden Land* (New York: Pantheon, 1975).

Hoskins, W. G. *The Making of the English Landscape* (London: Hodder & Stoughton, 1955).

Mitchell, W.J.T. (ed.), *Landscape and Power* (Chicago: University of Chicago Press, 1994a).

Mitchell, W.J.T. 'Imperial landscape' in Mitchell, W.J.T. (ed.), *Landscape and Power* (Chicago: University of Chicago Press, 1994b) pp. 5–34.

Rollins, W.H. 'Whose landscape? Technology, fascism and environmentalism on the National Socialist Autobahn' *Annals of the Association of American Geographers* **85** (1995) pp. 494–520.

Schama, S. *Landscape and Memory* (London: HarperCollins, 1995).

Short, J.R. *Imagined Country* (London: Routledge, 1991).

Taigel, A. and Williamson, T. *Parks and Gardens* (London: Batsford, 1993).

Tate, W.E. *The English Village Community and the Enclosure Movements* (London: Victor Gollancz, 1967).

Taylor, C.C. *Roads and Tracks of Britain* (London: Dent, 1979).

Turner, J. *The Politics of Landscape* (Oxford: Blackwell, 1979).

Turner, M. 'The Landscape of Parliamentary Enclosure', in Reed, M. (ed.), *Discovering Past Landscapes* (London: Croom Helm, 1984).

Williamson, T. *Polite Landscapes: Gardens and Society in Eighteenth-Century England* (Baltimore: Johns Hopkins University Press/Alan Sutton, 1995).

Williamson, T. and Bellamy, E. *Property and Landscape* (London: George Philip, 1987).

Young, A., *General View of the Agriculture of Norfolk* (Board of Agriculture, 1804).

6

The Evaluation of Landscape

There was a period around the start of the final quarter of this century when landscape evaluation attracted a great deal of attention. Laurie wrote that: 'Landscape evaluation may be defined as "the comparative relationships between two or more landscapes in terms of assessments of visual quality"; in this context, assessments are the "process of recording visual quality through an observer's aesthetic appreciation of intrinsic visual qualities or characteristics within the landscape"' (Laurie, 1975 p. 103). Each landscape has its own particular character and qualities and viewers will tend to evaluate landscapes according to their perceived merits, which will include aesthetic and ecological considerations as well as others, like cultural characteristics. In addition to the qualitative judgements made about landscapes in an informal context, landscape evaluation has also been practised as a deliberate exercise in assessment directed towards obtaining data that might be incorporated into planning or conservation strategies. Governmental concern with the assessment of landscape inspired an enormous amount of research into landscape evaluation during the 1970s and this area of study continues to receive considerable interest from workers engaged with the applied aspects of landscape study. Cosgrove noted that: 'Among British geographers interest in landscape was stimulated partly by perception studies, particularly the short-lived excitement over landscape evaluation for planning purposes which surrounded the 1973 reform of local government' (1985 p. 46). In both the informal and the research contexts there are difficulties associated with linking evaluation to subjective judgements, as, for example, in demonstrating why hilly countryside might be regarded as 'superior' to countryside which is flat.

Landscape and Taste

Not only are the human judgements about the merits of landscape difficult to substantiate according to objective criteria; they are also subject to change through the course of time. Linton wrote that:

In the course of historic time as man's knowledge and ingenuity have increased, the number of resources he has exploited or prized has also increased, and the values he has set upon them have undergone many changes, some up, some down. For something more than a century there have been people of sufficient sensibility to set store by scenic variety or splendour, and of sufficient wealth and leisure to travel in search of them. (1968 p. 219)

Earlier he noted that: 'Scenery is a natural resource. Scenery that charms, thrills or inspires is a potential asset to the land in which it is found. But like other natural resources it is a potential asset that becomes actual only when valued and exploited by a society that has reached a particular cultural and economic level' (Linton, 1968). Cultural factors and geographical origins will influence the intellectual development of a person and their taste in landscape; Nash wrote of the importance of the places where people were born and raised:

It is extremely meaningful to know that someone is a Westerner, a resident of New York City, a New Englander, a Texan, or from Dubuque. We instinctively sense that a people acquire certain mental and even physical characteristics from a particular locality . . . as the common heritage that everyone in a locality shares, landscape is an undeniably important factor in the development of common traits. (1975 p. 77)

Not only does popular taste in the type of landscape favour change, but so too may the standards by which landscape is judged:

Opportunities to experience landscape naively without some preconceived images are getting rare for everybody. In the nineteenth century expectations raised by black and white illustrations in travel books were likely to be surpassed by seeing the real scenery. But twentieth century expectations raised by stunning coloured photographs, travel agency posters and special television programmes by the National Geographic Society are much higher. (Johnson and Pitzl, 1981 p. 211)

Laurie considered that:

Beauty in landscape derives from two main sources which cannot be separated in assessments because they interact:
From the object The intrinsic formal qualities of individual object(s) whether natural or man-made (that is, shape, proportion, color, and the like); the aesthetic relationship between these individual objects (that is, their spacing, scale, composition, and so on); the relationship of an object or group of objects to a setting.
From the observer The inherent physiological, emotional, and psychological makeup of the observer; the relationship between the observer and society; the relationship between the observer and the object(s). (1975 p. 107)

He quoted from the English art critic, Eric Newton:

Beauty is a desirable commodity. But not all men are equally susceptible to it. Nor are all men agreed about its abode. Moreover it varies with period. It is subject to the laws that govern fashion . . . It also varies with its geographical position . . . Variation in national or racial standards of beauty are as noticeable as in period standards. (1950 p. 18)

So landscape preferences are unstable, a theme echoed by Lowenthal, who thought that: 'The tides of taste affected not just the popularity of mountains, ruins, lakes and waterfalls, but also whether these were more admirable from a distance or close at hand, in motion or in repose, from ground level or at a height, with the unaided eye or through binoculars, alone or in company' (1978 p. 383). He added that: 'approved landscape stances have ranged from aesthetic detachment to emotional involvement, moral reflection, scientific enquiry, physical exertion and risk taking. Favoured landscape types also reflect new forms of recreation and ease of access to remote spots' (1978 p. 383).

In the seventeenth and early eighteenth centuries, landscape taste was much different from that of today, and the rugged upland countrysides much favoured both by the late eighteenth-century

Figure 6.1 In the eighteenth century the landscaping taste of the educated classes was heavily influenced by the paintings of Claude, Poussin and Rosa. Elements from this painting, *Coastal View of Delos and Aeneas*, by Claude, were echoed in many new landscape parks of the time. (National Gallery, London)

disciples of the picturesque and today's lovers of scenery were regarded with awe and even loathing. Describing the mountains in south Wales encountered in 1724, Defoe wrote:

> We began with Brecknock, being willing to see the highest of the mountains, which are said to be hereabouts; and indeed, except I had still an idea of the height of the Alps, and of those mighty mountains of America, the Andes, which we see very often in the South Seas, 20 leagues from the shore: I say except that I still had an idea of those countries on my mind, I should have been surprised at the sight of these hills; nay, (as it was) the Andes and the Alps, though immensely high, yet they stand together, and they are as mountains, piled upon mountains, and hills upon hills; whereas sometimes we see these mountains rising up at once, from the lowest valleys, to the highest summits which makes the height look horrid and frightful, even worse than those mountains abroad; which though much higher, rise as it were, one behind another; so that the ascent seems gradual, and consequently less surprising. (1989 p. 131)

Defoe also found the landscape of the Lake District intimidating and about 1725 he wrote of the now much-cherished uplands:

> Nor were these hills high and formidable only, but they had a kind of unhospitable terror in them. Here were no rich pleasant valleys between them, as amongst the Alps; no lead mines and veins of rich ore, as in the Peak; no coal pits, as in the hills about Halifax, much less gold, as in the Andes, but all barren and wild, of no use or advantage either to man or beast. (p. 195)

He skirted the modern tourist Mecca of Windermere and wrote:

> Here we entered Westmoreland, a country eminent only for being the wildest, most barren and frightful of any I have passed over in England, or even in Wales it self; the west side, which borders on Cumberland, is indeed bounded by a chain of almost unpassable mountains, which, in the language of the country, are called Fells. (Defoe, 1989)

Lowenthal remarked that:

Figure 6.2   The orderly disposition of fields, hedgerows and hedgerow trees displayed in this air photograph from the Helperby locality of North Yorkshire would have appealed to the tastes of eighteenth-century country landowners. (Cambridge University collection)

Travellers who fancied crag and chasm the 'ruins of the world' and who considered mountains a hell where one died of cold had little use for Wales. Averse to mountains, Defoe in 1732 noted of Snowdonia only its 'monstrous height' . . . As late as 1768, 'dreary' was the sole adjective one traveller applied to Snowdonia, which others thought bleak, barren, and disagreeable. (1978 p. 386)

However, tastes swiftly changed:

From the 1770s, however, Wales in general, the mountainous north in particular, rapidly gained favour. 'Everywhere the rain-soaked uplands, sparsely populated and largely unploughed, were beautiful in the eyes of those who were reacting against their fathers' criteria for a beautiful landscape. By 1800 once 'barbarous Merionithshire', formerly the 'rudest landscape and roughest district in all Wales', had replaced civilised Kent as Britain's scenic ideal (Zaring, 1977, 403). Guides promised all the grand and stupendous scenery travellers could desire; not even Switzerland or North America could match North Wales's extravagant wildness and angry grandeur (Moir, 1964, 129). Wordsworth and Coleridge succumbed to Welsh charms; Peacock and Shelley spent a year in a Merioneth cottage. For artists, mountainous Wales was a land no less romantic than Italy; sketching trips to 'our British Alps' became *de rigeur* for aspiring landscape painters in the 1780s. (Lowenthal, 1978 p. 386)

With regard to the tastes of the preceding generations, Brandon explained that travellers of the early eighteenth century favoured undulating country where the complete humanisation of the natural world had endowed the landscape with many of the virtues conventionally associated with a garden. 'Such landscapes, especially where bordered by distant hills offering a contrast, were praised for their variety and for their suggestion of prosperous well-being, order and harmony, recalling to the mind the poetic imagery of the pastoral eclogue which was the main literary tradition of the time' (1979 p. 166). He noted the taste for trim, varied, orderly country-side in which farms were kept like gardens and remarked that one of the earliest surviving appraisals of the the scenic qualities of the lowland English landscape was written by John Dennis in 1717, who described the Wealden panorama seen from Leith Hill: 'all the

Figure 6.3   Wild and rugged countrysides, like this view of the Cuillins on Skye, were unattractive and threatening to the eighteenth-century mind. (Richard Muir)

wilds of Surrey and Sussex and a great part of that of Kent, admirably diversified in every part of them with woods and fields of corn and pastures . . . adorned by stately rows of trees' (1721 pp. 31–4). Then:

> A pleasurable sense that much of the South East was a delicately textured pattern of field, copse and hedgerow so well gardened that it resembled a work of art thus gradually entered into the consciousness of eighteenth-century travellers. The following century saw a deeper appreciation of the soft garden-like quality in the landscape, mainly among observers with a narrower field of vision who responded to the attractions of a particular locality or type of surroundings. (Brandon, 1979 p. 167)

By this time, however, the consensus in scenic taste favoured Snowdonia and the Lake District rather than Kent. These mountainous places are still highly favoured today, but it is important to remember that:

twentieth-century appreciation of Snowdonia contrasts strikingly with that of the eighteenth. The modern ascent is scenic, but scarcely sublime . . . changing religious and aesthetic views affected attitudes toward mountains, and vice versa: from loathed excrescences on the original smooth globe, mountains came to be inspiring locales, magnificently wild and irregular. (Lowenthal, 1978 p. 387)

He added that: 'Heavenly proximity, wilderness purity, hydro-logical utility, extensive panoramas, scenic configuration, architec-tural resemblances, stimuli to bravery and lessons for freedom are among the many motives since advanced for admiring mountains' (Lowenthal, 1978). Bourassa, too, has noted the major role played by painting and poetry in the development of modern attitudes towards mountain scenery. He acknowledged the 'importance of seventeenth century landscape painting in setting the stage for the appreciation of the Alpine landscape which developed in the eight-eenth century' (1991 p. 12), adding:

During this same period, poets began to describe mountains with terms of praise rather than disparagement . . . coupled with an increasing ease of travel across the Alps, these insights on the part of painters and poets contributed to a complete reversal of attitudes to mountains on the part of the general public: instead of invoking fear or disgust, the Alpine landscape came to be the apotheosis of sublimity (Bourassa, 1991).

Wordsworth, writing almost two centuries ago (Figure 6.4), was aware of the unstable nature of taste in scenery; in his *Guide to the Lakes* of 1810 he wrote:

A practice, denominated Ornamental Gardening, was at that time [around 1750] becoming prevalent over England. In union with an admiration of this art, and in some instances in opposition to it, had been generated a relish for select parts of natural scenery: and Travellers, instead of confining their observations to Towns, Manufactories, or Mines, began (a thing till then unheard of) to wander over the island in search of sequestered spots, distin-guished as they might accidently have learned, for the sublimity or beauty of the forms of Nature there to be seen. (1970 p. 69)

Plainly, tastes in landscape have evolved over time, while there is good reason to believe that tastes in landscape change from place to place and from culture to culture. Laurie wrote that:

Figure 6.4 From the time of Wordsworth and the Lake poets onwards, picturesque scenes, like this much photographed view of Ashness Bridge in Cumbria, have been widely regarded as the epitome of landscape beauty. (Richard Muir)

Differences in perceived landscape values have been found when there were significant differences between cultures (for example, differences in lifestyles and levels of economic subsistence) and their respective native landscapes (for example, from arctic to temperate and tropical landscapes) such as are found between Eskimos and Americans or between black West Indians and white Americans. Both of these studies suggest that environmental experience and landscape familiarity can be important factors in shaping perceptions of valued landscapes. (1975 p. 107)

American tastes in landscape are said to be characterised by a general preference for the wilderness over culturally modified scenery, for important and widely celebrated views and for spectacular landforms existing on the grandest of scales (Lowenthal, 1968), though a study of Philadelphians revealed enthusiasms for parkland with lawns and trees rather than 'natural' landscape (Rabinowitz and Coughlin, 1970). In England, however, the taste is for neat but rustic scenery which is picturesque and redolent of the past, while a survey of Hertfordshire residents indicated preferences for farmland and woodland with long views across unspoilt countryside (Penning-Rowsell *et al.*, 1977). While the English cherish references to the past in the landscape, in America 'with the Revolution came a new spirit: newness was not only tolerated but positively worshiped, and the lack of historical remains became a matter for self-congratulation' (Lowenthal, 1976 p. 91).

In addition to the spatial and temporal variations in taste there may also be a dimension of variation related to social class. Lowenthal and Prince considered that in a country such as England, with pronounced class differences, it is not safe or profitable to attempt to generalise about national attitudes. The loudest voice heard is of an upper or upper-middle class type with a pronounced rural bias, but the assumption that the English as a whole hold strong convictions about landscape need not be true: 'Indeed, many professed partisans of the countryside strive to show that they are a minority; they believe that the majority of their fellow countrymen, lacking their own appreciation of the landscape, are destroying it. Class lines are clearly drawn. Stories illustrating the supposed banality of popular taste spice the meetings of amenity societies' (Lowenthal and Prince, 1964 pp. 325–6).

Culture and class do not determine tastes and choices; lifestyle, personality and individual life experience can also be important; Greenbie wrote that:

To the corporate executive on the fortieth floor of an office tower, the urban landscape may not be aggressively threatening but aggressively exciting, a symbol of human purpose and power. He may enjoy the presence of trees on the street far below, but that enjoyment may have very low priority with him, especially if he has a lush home in a green suburb. (1992 p. 73)

Meanwhile:

To the clerk leaving an anonymous desk on a lower story, a walk through a park on the way home may be restorative; but he may prefer to elbow his way home by the shortest route to an apartment with a television set and a few potted plants on the window sill, or stop off in the purely social landscape of a local bar. (1992 p. 73)

Landscape tastes may provide a basis for a differentiation between classes, while these tastes also transmit messages about status:

In a society that does not officially sanction social stratification, individuals provide covert cues (such as speech, dress, and landscape tastes) rather than overt cues to their social status. Landscape tastes have been overlooked by students of social stratification. Yet they are a critical part of presentation of self for middle- and upper-class Americans, whose social interaction takes place to a great extent in the home landscape. (Duncan, 1973 p. 355)

In his study of landscape taste as a symbol of group identity in Bedford, New York, Duncan designated alpha and beta social classes. He found that: 'Alpha people are obviously anglophiles and appear to value the English upper-class style of studied seediness. Gardens as well as roads reflect that preference in their "natural" aura and their appearance of considerable age' (p. 343), and:

A member of the alpha landscape wants to stand in his garden and feel that he is out in the country, surrounded by nature, not by other houses. Distinguished is the alpha resident who has a long gravel driveway, possibly with a pair of stone posts at the entrance. In the beta landscape, however, the spacing of the houses and the openness of the landscape suggest that the resident wants to stand in his garden, to see and be seen, while a streetful of expensive houses and gardens similar to his own mirror his prosperity. (p. 344)

Landscape taste varies through time and between places and social classes. It may also vary between genders, while individual preferences are highly variable; Walmsley and Lewis noted that landscapes mean different things to different people, their symbolic values often generating strong attachments. How landscapes are interpreted:

can reflect the values and attitudes of the individuals concerned. Thus a capitalist may interpret landscape in monetary terms, an artist in aesthetic terms, a scientist in ecological terms, and a social activist in terms of disorder and injustice . . . a recreationist may interpret a landscape in terms of the extent to which it gratifies a desire for pleasurable experience. (1993 p. 208)

Landscape taste can be related to culture: 'Different cultures possess different *tastes* in cultural landscape; to understand the roots of taste is to understand much of culture itself', wrote Lewis (1979 p. 17), who added: 'if we ask why America's human land-scapes look the way they do, it may seem that we are asking simple-minded questions. In fact, we are also asking why do Americans possess certain tastes and not others? We are asking where those tastes came from and why they take hold in certain times and disappear at others' (p. 18). Variations in the response to landscape are largely related to the fact, highlighted by Meinig, that: 'any landscape is composed not only of what lies before our eyes but what lies within our heads' (1979 p. 34).

The question of where landscape tastes may come from was considered in an adventurous fashion by Orians (1986). He noted how much of human evolution had taken place in the savannahs of East Africa, where trees were scattered and where a high proportion of useful resources were to be found within two metres of the ground where it was accessible to people and to grazing and browsing animals, and also where most early human fossil sites in the water-deficient region were associated with riverside and lakeside loca-tions. He then offered certain predictions:

> First, savanna-type environments with scattered trees and copses in a matrix of grassland should be highly preferred environments for people and should evoke strong positive emotions. This prediction is borne out in the broad sense in that environments manipulated strictly or primarily for the pleasure they evoke are generally savanna types. (p. 11)

He added that: 'Parks and gardens in all cultures are neither closed forests nor open grasslands. In addition, great pains are taken in the creation of parks and gardens to create water or the illusion of water, or to enhance the quality and quantity of existing water resources'. He also predicted that: 'given the array of species from which early gardeners could select those to use in their manipulated environments, those with natural shapes more similar to the savanna models should have been preferred over those species with shapes more divergent from the savanna models'. Cosgrove, however, was unsympathetic to such ideas:

I do not doubt that as part of nature we intuit strong links between its processes and forms and those of our own bodies . . . But such intuitions are so transformed, overlain and mediated by social, cultural and economic as well as personal meanings historically, that to trace the bio-physiological bases of environmental (*not* landscape) response seems futile at best, and at worst pandering to the most dangerously idiological interpretation of 'human nature'. (Orians, 1986 p. 23)

Other biologically-based interpretations of human landscape preferences were offered by Appleton in the form of *habitat theory* and *prospect-refuge theory* (which are discussed at greater length in Chapter 8). According to habitat theory: 'aesthetic satisfaction, experienced in the contemplation of landscape, stems from the spontaneous perception of landscape features which, in their shapes, colours, spatial arrangements and other visible attributes, act as sign-stimuli indicative of environmental conditions favourable to survival, whether they really *are* favourable or not' (1996 p. 62). He added that: "Ingestive" requirements, for instance, are very directly suggested by the smiling cornfields, the browsing flocks and the limpid brooks of the classical poets and their latter-day disciples' (pp. 62–3), and he deduced that:

'Habitat theory' thus asserts that the relationship between the human observer and the perceived environment is basically the same as the relationship of a creature to its habitat. It asserts further that the satisfaction which we derive from the contemplation of this environment, and which we call 'aesthetic', arises from a spontaneous reaction to that environment as a habitat, that is to say as a place which affords the opportunity for achieving our simple biological needs. When we attain a sufficient control over our environment to render the mechanisms by which we make this spontaneous appraisal of it no longer essential to the achievement of these biological needs, the mechanisms do not immediately die out in the species but continue to be transmitted from one generation to another and may, if needed, be called upon again to discharge their primitive function. (1996 p. 63)

Once released from functions needed to ensure the survival of the species 'we are then able to enjoy the satisfaction which results from the perception of a biologically favourable environment without uncomfortably exposing ourselves to the hazards against which this sensitivity to our surroundings would protect us in a "state of nature"' (Appleton, 1996).

Appleton's prospect-refuge theory asserts that the landscapes which seem most fulfilling to humans are those which provide us with an ability to prospect or see without ourselves being seen. Walmsley and Lewis noted that:

> both prospect and refuge can be characterized symbolically: the former by light, open areas (e.g. sea-shores) and the latter by dark, impenetrable areas (e.g. woodland). In short, prospect-refuge theory argues that the sensitivity which humans experience in regard to a landscape, whether it be a painting or the real world, hinges on whether the landscape in question provides them with an ability to see without being seen and that this, in turn, derives from behavioural mechanisms which are innate. (1993 p. 209)

Appleton wrote:

> A creature *hunting* says to itself, 'If I wish to catch my quarry I must do so before it can reach a place which is inaccessible to me. Such a place may be a hole in the ground, a pond, a tree top, or simply, if the quarry has greater speed and stamina than I, a distant location from which it can move further as I approach. To minimise its chances of doing this I must approach as close as possible before it sets in motion the mechanism for achieving this escape, which means, in practice, before it notices me.' *Per contra* a creature *escaping* says to itself, 'If I am to escape successfully, I must ensure that I can reach a place inaccessible to my pursuer before he can prevent me. When, therefore, I am engaged in activities such as feeding, which involve the diversion of my attention from the activities of a potential pursuer, I must so position myself, if possible, that either he will not see me or, if he does, I will perceive him threatening me while I yet have time to reach safety'. (1996 p. 64)

According to this theory these innate mechanisms will remain even though we may cultivate our appreciation of landscape, while our needs for natural vantage points and refuges will prevent us from ever fully enjoying unnatural settings. In short:

Habitat theory postulates that aesthetic pleasure in landscape derives from the observer experiencing an environment favourable to the satisfaction of his biological needs. Prospect-refuge theory postulates that, because the ability to see without being seen is an intermediate step in the satisfaction of many of those needs, the capacity of an environment to ensure the achievement of *this* becomes a more immediate source of aesthetic satisfaction. (p. 66)

Cosgrove (1978) also objected to these ideas, and while *Homo habilis* and his descendents may have survived as hunters (or scavengers), our more distant, australopithecine forebears appear to have existed as gatherers who consumed much vegetable matter. 'It also flies in the face of the observation that most recreationists seem able to find enjoyment in a wide variety of landscapes. Moreover, the attraction that beaches hold for recreationists can presumably be explained without resort to prospect-refuge theory' (Walmsley and Lewis, 1993 p. 209). Another socio-biologically based approach was developed by the environmental psychologists, S. and R. Kaplan (1978), and all are explored in more detail in Chapter 8.

Techniques for Landscape Evaluation

Much of the interest directed towards questions of landscape evaluation in Britain during the decades following the Second World War derived from planning legislation which required that local authorities should evaluate landscape quality to provide a basis for the formation of policies for environmental protection and enhancement. In the UK the 1947 Town and Country Planning Act and the 1949 National Parks and Access to the Countryside Act made landscape evaluation a statutory duty for both local and central government. Zube, Sell and Taylor remarked that:

The major impetus for systematic analyses and studies of landscape beauty and amenity occurred during the decade of the 1960s and the early 1970s. A substantial body of legislation was enacted during this time both in the U.S.A. and Great Britain that directed attention to the identification and management of scenic resources. (1982 pp. 1–2)

Meanwhile: 'Legislation in the U.S.A. addressed the subjects of wild and scenic rivers, scenic and recreational trails, scenic highways, environmental impacts of major development projects including aesthetic impacts, coastal zone management and natural resources planning' (Zube, Sell and Taylor, 1982). They noted that in Britain, the Countryside Act of 1968 stated: 'in the exercise of these functions relating to land under enactment every Minister, government department and public body shall have regard to the desirability of conserving the natural beauty and amenity of the Countryside'. Subsequently, they pointed out, attention was directed towards concerns of an aesthetic nature associated with agriculture, forestry, recreation and designated Areas of Outstanding Natural Beauty, National Parks and Heritage Coasts.

Two styles of study derived from this growing official involvement with the evaluation of landscape: 'On the one hand, there were attempts to quantify landscape quality by allocating points for the presence/intensity of designated features (see Fines 1968). This approach has attracted stern criticism, not least because of the subjectivity involved (Brancher 1969)' (Walmsley and Lewis, 1993 p. 207). Consequently an alternative approach came to be widely adopted.

This has involved using photographs as surrogates for actual visits to landscapes, and then assessing them with the help of panels of 'experts' (see Jacques 1980). This too has proved problematical. Aside from the predictable problem of ensuring that all photographs are of similar quality (e.g. light, angle, exposure, focus), the approach is fundamentally flawed because it is not known to what extent the views of 'experts' and 'non-experts' coincide (Harrison and Howard 1972). (Walmsley and Lewis, 1993 pp. 207–8)

In the field of landscape evaluation an opposition between the advocates of quantitative and qualitative methodologies became well established, the work of the quantifiers sometimes seeming exact but irrelevant, while that of the qualitative students could be more relevant but was supported only by intuition.

Planners engaged on studies in landscape evaluation may use their own judgements or those of other professionals to justify planning recommendations. Alternatively, they may employ questionnaires or other sampling methods in order to discover the nature of public landscape preferences. 'The two forms of enquiry are often confused because landscape evaluators often claim that their surveys take account of popular judgements. But the claim is seldom valid; the line between "expert" landscape evaluation and public appraisal is usually clear and distinct' (Lowenthal, 1978 p. 389). Lowenthal was scathing in his criticism of the application of techniques of landscape evaluation by planners:

> Landscape evaluation studies neither ascertain landscape tastes nor assess public preferences; they tell us nothing about what landscapes the public values or why. Indeed, they are not a form of research at all but a planning tool to help determine how to use land, where to site motorways and reservoirs, when to spend money on development or protection. Landscape evaluation is not a way to learn about attachment to locales, but a practical means to a policy end. (Lowenthal, 1978)

Penning-Rowsell (1975) identified four main objectives associated with landscape evaluation programmes. Of these, *landscape preservation* was the most important:

> Here evaluations provide primary data for identifying areas of countryside which can be designated as being worthy of preservation in as near their existing conditions as possible. Behind this type of policy lies the philosophy which led to the designation of Areas of Outstanding Natural Beauty (A.O.N.B.), although their designation was not based on any systematic application of landscape-evaluation methods, but rather on the considered opinions of local planning department and Countryside Commission personnel. (p. 149)

Allied to the goal of landscape preservation is *landscape protection*:

> The application of landscape-evaluation methods to this area of planning involves linking development-control decisions to available landscape resources. Clearly, two options are open: either one allows new residential or other land uses in localities with high landscape quality, on the basis, for example, that these represent favourable residential locations, or one takes the opposite viewpoint and sites the developments away from areas of high

landscape quality and reserves these for recreation-based land uses which will be less destructive in landscape terms. The decision as to which line to adopt will again depend on the priorities of local planners and the public, but the necessity for a systematic appraisal of landscape resources on which to base the decision is hard to deny. (p. 150)

Third, *recreation policy* was an objective of local authority landscape evaluation programmes:

Here the same two objectives that exist in planning for landscape protection create more difficulties for decision-makers, when reviewing the constraints on locating recreational facilities. Either the high landscape quality areas, when identified by some evaluative technique, are preserved as sanctuaries with little encouragement for recreational provision . . . or they are developed into foci of mass recreation with the planning authority exercising a positive rather than a passive role in this development. (pp. 150–1)

The fourth objective of landscape evaluation work by planning authorities was *landscape improvement*:

The basis of improvement policies is the type of evaluation which allows the identification of landscape elements and components which are considered to detract from landscape quality. Existing legislation can then be used to remove or modify the offending eyesores, especially within A.O.N.B.s, or alternatively liaison with local industry, national undertakings and local government departments can yield useful results . . . The emphasis given to landscape improvement within landscape-evaluation programmes is in general not as great as the emphasis on landscape protection and preservation. This is primarily because unfortunately landscape-evaluation techniques have always been seen as a means of identifying high rather than low quality landscape areas, whereas following the designation of the National Parks and the numerous A.O.N.B.s the latter function is perhaps of greater importance. (p. 151)

Each of the four planning policy areas had its own problems of linking particular landscape evaluation results to planning policy objectives and no one technique was considered to be appropriate for all four policy areas. The major constraints affecting the suitability of the techniques for the different applications were: (a) the *type* of landscape evaluation undertaken, concerning the level of detail at which the data was collected and the extent to which landscape users or consumers were involved in the landscape appraisal; (b) the *scale* of the survey unit, whether this was field based or cartogaphically based and (c) the *ease of up-dating* the results of landscape evaluation (p. 151).

The progress of landscape appraisal research from the mid-1960s to 1980 was also charted by Penning-Rowsell (1981), who noted how this period witnessed a sustained effort to devise techniques to quantify the scenic value of rural landscapes:

> This movement was inspired by growing awareness of landscape deterioration through urban expansion or inadequate management, and a perceived need for increased protection of those areas of greatest landscape quality. Many methods of landscape evaluation were devised in Britain, the United States and elsewhere, all intended to provide a foundation for more systematic landscape planning and management than had previously been possible. (Penning-Rowsell, 1981 p. 25)

He believed that three clear stages in attempts to evaluate landscapes could be identified, each linked to a different approach to assessing landscape value and locating valued landscapes: 'first, an early emphasis on *intuitive* methods; second, the development of complex *statistical* approaches to landscape quality prediction; third, an emphasis on landscape *preferences* and the development of a greater understanding of personal feelings and attachments towards valued landscapes' (p. 26).

According to Penning-Rowsell (1981), intuitive methods of landscape evaluation were characteristic of the period 1967–71: 'The earliest techniques simply classified landscape tracts according to the intuitive judgements of planners and landscape architects concerned to determine relative landscape value or quality' (p. 27). Such methods were criticised for their subjectivity because some felt that planners should not impose their private values on the public resource of landscape, and also because of variations in the assumptions and methods employed by the different local planning departments. Around 1970, simple mathematical techniques were employed to organise the varied landscape elements into indicies of landscape value: 'Planning departments found these "mathematical" methods more acceptable than the earlier purely subjective judgements, mainly because the basic resource assessments were more mechanical, and therefore supposedly more scientific, objective and valid' (p. 28).

The continuing criticisms of subjectivity favoured the adoption of more complex statistical techniques in the years 1971–6, though the techniques developed became more rather than less controversial. Much interest was attracted by the 'Coventry–Solihull–Warwickshire' (C–S–W) technique:

> The main reason for choosing the C–S–W technique is the clear way it distinguishes between the three basic stages in the landscape evaluation process: (a) the measurement of the elements which together form the landscape: landform, land use and land features such as rivers; (b) the measurement of individual or group preferences for landscape; and (c) the expression of landscape preferences in terms of measured components in the final evaluation. This gives the technique great flexibility and allows considerable scope for future modfication and improvement. (Blacksell and Gilg, 1975 p. 137)

However, the technique had several disadvantages:

> The visual quality assessments are made on a scale from 0–26 and the only clue to where a particular type of landscape ought to be placed within this range is the suggestion that good quality, flat farmland should be awarded a score of 8. Such a large scale, with so little guidance on how it ought to be interpreted, seems unnecessarily crude. (Blacksell and Gilg, 1975).

Criticism of statistical approaches to landscape evaluation grew during the 1970s, some criticisms concerning the statistical bases of the studies, and some concerning the fact that the quantitative techniques did not take account of the ways in which people perceive landscape and the use of narrowly visual assessment criteria. Writing in 1975, Penning-Rowsell found that:

> There has been a tendency in the landscape-evaluation work of local planning authorities to devise new measures of landscape quality for their own sake, each new one supposedly more

accurate and sophisticated than its predecessors. As well as neglecting the possibility of incorporating landscape-used or consumer attitudes into evaluative methods, planning authorities have not attempted to link evaluative method with the potential application of results. The result of this lack of consideration for the application of evaluations has been the use by many local authorities of the results of a single method in many contrasting policy areas, some objectives of which cannot be met with the results obtained. (p. 154)

In 1981 he noted that commentators had usually regarded statistical approaches to landscape evaluation as being too complex, too abstract and too expensive. He thought the last point to be particularly pertinent, since one stated objective of the statistical approach was its potential for saving money (pp. 30–1).

From the mid-1970s, a preference-based approach came to the fore, focusing on the preferences concerning total landscapes expressed by panels of observers, these preferences often related to tracts of landscape as depicted in photographs. Judgements about landscape preferences were frequently derived from the consensus opinions of ordinary members of the public, leading to criticisms that such evaluations were rooted in past landscape values and were tied to the common denominator of popular taste, which might not be the best yardstick for judging landscape value.

The clear concern of the preference approach is with the views of the man in the street . . . The public preference approach has its own problems of tapping landscape perceptions. The use of photographs as surrogates for real landscapes 'felt in the blood' has attracted criticism. Possible biases in question design may limit the validity of social survey valuations of landscape (Lowenthal, 1978, 30). Indeed the bases of landscape perceptions and attachments may not be discernible by asking the public questions, since they may not understand the questions or know the answers. Moreover, landscape evaluations based only on visual preferences, without analysis of the causes of perceptions, can take a narrow view of landscape: areas which are not 'preferred' may be otherwise valuable for their rarity or historical associations. (Penning-Rowsell, 1981 p. 32)

He concluded that: 'Perceiving both a decline in the area of rural land owing to rapid urban expansion, and threats to wilderness or

heritage landscapes from motorways and other developments, planners and academics alike sought refuge in "scientific" assessment
techniques to support plans that would further restrict landscape
change' (p. 37). Subsequently it was found that rather than removing controversy from the arenas of environmental decision-making,
the new techniques created new problems. Yet since some forms of
landscape quality assessment had come to be favoured by government and were sometimes required by statute, these positivist
techniques endured in the face of widespread scholarly, bureaucratic
and public disenchantment. 'Unfortunately this attempt at techni-
cally-based landscape planning, pursuing objectivity at the expense
of validity, also drew attention away from the fundamental economic and political forces promoting landscape change and from
the reactions, perceptions and attachments of people for the ordinary and extraordinary joys of landscape' (Penning-Rowsell, 1981).

Reviewing the situation in 1993, Walmsley and Lewis considered
that: 'it is not surprising that work on quantifying environmental
quality has not progressed much. Instead research attention has
been directed to landscape *interpretation* and to landscape *aesthetics*'
(p. 208). The work on landscape interpretation had attempted to
identify what gives landscapes their value: 'This is no easy task. As a
result researchers are far from being able to say what constitutes a
good view or a beautiful landscape, nor have they found a satisfac-
tory means by which to articulate the nature and significance of the
intimate attachments that people develop for landscape' (Walmsley
and Lewis, 1993). However, prominent amongst the qualities associated with valued landscapes are those which evoke the past and
which may therefore offer an escape from the present. In terms of
landscape aesthetics:

> Basically there are three elements whereby the aesthetic quality of
> a landscape can be assessed: unity (do the components of the
> landscape cohere into a single harmonious unit?); vividness (does
> the landscape have features that make it distinct and striking);
> and variety (does the landscape have enough variety to engage
> human interest without so much complexity as to make it
> chaotic?) (Litton 1972). (Walmsley and Lewis, 1993)

Doubts about the techniques employed in landscape evaluation
have remained. Relph was critical of systematic approaches to
landscape evaluation. He wrote that: 'Trying to investigate places

and landscapes by imposing standardized methods is like studying
ballet by putting the dancers in straitjackets, or judging wines by
measuring their alcohol content – the information obtained may be
accurate but it seriously misrepresents the subject matter' (1989
p. 149). He added:

> There are people who measure what they call landscape quality
> and attachment to place by means of a complex apparatus of
> photographs divided into grids, psychological tests, question-
> naires and statistical analyses. The results of all this have the
> same mathematical form as a measure of alcohol content and are
> therefore enthusiastically received by bureaucrats and others who
> prefer a whole number to a clear thought, but as the entire
> procedure is based on arbitrary definitions of landscape and
> places being studied (just where do you draw a boundary around
> landscape?) the results can in fact mean anything one chooses.
> This must be the sort of approach the philosopher Ludwig
> Wittgenstein was referring to when he wrote of psychology that
> it has 'experimental methods and conceptual confusion'. (pp. 149–
> 50)

He contrasted the systematic and scientific methods – imposed on
the subject matter and wringing information from it – with responsive methods which were phenomenological and artistic and which
were adapted to the form and character of the subject. The
responsive methods were appropriate to investigating the landscape:
'It is all too easy to follow intellectual fashions, or to work with
abstract models, and then to impose these on to places and
environments encountered only vicariously through a haze of words
or statistics or formulae' (p. 161) while:

> The uses of responsive methods as qualified by the geographical
> imagination are these: by teaching, to encourage and to direct
> others to experience landscapes and places for themselves, and so
> to arrive at a better self-understanding; by writing (or any other
> medium), to illuminate the places and environments of the world,
> and to interpret them, good or bad, so that others can appreciate
> their significance. (Relph, 1989 pp. 161–2)

Despite reservations such as these, systematic investigations of
landscape evaluation have remained popular in the literature of

applied landscape studies and planning. Orland (1992) compared the rural scenic preferences of rural residents of Arizona and urban residents of Tucson. Both groups were asked to evaluate a series of slides in terms of their scenic beauty and both showed similarities in their responses, but the rural group responded more favourably to the scenes than did the urban group, presumably because the rural group were more familiar with rural settings. It was suggested that:

> Two effects of importance to the planning of rural-landscape development have been noted in this study. First, the presence of human influences in otherwise 'natural' landscapes may dispose viewers to regard the whole natural/human influenced composite as human-influenced and hence perceive it as relatively less attractive than a purely natural landscape . . . Second, responses to certain types of landscape settings are to some degree influenced by the place of residence of the respondent . . . grassland scenes received relatively higher ratings from rural respondents when compared with the respondent's similarly high ratings of natural scenes. (p. 377)

Kaplan and Herbert (1992) compared the reactions of Australians and residents of Michigan to rural scenes from Michigan. The preferences expressed by the two groups were very similar and both responded favourably to vegetation and manicured landscapes. Though evidence of a preference for the familiar was at first thought to have emerged, with the Michigan residents responding more favourably than the Australians, the Australians responded relatively unfavourably to pastoral/open rural scenes of a type which would have seemed familiar to them. Thus there was evidence both for and against a preference for the familiar.

The enthusiasm for landscape evaluations continues and it embraces support for communal surveys. Roberts suggested that the term 'cultural landscape' appeared to enter popular parlance in Britain at about the time, after 1945, that the mechanisation of agriculture was displacing human toil from the countryside so 'in the best sibylline traditions, our interest in these landscapes grew as they became scarcer and more precious' (1994 p. 134). He noted that Guidelines prepared under the provisions of the Wildlife and Countryside (Amendment) Act of 1985 acknowledged that people value a place for its associations, and that places associated with particular novelists, poets, painters and musicians become imbued with special significance; he added:

> the appreciation of a 'cultural' landscape is not limited to a mere understanding of the physical *marks* left by society on the land but also demands our awareness of the attachment or *associations* that people can have for their home ground. This suggests that a proper appreciation of this latter, more abstract quality, comes only with time and commitment to place. Perhaps we should invest more time and effort in encouraging communities to undertake appraisals of their own landscapes and be less prescriptive in the way we expect landscapes to be 'managed'. (Roberts, 1994 p. 135)

A decade earlier, Zube had argued for perspectives that recognised humans as participants in landscape rather than as detached observers. Noting that most professional paradigm models regarded the human as an observer of the landscape, and that much of the behavioural research treated people either as observers or as thinkers (as processors of information about the landscape), he urged: 'If we are to gain better understanding about the meanings of landscapes and the significance of landscape experience, the human must be treated as an active participant with and in the landscape. It is from this perspective that the humanistic paradigm should be viewed' (1984 p. 108). He pointed out that reviewers had regarded landscape assessment as atheoretical or else had described the field as being made up of diverse theories that were imbedded, but not always explicit, in much of the work (Zube, Sell and Taylor, 1982). Bearing these factors in mind, he considered that a general theory for landscape assessment should:

(a) provide a framework for encompassing and bridging the professional, behavioural, and humanistic paradigms (that is, contribute to the doing of landscape assessment and the understanding of human/landscape interactions);
(b) recognise the need for and relationships between quantitative and qualitative information;
(c) encompass interests in both urban and natural landscapes;
(d) encompass diverse geographic scales ranging from the site to the region.

Difficulties remain, and a review by Uzzell (1991) identified:

> various methodological problems with research on landscape
> perception, assessment and preferences. It has been subject to
> methodological conservatism with too great an emphasis on
> reductionist quantitative techniques. This is not to say that
> quantitative studies are inappropriate. Far from it, they offer a
> certain rigour and comparability that is difficult to achieve in
> qualitative studies. The two should not be seen as mutually
> exclusive but complementary. (p. 8)

He added that: 'Another problem with a reductionist approach is
that it often ignores the social and cultural meanings that inform
and condition any response and interpretation of landscape'. In
addition: 'Many studies involve assessing photographs rather than
experiencing places. It seems highly likely that the preferences
expressed on the basis of two-dimensional photographs are different
to those which might be made *in situ*' (p. 9). Uzzell concluded with
an appeal to:

> reinstate the person into the landscape – a human who is not just a
> bundle of personality traits nor a set of motor neurone receptors
> ready to respond to environmental stimuli. Even when we do
> respond to the physical or aesthetic characteristics of the land-
> scape such as water, pattern or colour, it has to be recognised that
> water, pattern and colour have a cultural history and meaning for
> the individual and the social group. We need theories of landscape
> perception, assessment and preference which recognise individual
> and social action and intention and which see person–environ-
> ment relations in transactional and goal directed ways. (Uzzell,
> 1991)

References

Appleton, J. *The Experience of Landscape*, 2nd edn (Chichester: John Wiley,
    1996).
Blacksell, M. and Gilg, A. F. 'Landscape evaluation in practice – the case of
    south-east Devon' *Transactions of the Institute of British Geographers* **66**
    (1975) pp. 135–40.

Bourassa, S. C. The *Aesthetics of Landscape* (London: Belhaven Press, 1991).

Brancher, D. W. 'Critique of K. D. Fines' *Regional Studies* **3** (1969) pp. 91–2.

Brandon, P. F. 'The diffusion of designed landscapes in South-east England' in Fox, H. S. A. and Butlin, R. A. (eds), *Change in the Countryside: Essays on Rural England 1500–1900*, Institute of British Geographers Special Publication No. 10 (London: Institute of British Geographers, 1979) pp. 165–87.

Cosgrove, D. 'Place, landscape, and the dialectics of cultural geography' *Canadian Geographer* **22** (1978) pp. 66–72.

Cosgrove, D. 'Prospect, perspective and the evolution of the landscape idea' *Transactions of the Institute of British Geographers* NS **10** (1985) pp. 45–62.

Defoe, D. *A Tour Through the Whole Island of Great Britain* (ed.) Rogers P. (Exeter: Webb & Bower, 1989).

Dennis, J. *Original Letters* (1721).

Duncan, J. S. 'Landscape taste as a symbol of group identity' *Geographical Review* **63** (1973) pp. 334–55.

Fines, K. D. 'Landscape evaluation: a research project in East Sussex' *Regional Studies* **2** (1968) pp. 41–55.

Greenbie, B. B. 'The landscape of social symbols' in Nasar, J. L. (ed.), *Environmental Aesthetics, Theory, Research, and Applications* (Cambridge: Cambridge University Press, 1992) pp. 64–73.

Harrison, J. and Howard, W. A. 'The role of meaning in the urban image' *Environment and Behaviour* **3** (1972) pp. 389–411.

Jacques, D. L. 'Landscape appraisal: the case for a subjective theory' *Journal of Environmental Management* **10** (1980) pp. 107–13.

Johnson H. B. and Pitzl, G. R. 'Viewing and perceiving the rural scene: visualization in human geography' *Progress in Human Geography* **5** (1981) pp. 211–33.

Kaplan, R. 'Some methods and strategies in the prediction of preference' in Zube, E. H., Brush, R. O. and Fabos, J. G. (eds), *Landscape Assessment, Values, Perceptions and Resources* (Stroudsburg, Pa: Halsted Press, 1975).

Kaplan, S. and Kaplan, R. (eds), *Humanscape: Environments for People* (Belmont, Calif.: Duxbury, 1978).

Kaplan, R. and Herbert, E. J. 'Familiarity and preference: a cross-cultural analysis' in Nasar, J. L. (ed.), *Environmental Aesthetics: Theory, Research, and Applications* (Cambridge: Cambridge University Press, 1992) pp. 379–89.

Laurie, I. C. 'Aesthetic factors in visual evaluation' in Zube, E. H., Brush, R. O. and Fabos, J. G. (eds) *Landscape Assessment: Values, Perceptions and Resources* (Stroudsburg, Pa: Halsted Press, 1975) pp. 102–17.

Lewis, P. F. 'Axioms for reading the landscape' in Meinig, D. W. (ed.), *The Interpretation of Ordinary Landscapes* (New York: Oxford University Press, 1979).

Linton, D. L. 'The assessment of scenery as a natural resource' *Scottish Geographical Magazine* **84** (1968) pp. 219–38.

210   *Approaches to Landscape*

Litton, R. B. 'Aesthetic dimensions of the landscape' in Krutilla, J. V. (ed.), *Natural Environments* (Baltimore: Johns Hopkins University Press, 1972) pp. 262–91.
Lowenthal, D. 'The American scene', *Geographical Review* **58** (1968) pp. 61–88.
Lowenthal, D. 'The place of the past in the American landscape' in Lowenthal, D. and Bowden, M. J. (eds), *Geographies of the Mind* (New York: Oxford University Press, 1976) pp. 89–117.
Lowenthal, D. 'Finding valued landscapes' *Progress in Human Geography* **2** (1978) pp. 373–418.
Lowenthal, D. and Prince, H. C., 'The English landscape' *Geographical Review* **54** (1964) pp. 309–46.
Meinig, D. W. 'The beholding eye' in Meinig, D. W. (ed.), *The Interpretation of Ordinary Landscapes* (New York: Oxford University Press, 1979) pp. 33–48.
Moir, E., *The Discovery of Britain: The English Tourists 1540 to 1840* (London: Routledge & Kegan Paul, 1964).
Nash, R. 'Qualitative landscape values: the historical perspective' in Zube, E. H., Brush, R. O. and Fabos, J. G. (eds), *Landscape Assessment: Values, Perceptions and Resources* (Stroudsburg, Pa: Halsted Press, 1975) pp. 10–17.
Newton, E. *The Meaning of Beauty* (London, 1950).
Orians, G. H. 1980 'Habitat selection: general theory and applications to human behaviour' in J. Lockard (ed.), *Evolution of Human Social Behaviour* (New York: Elsevier, 1980) pp. 49–66.
Orians, G. H. 'An ecological and evolutionary approach to landscape aesthetics' in Penning-Rowsell, E. C. and Lowenthal, D. (eds), *Landscape Meaning and Values* (London: Allen & Unwin, 1986) pp. 3–25.
Orland, B. 'Aesthetic preference for rural landscapes: some resident and visitor differences' in Nasar, J. L. (ed.), *Environmental Aesthetics: Theory, Research, and Applications* (Cambridge: Cambridge University Press, 1992) pp. 364–78.
Penning-Rowsell, E. C. 'Constraints on the application of landscape evaluations' *Transactions of the Institute of British Geographers* **66** (1975) pp. 149–55.
Penning-Rowsell, E. C. 'Fluctuating fortunes in gauging landscape value' *Progress in Human Geography* **5** (1981) pp. 25–41.
Penning-Rowsell, E. C., Gullet, G. H., Searle, G. H. and Witham, S. A. *Public Evaluation of Landscape Quality* (Enfield, Middlesex: Middlesex Polytechnic Planning Research Group Report No. 13, 1977).
Rabinowitz, C. B. and Coughlin, R. E., *Analysis of Landscape Characteristics Relevant to Preference* (Philadelphia: Regional Science Research Institute, Discussion Paper No. 38, 1970).
Relph, E. 'Responsive methods, geographical imagination and the study of landscapes' in Kobayashi, A. and Mackenzie, S. (eds), *Remaking Human Geography* (Boston: Unwin Hyman, 1989) pp. 149–63.
Roberts, G. 'The cultural landscape' *Landscape Research* **19** (1994) pp. 133–6.

Uzzell, D. L. 'Environmental psychological perspectives on landscape' *Landscape Research* **16** (1991) pp. 3–10.

Walmsley, D. J. and Lewis, G. J. *People and Environment: Behavioural Approaches in Human Geography* (Harlow: Longman, 1993).

Wordsworth, W. *Guide to the Lakes* (Oxford: Oxford University Press, 1970).

Zaring, J., 'The romantic face of Wales' *Annals of the Associations of American Geographers* **67** (1977) pp. 397–418.

Zube, E. H. 'Themes in landscape assessment theory' *Landscape Journal* **3** (1984) pp. 104–9.

Zube, E. H., Sell, J. L. and Taylor, J. G. 'Landscape perception: Research, application and theory' *Landscape Planning* **9** (1982) pp. 1–33.

7
Symbolic Landscapes

Long-established approaches to the historical study of landscapes have been concerned with investigating the evolution of the form and cultural contents of the landscape and with interpreting how landscapes have evolved to attain their present appearance. Much newer are the attempts to identify the symbolic meanings and messages contained in landscape. Penning-Rowsell noted that: 'Landscapes . . . carry symbolic meanings that are not so wholly innocent as might at first be thought. Created landscapes can be assertions of power – over nature or over neighbours – and our cognition of landscapes is selective and sometimes deliberately distorted in the pursuit of our own interests' (1986 p. 115). He added that:

> Landscapes may have an ideological function in mystifying rather than revealing: confusing by distortion or other emphases, rather than providing simple and accessible patterns. Thus our ways of seeing and knowing (perception and cognition) are influenced by the social relations inherent in the landscapes we view. Testing this empirically is difficult but historical evidence shows, for example, how 18th-century landscape gardens were created as expressions of political (Whig) dominance. In a similar way grouse moors and farmed landscapes are expressions of capitalist society today, and city landscapes are manipulated to proclaim the loudest social messages.

A Way of Seeing?

According to Butlin, the exploration of the symbolic associations of landscape is related to the ebb and flow of larger academic tides. The development of a new set of perspectives on landscape and its representation could partly be explained by a decline in interest in positivist approaches to the study of society and to the adoption of more humanistic perspectives. Thus:

A different kind of problematic has emerged, more focused on such notions as social justice, symbolism, and the relationship of landscape to a very wide range of cultural issues and perspectives. This new set of approaches renders all landscapes and landscape elements symbolic, so that it turns landscape into a subject rather than an object. (1993 p. 137)

Hence, to those initiated in these arts: 'the landscape, in past and present form, may be seen as a symbol of changing social orders, including feudalism and capitalism in their various temporally and spatially located and experienced forms' (1993).

The theme of an intellectual shift to a more humane geography was expressed by Cosgrove, who wrote:

Such an approach has begun to emerge among a small number of human geographers since the early 1970s . . . As with all shifts in the direction of geographical research, this change is related to broader social movements: protests against environmental exploitation and pollution, unease with megascale planning and the anonymous landscapes of urban redevelopment, the growing voice of organised women challenging the dominance of male culture and the failure of the post-war social and political consensus have all played their part in nudging human geography towards *humanistic* geography. (1989 p. 121)

Earlier he had written:

Over the past decade the view of geography as a positive science has been challenged by writers favouring a 'humanistic' approach to understanding relations between humans and their world. Landscape has re-emerged in their writings as an important term because its affective meaning seems to allow for an escape from the outsider's position and for the incorporation of sensitivity to human engagement with particular places and areas. (1984 pp. 33–4)

Ley considered that humanistic geography: 'represented a reaction against the quantitative juggernaut of spatial analysis as it gathered speed in the 1960s' (1981 p. 250). The early quantitative work, with its determinism, economism, and abstraction of the early quantitative publications, seemed to eradicate humanity, culture, human variability and free will. Given this intellectual climate it was to be expected that:

> a counter current would emerge which would highlight the distinctively human components of mind, consciousness, values, or more briefly perception, which would seek affinities with the humanities, including artistic and literary endeavours, and which would adduce a philosophical underpinning in such philosophies of meaning as phenomenology, existentialism, and pragmatism. (1981 p. 251)

The ideas about symbolism and landscape now current are heavily influenced by the work of post-modernist scholars (whose writings employ terminology which may be incomprehensible and alienating to outsiders), with the work of the French theorists, Roland Barthes and Michel Foucault, being particularly influential. Earlier and less intricate identifications of the symbolic associations of landscape were suggested by Meinig (1979), who noted that: 'Every mature nation has its symbolic landscapes. They are part of the iconography of nationhood, part of the shared set of ideas and memories and feelings which bind a people together' (p. 164). He mentioned how pictures of buildings like the White House are employed to prompt a symbolic connection with national institutions and history, but showed that:

> There are also landscape depictions which may be powerfully evocative because they are understood as being a particular kind of place rather than a precise building or locality. Among the most famous in America is the scene of a village embowered in great elms and maples, its location marked by a slender steeple rising gracefully above a white wooden church which faces on a village green around which are arrayed large white clapboard houses which, like the church, show a simple elegance in form and trim. (p. 165)

The symbolic significance of such a scene is considerable, and Meinig thought that such scenes bore connotations of continuity amounting to a visible bone between past and present along with messages of stability, quiet prosperity, cohesion and intimacy:

'Taken as a whole, the image of the New England village is widely assumed to symbolize for many people the best we have known of an intimate, family-centred, Godfearing, morally conscious, industrious, thrifty, democratic *community*' (Meinig, 1979).

Meinig noted other symbolic landscapes. There was the Main Street of Middle America, lined with three or four storey red brick business blocks with their ornate nineteenth-century fenestrations and cornices and with the offices of lawyers, doctors and dentists set above the shopfronts, and there was California Suburbia, with its low, wide-spreading, single-storey houses set on broad plots fronted by perfect green lawns. Having identified the symbolic landscapes, however, he added:

> We may feel we know them well, but perhaps we have been deluded by the very power of the symbols. When we attempt to penetrate the familiar generalizations and clichés about the New England Village, Main Street, and Suburbia, we may be startled at how narrow and uneven are the foundations upon which these stereotypes rest. (p. 173)

A feature of the newer approaches to landscape study concerns the treatment of landscape as text. Some of the earliest formulations of this idea were provided by W. G. Hoskins; two of his less well-known articulations follow. First, discussing holidays enjoyed as a boy in the Devon countryside, he wrote: 'Even then I felt that everything I was looking at was saying something to me if only I could recognise the language. It was a landscape written in a kind of code' (1973 p. 5). In 1978 he wrote: 'When I was young – and I have spent a lifetime of study since – I felt in my bones that the landscape itself was speaking to me, in a language that I did not understand, and I had to find out how to read it' (p. 10). Now, a more complex view is taken, with text being regarded as having multiple layers of meaning:

> The landscape as ideology, symbol and as a moral statement are elements of this new cultural/historical geography of landscape (Figure 7.1). In effect, they represent in part attempts to answer questions about the kind of past or pasts that we seek to recover or reconstruct. Landscape thus becomes not just a book with statements that can be read only one way, but a text to be read in a variety of different ways, subject to a wide range of interpretations. (Butlin, 1993 pp. 136–7)

Figure 7.1   Landscapes contain symbols of many kinds; some can be translated, but some of the symbolism, like that associated with this Cumbrian stone circle, is mysterious. (Richard Muir)

Duncan and Duncan have drawn landscape into the debate concerning post-modernism by applying to the landscape the post-structural concepts of text and intertextuality, which originated in literary theory; they wrote that 'literary theory provides us with ways to examine the text-like qualities of landscape, and to see them as transformations of ideologies' (1988 p. 117) and they added that: 'As geographers, the textualised behaviour that concerns us is the production of landscapes; how they are constructed on the basis of a set of texts, how they are read, and how they act as a mediating influence, shaping behaviour in the image of the text' (pp. 120–1). (The concept of intertextuality was proposed by Julia Kristeva in 1966 and denotes the fact that a text does not exist in isolation but is composed from a mosaic of quotations, so that any text is the absoption and transformation of another: the text has an interdependence with a mass of other texts which have preceded it.)

According to Duncan and Duncan (1988):

It can be argued that one of the most important roles that landscape plays in the social process is ideological, supporting a set of ideas and values, unquestioned assumptions about the way a society *is*, or should be organized . . . If landscapes are texts which are read, interpreted according to an ingrained cultural framework of interpretation, if they are often read 'inattentively' at a practical or nondiscursive level, then they may be inculcating their readers with a set of notions about how the society is organized: and their readers may be largely unaware of this. If, by being so tangible, so natural, so familiar, the landscape is unquestioned, then such concrete evidence about how society *is* organized can easily become seen as evidence of how it *should*, or *must* be organized. (p. 123)

Duncan wrote: 'The landscape, I would argue is one of the central elements in a cultural system, for as an ordered assemblage of objects, a text, it acts as a signifying system through which a social system is communicated, reproduced, experienced, and explored' (1990 p. 17). Much of recent work in this area has had the effect of rendering a subject which has long attracted and fascinated a broad spectrum of enthusiasts inaccessible and irrelevant. Strands of thinking in the post-modern treatment of landscape were brought together in 1991 in the book *Writing Worlds: Discourse, Text and Metaphor in the Representation of Landscape* by Barnes and Duncan:

The essays adopt different textual strategies in order to begin to deconstruct traditional forms of representation within geography. Although the subject of the volume is the representation of landscape, the term landscape as used in the volume is itself unstable, at times referring to concrete places, at other times to intellectual sites. In this respect the authors acknowledge the manner in which the term landscape has, through metaphor, escaped the confines of geography and art criticism. (Duncan, 1993 p. 375)

When terminology itself becomes unstable the reader is likely to be offered confusion in large measures.

Duncan has described two quite different uses of the term 'landscape':

In the first usage landscape is defined as a way of seeing. This definition has been introduced into geography primarily through the work of Cosgrove (1984) and Daniels (1993; Cosgrove and Daniels, 1988). In their accounts, landscape is a painterly way of seeing the world that creates a picturesque view. Such a painterly way of seeing, as they point out, is an élite way of seeing, not only because it was the wealthy classes of Europe who commissioned paintings but also because there developed a dialectical relationship between the rural landscape and painting. Wealthy estate owners paid landscape architects to design their properties to look like landscape paintings and then had them painted. (1995 p. 414)

He added that:

The other principal definition of landscape is closer to popular usage in that landscape is a portion of a natural and cultural environment – it is material. Although it is seen, it is 'out there', so to speak, rather than in one's head. This definition of landscape originated in nineteenth-century Germany and was introduced into American geography through the work of the Berkeley school. (1995 p. 414)

Duncan believed that:

The painterly tradition is good at showing us that the landscape is a way of representing the world and that representations have very real political consequences. A limitation of this approach is that it is focussed on Europe and is not (nor should it be) translated to other cultures. It should be noted, however, that this is a critical theory and as such its focus on Europe and on élite classes does not make it either eurocentric or élitist as some commentators have been too quick to assume. (1995 p. 415)

Cosgrove had written that: 'the landscape idea represents a way of seeing – a way in which some Europeans have represented to themselves and to others the world about them and their relationships with it, and through which they have commented on social relations' (1984 p. 1). He added:

Landscape is a way of seeing that has its own history, but a history that can be understood only as part of a wider history of economy and society; that has its own assumptions and consequences whose origins and implications extend well beyond the use and perception of land; that has its own techniques of expression, but techniques it shares with other areas of cultural practice.

He thought that:

Landscape . . . is an ideological concept. It represents a way in which certain classes of people have signified themselves and their world through their imagined relationship with nature, and through which they have underlined and communicated their own social role and that of others with respect to external nature. (1984 p. 15)

Later, he described a unifying principle deriving from the active engagement of the human subject with the material object, and wrote:

landscape denoted the external world mediated through subjective human experience in a way that neither region nor area immediately suggest. Landscape is not merely the world we see, it is a construction, a composition of that world. Landscape is a way of seeing the world. For all its apparent objectivity and foundation in the historical record the landscape described in *The Making of the English Landscape* possesses an affective meaning, it represents W. G. Hoskins's (1955) way of seeing England. It is this which informs his interpretation of how people in the past saw and remade the land. In Yi-Fu Tuan's words (1971 p. 183), the landscape 'is somewhat analagous to the interior of the house, in that its totality reveals purposes and ends that have directed human energy'. (pp. 13–14)

(This is all very well, but Hoskins made an earnest attempt to *explain* the evolution of cultural landscapes, and in doing so he drew upon an impressive array of painstakingly accumulated professional techniques and skills. The results of his work could be tested objectively and were exposed to scrutiny by other experts, similarly endowed with genuine expertise, and as a result the understanding of landscape history has been advanced.)

Elsewhere Cosgrove wrote: 'Landscape is in fact a "way of seeing", a way of composing and harmonising the external world into a "scene", a visual unity' (1989 p. 121) and:

I have argued that landscape is a social and cultural product, a way of seeing projected on to land and having its own techniques and compositional forms; a restrictive way of seeing that diminishes alternative modes of experiencing our relations with nature. This way of seeing has a specific history in the West, a history I have outlined in the context of the long process of transition in western social formations from feudal use values in land to capitalist production of land as a commodity for the increase of exchange value. (1984 pp. 269–70)

Having commented on the development of a new relationship between humans and their environment at the time of the Renaissance, with the establishment of perspective, sophisticated map projections, landscape painting and the construction of rational human landscapes, he added: 'Landscape is thus intimately linked with a new way of seeing the world as a rationally-ordered, designed and harmonious creation whose structure and mechanism are accessible to the human mind as well as the eye, and act as guides to humans in their alteration and improvement of the environment'. A clarification of key concepts was provided by Pringle, who wrote:

At the simplest level *landscape* denotes simply a subjective 'way of seeing'. It is however also a social product, the result of the collective transformation of nature. From this dichotomy landscape is invested with a dialectical tension. It is effectively a historically specific *process*, one in which social groups experience, reflect upon and structure the world around them. (1991 p. 43)

Cosgrove pointed out that landscape in human geography has long been associated with culture. In the cultural geography of Carl Sauer there was a concentration on the visible forms of landscape, like farmsteads and field patterns, and culture was regarded as a fairly unproblematical concept: a set of shared practices common to a particular human group, practices that were learned and passed down the generations.

Culture seemed to work *through* people to achieve ends of which they seemed but dimly aware. Critics have called this 'cultural determinism' and have stressed the need for a more nuanced cultural theory in geography, particularly if we are to treat contemporary landscapes and sophisticated modern culture. A revived cultural geography seeks to overcome some of these weaknesses with a stronger cultural theory. It would still read the landscape as a cultural text, but recognises that texts are multi-layered, offering the possibility of simultaneous and equally valid different readings. (1989 pp. 122–3)

He then identified three ways in which modern cultural geography advances theoretically beyond former approaches. First, in the realms of culture and consciousness he noted that rather than being something that works through human beings, culture has to be constantly reproduced by them in their actions, mostly in mundane day-to-day activities. Culture always retains the potential of being brought to the level of conscious reflection and communication, 'So culture is at once determined by and determinative of human consciousness and human practices' (p. 123). Second, in terms of culture and nature he asserted that any human intervention in nature involves its transformation to culture: for instance, the act of preparing a tomato as human food converts it into a cultural object that has been layered with meaning. Third, in terms of culture and power he argued that the study of culture is closely connected with the study of power:

A dominant group will seek to establish its own experience of the world, its own taken-for-granted assumptions, as the objective and valid culture of all people. Power is expressed and sustained in the reproduction of culture. This is most successful when least apparent, when the cultural assumptions of the dominant group appear simply as common sense. (p. 124)

Cosgrove explained that an understanding of the expressions written into its landscape by a culture demanded an understanding of the 'language' employed, that is to say the symbols and their meaning within that culture:

All landscapes are symbolic, although the link between the symbol and what it stands for (its referent) may appear very tenuous. A dominating slab of white marble inscribed with names, surmounted by a cross and decorated with wreaths and flags standing at the heart of a city is a powerful symbol of national mourning for fallen soldiers, although there is no link between the two phenomena outside the particular code of military remembrance. (p. 125)

He added that much of the symbolism in landscape is far less apparent than the symbolism in these examples, but it still serves the purpose of reproducing cultural norms and establishing the values of dominant groups across all of society. In this way the municipal parks in English provincial towns still symbolise the ideals of propriety and decency which were held by members of the Victorian bourgeoisie and the park founders' intention of advancing the physical and spiritual welfare of the labouring classes. Cosgrove wrote:

> All landscapes carry symbolic meaning because all are products of the human appropriation and transformation of the environment. Symbolism is most easily read in the most highly-designed land- scapes – the city, the park and the garden – and through the representation of landscape in painting, poetry and other arts. But it is there to be read in rural landscapes and even in the most apparently unhumanised of natural environments. (1989 p. 126)

The many-layered meanings of symbolic landscapes can, it is claimed, be decoded, a prerequisite being the close and detailed reading of the text, that is to say the landscape in all its expressions. The evidence to be studied will encompass any source that provides information about those who created, changed, sustained or visited the landscape. According to Cosgrove:

> The kind of evidence that geographers now use for interpreting the symbolism of cultural landscapes is much broader than it has been in the past. Material evidence in the field and cartographic, oral, archival and other documentary sources all remain valuable. But often we find the evidence of cultural products themselves – paintings, poems, novels, folk tales, music, film and song can provide as firm a handle on the meanings that places and land- scapes possess, express and evoke as do more conventional 'factual' sources. All such sources present their own advantages and limitations, each requires techniques to be learned if it is to be handled proficiently. Above all, a historical and contextual sensi- tivity on the part of the geographer is essential. We must resist the temptation to wrench the landscape out of its context of space and time, while yet cultivating our imaginative ability to get 'under its skin' to see it, as it were, from the inside. (1989 p. 127)

Daniels and Cosgrove (1988) have referred to the 'iconography of landscape' and they noted that the term was revived during the present century, initially in the interpretation of Renaissance imagery by the school of art history associated with Aby Warburg for which iconographic study sought to explore meanings in a work of art by viewing it in its historical context and attempting to interpret the ideas embodied in its imagery. They thought that:

> by definition, all art history translates the visual into the verbal, the iconographic approach consciously sought to conceptualise pictures as encoded texts to be deciphered by those cognisant of the culture as a whole in which they were produced. The approach was systematically formulated by Warburg's pupil, Erwin Panofsky. (p. 2)

Panofsky was a scholar of Renaissance art. The first important critic and art historian to address the tradition of landscape painting was John Ruskin. According to Daniels and Cosgrove:

> In landscape Ruskin sought a stable ground in which a consistent order of divine design could be recognised in underlying form. Landscape he treated as a text, taking his method from biblical exegesis, seeking the reassurance of order in the face of the apparent chaos of industrialising Britain. Thus the central purpose of his first great text, *Modern painters* (1843), was to locate landscape in a broader context than the study of form and the history of style. The 'higher landscape' depended upon a humble submission of men to the great laws of nature, a close observation of the natural world and the application of the greatest skill and imagination in its representation. In the hands of a master like Turner, landscape became in Ruskin's eyes a suitable subject for examining the deepest moral and artistic truths, rather as history painting had been viewed within the academic tradition (p. 5).

They justified the iconographic model in contemporary cultural enquiry:

> The post-modern apprehension of the world emphasises the inherent instability of meaning, our ability to invert signs and symbols, to recycle them in a different context and thus transform their reference. Earlier and less commercial cultures may sustain

more stable symbolic codes but every culture weaves its world out of image and symbol. For this reason the iconographic method remains central to cultural enquiry. (pp. 7–8)

They concluded that:

From such a post-modern perspective landscape seems less like a palimpsest whose 'real' or 'authentic' meanings can somehow be recovered with the correct techniques, theories or ideologies, than a flickering text displayed on the word-processor screen whose meaning can be created, extended, altered, elaborated and finally obliterated by the merest touch of a button. (p. 8)

Much work relating to symbolism in the landscape is said to be informed by semiology (or semeiology), associated with the linguist, Ferdinand de Saussure, and developed by the writer, Roland Barthes, and by semiotics, associated with C. S. Pierce. These sciences of signs and systems of signification relate to the ways in which signs are produced and ascribed meanings. Individually and collectively, humans seek to communicate, not only through language but also via gestures, music, dress and in other ways, and landscapes are said to be amongst these systems of signification. Hopkins claimed that:

Offering potential theoretical and methodological insights into the communicative function of landscape and the reproduction and perpetuation of social relations and human actions, linguistic metaphors (reading the landscape as 'text'), semiotic terminology ('signs,' 'symbols,' 'signification,' 'myth'), and semiotic analyses are being adapted by geographers with increasing frequency to assist in landscape interpretation. (1990 p. 3)

Among those geographers who venture out into the 'field' to engage in landscape interpretation one strongly suspects that such concepts are unknown.

Symbols in the Landscape

The search for the symbolic meaning of landscapes can be exemplified by several specific studies. Among the most obviously symbolic landscapes are burial grounds. Lowenthal wrote:

cemeteries mark no significant event in most people's lives; we seldom die in them, but are simply put there for memorial convenience. Cemeteries matter less as repositories for the dead than as fields of remembrance for the living; the unmarked grave goes unseen . . . cemeteries are assemblages of personal memorials. Often the collective quality of memorialization stands out: in military cemeteries, the massed and uniform crosses, the anonymity of the graves, evoke not individual soldiers but the Great War in which they died. (1979 p. 123)

Sometimes a portion of a territory is presented as a symbol of the essential essence of the territory in its entirety. Nash (1993) described how, in the early years of this century, the province of Connaught and the western seaboard of Ireland came to symbolise the whole of Ireland in the minds of many Irish nationalists. Nationalist writers found the region attractive as its stark, rugged landscapes were little touched by the processes of Anglicisation, and they felt that a national sense of identity might be rebuilt in places which differed greatly from the gentle and mellow countrysides of England. The people of western Ireland, closely bonded to their land, steadfast and strong, contrasted with the English stereotype of the feckless Irish and they were presented by the nationalist writers as embodiments of the Irish identity.

The symbolism associated with a landscape need not be a true reflection of its personality and characteristics. Edward Said (1978) studied the western perceptions of the Muslim Near East and North Africa which gave rise to a body of texts and shared assumptions which he termed 'Orientalism'. The Orient was regarded as a corrupt, decadent and violent place which was peopled by savages under the leadership of tyrants; as visitors interpreted what they encountered in terms of such images, and as they projected their own fantasies on to the Orient, so an imagined geography was created. Thus Orientalism expressed the values of the cultures which produced it.

Hence it is possible to suggest that the 'sense of place' produced by Orientalism, and through which western visitors to that area interpreted what they saw, did not offer a sense of the Orient on its own terms but rather established the Orient as an exotic place against which a European 'home' was defined, usually as all the more favourable. The meaning of (Christian) Europe thus

Figure 7.2   It has been suggested that megalithic tombs, like this one at Poulnabrone in Co. Clare, had strong symbolic associations. To outsiders they symbolised the fact that land had been held for generations by the community whose ancestors were contained in the tombs. They may also have symbolised the restoration of energy and resources to the earth when a leader was buried, perhaps compensating the land for the goodness robbed by cultivators. (Richard Muir)

depended on its image of an (Islamic) Orient against which it could identify itself. (Rose, 1995 p. 95)

To Said, the Orient was the *Other* of the West and was thus defined in terms of the ways that it was thought to differ from the West: a symbolic landscape representing the antithesis of the Western identity. It embodied the spirituality of desert people, which Westerners envied, and the Oriental customs, which they despised. Because the Orient was regarded as less civilised than the West, Orientalism justified European attempts to colonise and exploit the region.

Cosgrove briefly described a polar landscape whose cultural significance derives from its savage unconquerability by humans:

During the period of the great polar expeditions at the turn of the century the landscape of ice, crevice [crevasse?], snowstorm, polar bear and green seas became the very paradigm of a Boys' Own world, the setting for a British upper-class male cultural fantasy. Scott's death in 1912 made a corner of Antarctica 'forever England'. Imperial themes of military heroism taking strength from a barren and hostile environmental setting were revived in 1982, as British troops 'yomped' across the South Atlantic islands during the Falklands–Malvinas war. (1989 p. 126)

A more detailed investigation of the ideological messages conveyed by the polar landscape over the last 150 years was undertaken by Pringle (1991). In 1864 Sir Edwin Landseer exhibited a painting entitled *Man Proposes, God Disposes*. It depicted an Arctic landscape in which two polar bears were scavenging on human remains around the wreckage of one of the ships which had sailed with the ill-fated John Franklin in 1845 in search of a north-west passage around the pole. The image troubled contemporary society, the Victorians being reminded of Darwin's exposure of the links between humankind and animals. Rumours that starving expedition members had resorted to cannibalism raised disquieting thoughts about the animality lurking within humans and Pringle felt that: 'While recognising the natural behaviour of Landseer's bears, Victorian polite society feared that such regressive behaviour could be metaphorically paralleled by the working classes. Brutality to beasts was explicitly linked in parliament to social revolution and political violence' (p. 45). Interpreting the image it emerged that:

Here an Arctic image carried an implicit ideological commentary on the British social order. In doing so it demonstrated one of the frequently forgotten traits of imperialist imagery – its ability to influence not only subjugated regions but the British homeland itself. Like Shelley's Frankenstein Landseer's image was indeed clearly rooted in a distant landscape charged with metaphorical vision. (Pringle, 1991)

In 1912, Scott's party perished after failing in their imperialistic attempt to be first to reach the South Pole. Their courage was celebrated by the popular media, while in 1911 and 1915 the cigarette manufacturer, John Player, produced sets of cigarette cards devoted to the history of polar exploration. A comparison of the two series of cigarette cards shows how the presentation of symbolic polar landscapes had changed dramatically following the outbreak of the Great War:

> the ideological nature of the Player's polar exploration series was related not simply to its content, but to the *context* within which it appeared . . . The issue of a second series, centred on the almost mythical Captain Scott, during a bloody European war drew the public's attention to the qualities that were expected of Britons both on the front and at home . . . it was intended to stir English hearts. (p. 46)

Pringle added: 'Like Scott's dying statement to the public these polar images called upon a heroic past to fortify the nation's future. As with images of Franklin's earlier expedition, the harsh polar landscape provided the stage upon which an old patriotic model could be projected, reconstructed and re-presented'. He described how the recent exhuming of bodies of Franklin's crewmen from the permafrost recreated links with an imperial past and lent it an intimation of immortality and noted that: 'It is a living, nationalist imperial past which persists in our contemporary polar imagery' (p. 48).

Other associations with an imperial past are evoked by the British hill stations in India. Kenny wrote that: 'As a derivative of Western colonial experience, the hill station's institutional complex and morphological images included Christian churches, private schools taught in the English language, the administrative headquarters of district and state government, and the kinds of recreational facilities usually associated with British country life or an English spa' (1995 p. 694). Approximately 80 such settlements were built by the British in India to serve as mountain retreats from the hot season on the plains, the first being established in 1819. From the 1860s, certain hill stations also functioned as summer capitals, with the administrators conducting government from remote locations for six or eight months of the year.

> Although the Anglo-Indian sense of self was not divorced from the Indian as colonial subject, the rulers could 'overlook' indigenous elites and subalterns while in the hills. The hill stations thus served a particular role within the imaginative geographies of imperial discourse, a role that enabled the imperialist 'mind [to]

intensify its own sense of itself by dramatizing distance and difference' (Said 1978: 55) from the centers of Indian population in the plains. (Kenny, 1995 p. 696)

Explaining the reference to 'discourse', Kenny pointed out that: 'Discourses can be defined as social frameworks that enable and limit ways of thinking and acting' (p. 695). A discourse is an assemblage of social practices through which the world is made meaningful and intelligible to oneself and others, defined by Barnes and Duncan as 'frameworks that embrace particular combinations of narratives, concepts, ideologies and signifying practices, each relevant to a particular realm of social action' (1991 p. 8). The story of the hill station landscape focused on the stories that the British told about themselves: 'In the summer capitals of the Raj, the relative isolation of the hill station afforded the British a stage with "homelike" qualities on which to define their difference and to confirm, in appropriately British terms, their identity as rulers of India' (Kenny, 1995 p. 696). The discourses on race and climate maintained that races were differentiated by their physical and mental attributes with each one occupying its own salubrious zone: Europeans had evolved in a physical environment that produced 'superior beings' destined to preside over others, but, according to the discourses, an Englishman established in the torrid lowlands of India would deteriorate and his descendents would degenerate.

In the case of one hill station:

The 'founder' of Ootacamund, John Sullivan, set out to make the station an Indian Utopia with an English landscape by introducing not only European trees, flowers, fruit and vegetables, but also the serpentine lake of a country estate. Later visitors to the hill station commented on the remarkable similarities between the landscape and *home*. (Kenny, 1995 p. 702)

Having reviewed the symbolic landscape of the hill station, Kenny concluded that:

It is a widely accepted tenet in cultural geography that landscape constitutes a culturally produced expression of social order. That was what one govenor's wife had in mind in describing Ootacamund as 'an island of British atmosphere hung above the Indian plains' (Pentland 1928). Her imagery splendidly naturalizes the social world of Ootacamund and its separation from the Indian centers in the plains. Both the nineteenth-century imperial discourse and the discourse of climate served to reflect and reinforce the emerging belief in racial difference . . . The Victorian social, political and aesthetic values inscribed on these resort settlements and summer capitals raise issues today that defy easy resolution when weighed against the goals of a socialist India. The hill stations are no longer enclaves of a foreign power and yet the question of their future retains symbolic significance in light of their past. (p. 711)

Jackle (1985) has explored the iconic status of the New York skyline, while the sky itself was studied by Gruffudd in his study of the air and English cultural nationalism. He noted the importance of the sky and cloud effects in the landscape paintings of Constable and Turner and how the RAF exploited the rural idyll for recruiting purposes: 'one advert showing an officer standing at the gate (the rusticated bars of which spell RAF) to a lush landscape and beckoning the young recruit to enter in search of a brighter life' (1992 p. 20). After the 1939–45 War, however, the symbolic significance of the skies to the English changed as the post-war sky lost its innocence:

The 1930s and 40s were perhaps the last flowering of a modernist notion of the rural landscape, confident enough to accommodate aesthetic change in a reconciliation between tradition and modernity. Wartime was also an era when landscape and sky were one in artistic representation; the culmination of a movement which at least in part originated with Constable. Now the sky is anything but reassuring, and a whole new realm of symbolism is attached to it. (p. 24)

According to Cosgrove, Roscoe and Rycroft (1996) there has recently been an upsurge of academic interest in Englishness and British national identity, with a variety of writers underlining the crucial role played by landscape representations of the countryside, of pictorial, cartographic or textural natures, in constructing Englishness (Figures 7.3, 7.4):

Accompanying such celebration of the countryside as the seat of national virtue has been the fear of it being under continuous threat from processes of change, either external in the case of military conflict or, more commonly in England, internal, from the alienating and destructive forces of modern progress, generally identified as originating in the city. (p. 536)

They add that geographers have:

long recognised that national identity is constructed in the context of local identities which cut across both it and each other in complex ways. But it is arguable that different kinds of regional landscape play distinct roles in the complicated discourse of national identity. Constructing a regional geography of England's (let alone Britain's) symbolic landscape is a research task yet to be systematically engaged.

The pro-rural sentiments echo those described by the political geographer, P. J. Taylor:

The Anglo-British 'discovery' of rural England was . . . part of the national regeneration of the late nineteenth century. The crisis that England was facing, relative economic decline, was interpreted as an urban crisis. Urban surveys of poverty brought forth 'racial' worries about the quality of the national stock. Despite the fact that rural poverty was at least as bad as its urban counterpart, the countryside became viewed as the ideal location in which to breed a healthy moral race . . . In history the anti-urban bias was reflected in a rewriting of the national history to highlight the 'golden Elizabethan age'. Here a pre-industrial but early imperialist England was discovered as the basis of subsequent national greatness. This 'authentic state of Merrie England' was a Tudor world that was 'truly rural' (Hawkins 1986, 71) but which had been transformed out of all recognition by the industrial revolution and consequent urbanisation. (1991 p. 153)

Cosgrove, Roscoe and Rycroft (1996) proposed an 'iconic landscape structure' of Britain. The country was divided into two concentric zones centred on London. First there were:

the landscapes that some writers have called 'Deep England': the cultivated lowland regions of scarps and wide river valleys with small, hedged fields, tight villages and occasional country houses

Figure 7.3

set in parkland are overwhelmingly located in an arc of lowlands around London, with outliers in such areas as the Vale of York and the Cheshire Plain . . . These are the landscapes of what Taylor (1991, 150) has called the 'Crown Heartland'.

Nationally, the most powerful symbolic associations of these places were with English domesticity, agrarian productivity and secure, conservative, stable social order (Figure 7.5). Second, beyond this so-called English Heartland zone was a zone of wild and upland Britain:

Figure 7.4

It is said that landscape is a way of seeing. The pictures of Ely cathedral and the churchyard show how the way of seeing would be difficult were our eyes to be made sensitive to the infra-red radiation associated with living creatures and plants. (Richard Muir)

> Here, rural landscapes are typified (not with consistent accuracy) as upland, often moorland and pasture rather than ploughland and, characteristically, they are stereotyped as rougher and less domestic than the 'champion' lands of the southern and midland shires . . . These landscapes are characteristically associated with nature rather than human community, despite their significant rural economy and society. (pp. 536–7)

P. J. Taylor's Crown Heartland formed part of a not dissimilar division and characterisation of Britain. Crown Heartland, Upper England or the Home Counties were regarded in a paradoxical way:

> The pioneer of industrialization and the most urbanised country in the world is idealized in rural terms: thatched cottages around a village green is the archetypical English scene. Such anti-urban images are themselves quite common in the national landscapes of peoples. The difference for the English is that they are not featured in their own landscape. (Taylor, 1991 p. 151)

Figure 7.5 The powerful symbolic associations of landscape are often exploited in advertising and publicity. Here an idyllic passage of ancient countryside is invoked to represent Britain on the cover of a booklet concerning information technology and the British Library. (Andrew Jones/British Library)

He added that:

The Anglo-British became a non-rural people with an ideal rural image. Of course, the rural image was not any non-urban picture of England. Wild country, the moors of Northern England for instance, was never deemed typically English. England became defined as a green and pleasant land situated in southern rural England where an idealised ordered society was reflected in a neat ordered landscape. Unlike real urban industrial England, this was a tranquil world, unchanging and non-threatening. It was not a land of the 'people' but a conservative paradise where everybody knew their place. (p. 153)

Inglis interpreted the English involvement with their countryside in the following manner:

Landscape in our society is counterposed to townscape much as leisure is counterposed to work. Landscape, we may say, is allocated to the realm of private feeling, townscape to the realms of public business. No doubt this is why the standard reproductions in department stores, or the busy trade in tiny little water-colours sold in tens of thousands along the tourist trails, are always idealised glimpses of the local countryside, and rarely townscapes. (1990 p. 198)

Short, too, noted the primacy of the rural in the national iconography:

The countryside became, and still is, the most important land-scape in the national environmental ideology. It holds pride of place. In England the two meanings of country, as countryside and nation, are collapsed into one another; the essence of England is popularly thought to be the green countryside – the enclosed fields, the secluded/excluded parklands of the country houses, and the small villages. The nineteenth-century landed elite may have lost economic power in the twentieth century but their symbolic power is still evident in this view, which is widely believed at home and increasingly marketed abroad. The countryside has become 'real' England, the 'unchanging' England. It has become the land of retreat from an increasingly urban and overwhelmingly indus-trial society, the place to escape modernity. (1991 p. 75)

Symbolic landscapes figure prominently in the English vision of England. John Taylor (1990 p. 193) has quoted from a popular countryside book published by Batsford in 1915 where this vision was articulated:

> It is the past which has made the England of today, and the present is but its continuation. Prehistoric trackway, ancient village, sleepy town, the farmhouse in the hollow, the sheepfold on the hill – all have rendered their share in the making of England, and in the building up of that race whose sons are emulating on the battlefield the deeds of their forefathers set forth in quaint inscriptions on the walls of many a village church or in the mouldering records of ancient boroughs. (Pulbrook, 1915 afterword n.p.)

The symbolic landscapes of the imagination come in many forms; Woolf has explored the image of Europe harboured in the American mind. He wrote that:

> Europe is seen consistently in an ambiguous form, an uneasy amalgam of decadence and dream, a version of a kingdom made by magic. Economic or political reality tends to remain shadowy and insubstantial. Europe acts as an introspective device: a landscape in which mental possibilities can be realized in concrete geographical shapes; a kind of objective correlative for aspects of the American imagination. (1996 p. 35)

He examined the character of Europe in the American mind through two metaphors, that of 'Disney's Magic Kingdom' being one, while 'the figure of the European princess, shaped by Henry James and wildly parodied by Henry Miller, offers a model for that which has been radically changed in the perception of Europe in the America mind'. He explained that:

> Contained within the notion of a kingdom of magic is an idea of Europe as a world less real than America, a poetic device formed more by the imagination than by political, economic or geographical realities. The princess represents a view of Europe as socially complex and stratified in ways not found in America. (Woolf, 1996)

As to the first metaphor:

The Magic Kingdom is a version of Europe invented in the USA and re-exported to Euro-Disney. It is a quasi-romantic fiction: Europe as a landscape dreamed of and invented in America, modelled out of Grimm's fairy tales, populated by the princes and princesses of the imagination, inhabiting romantic castles of dreams. (Woolf, 1996)

In his *Fields of Vision* (1993) Daniels studied important British and American landscape painters of the eighteenth and nineteenth centuries and what their work reveals about national identity:

he demonstrates how these paintings have been interpreted from their first showings to the present and how contemporary themes, such as patriotism, heritage and consumerism, re-encode each artist's work. There are few in any field who are as skilled as Daniels at decoding the cultural politics of landscape painting. (Duncan, 1994 p. 363)

Daniels wrote that:

National identities are co-ordinated, often largely defined, by 'legends and landscapes', by stories of golden ages, enduring traditions, heroic deeds and dramatic destinies located in ancient or promised home-lands with hallowed sites and scenery. The symbolic activation of time and space, often drawing on religious sentiment, gives shape to the 'imagined community' of the nation. Landscapes, whether focusing on single monuments or framing stretches of scenery, provide visible shape; they picture the nation. As exemplars of moral order and aesthetic harmony, particular landscapes achieve the status of national icons. Since the eighteenth century painters and poets have helped narrate and depict national identity, or have had their work commandeered to do so; scholars and professionals have been enlisted too: historians, map-makers, geographers, engineers, architects and archaeologists. There is seldom a secure or enduring consensus as to which, or rather whose, legends and landscapes epitomize the nation. While most nationalists recognize several represenative histories and geographies, all, by definition, reject others, including those of people dwelling within their own national borders. The very process of exclusion is integral to the nationalist enterprise. (Daniels, 1993 p. 5)

In examining how landscapes have articulated national identities Daniels discovered a relationship between imperialism and national introspection. As English imperialism reached into distant lands a countervailing affinity for the cosy domestic scenery of the thatched cottage, gardens and pastoral countryside arose which provoked Daniels to observe that inside Great Britain, Little England lurked:

> At the same time in the 1880s as Greenwich was taken as the Prime Meridian, as the British public gazed at global maps centred mathematically on Britain, with dominions coloured red to show an empire on which the sun never set, and margins illustrated with exotic human figures, fauna and flora, so the very picture of rustic England, Constable's *Hay-wain*, entered the National Gallery and, through reproduction, the national imagination. By the First World War, the *Hay-wain* was upheld as an epitome of the country it was worth dying to defend. (1993 p. 6)

Elsewhere Daniels wrote: 'The experience and memory of the trenches enhanced the allure of pastoral England as a refuge, and arguably a securely realistic one, from the absurd theatre of Flanders, a boundless, discomposed land, a no-man's land, an anti-landscape' (1991 pp. 12–13).

Landscape played an important role in the imperial process and Daniels suggested that:

> Imperial nationalists, almost by definition, have been intent to annex the home-lands of others in their identity myths. They have projected on these lands and their inhabitants pictorial codes expressing both an affinity with the colonizing country and an estrangement from it. It is often the very 'otherness' of these lands which has made them appear so compelling. (1993 p. 5)

Ryan studied several Victorian colonial expeditions and concluded that:

> these case studies testify to the significance of landscape, as a way of seeing, in the cultural representation of imperialism. Landscape, as produced by these expeditions, was framed in various ways by the cultural and material value projected onto the environments being explored by the explorers. Furthermore, in the process of visually mapping landscapes these expeditionary practices were simultaneously globalising a particular landscape vision. Indeed, the very idea of empire in part depended on an

idea of landscape, as both controlled space and the means of representing such control, on a global scale. (1995 p. 74)

Symbolism can be studied at many different scales. It is found in the 'icon Earth' images of the Earth as seen from space (Cosgrove, 1994), in symbolic images of the national homeland, in regional and local images, in landscape components (as exemplified by Daniels's study (1988) of the political iconography of woodland and even in the evocative symbolism of different types of tree (Davies, 1988). Though the study of symbolic landscapes could take many forms, the 'landscape as text' model dominates current thinking, though Butlin warns that:

Such approaches offer some exciting prospects for historical and cultural geographers, but they do also have attendant problems, including the difficulty of finding appropriate criteria by means of which the freer 'textual' interpretations of text and landscape themselves may be judged and evaluated, sceptics seeing the subjective interpretations of texts (and presumable also land-scapes as texts) as 'a hall of mirrors reflecting nothing but each other and throwing no light upon the "truth", which does not exist' (Stone, 1991, 217). This is, of course, one of the significant dilemmas of post-modernism as a whole. (1993 p. 138)

The origins of symbolic landscapes may be known, as with the battlefield of Culloden where the ancient culture of the Highlands perished in 1746, or the sources of the landscape imagery may be mysterious:

Like the words employed to describe or explain a landscape, the original authors, contexts, and meanings of landscape images are often lost, but residual as contexts for the making of some ersatz or otherwise loaded image. The image may become, as it were, part of the media for the making of its likeness in the impressions of others. Here too, however, the image acquires an objective content as it is shared, promulgated, and changed by other authors to suit their own purposes. The image may become part of the media for the making of shared landscapes. (Samuels, 1979 p. 72)

Also, the symbolic associations of landscape may change: 'In the mid-nineteenth century, when the path of industry is growing grimly clear, wild nature ceases to denote privation and becomes a sanctuary. Consolation is found in communion with her such as is not felt amid the works of man' (Walbank, 1941 p. 105). Similar ideas were proposed by Short, though his time scale was rather different:

> With the rise of agriculture, wilderness became an ambiguous concept. On the one hand, its defeat was a marker of human progress. On the other hand, it became a symbol of an earthly paradise, the place of before the fall where people lived in close harmony and deep sympathy with nature. Uncultivated land was something to be revered, part of God's work untouched by human intervention. (1991 p. 10)

An interest in the symbolic aspects of landscapes crosses cultural divides, and Nature pervades the art, myth, legend, and religions of the Indian subcontinent. Nature itself, or certain of its elements of it, is considered both sacred a source of aesthetic pleasure:

> As sacred, it contains the essence of divinity, manifesting it in varied forms ranging from the material to the symbolic. The landscape, flora, and fauna of the Indian subcontinent have been incorporated into the myths and legends of the vast pantheon of Hindu gods and goddesses. In the location of pilgrimage sites and temple complexes the landscape, as a source of sacred power, has played an important role. (Sinha, 1995 p. 3)

Different facets of the landscape have different symbolic associations. Water, being formless, symbolises fertility as it is regarded as a reservoir of all possibilities of existence. Immersion in a body of water is symbolic of regeneration. Mountains are regarded as the cosmic axis linking earth to heaven and celestial beings populate their summits. Trees represent life and continuity in the material world, while different deities are associated with different tree species (Vishnu with basil and Shiva with the bel tree) and: 'The close association of pilgrimage centers with sites of natural grandeur draws the Hindu culture closer into the bosom of nature, thereby transcending the duality between nature and culture' (p. 9).

Moving further to the east:

> Chinese painting is particularly associated with landscapes . . . an emphasis that has its roots in the various religious and philosophical sources of Chinese culture. The idea that wisdom and peace

can be found in the viewing of mountains and rivers, indeed the vitality of various forms of nature and their connection with the spirit world is central to both Taoism and Buddhism. (Lai, 1992 p. 32)

Chinese painting does not conform to Western conventions and will present many unfamiliar aspects. Scenes depicted need not be landscapes viewed from a specific vantage point, but rather representations of passages of scenery encountered in the progress of a ramble, while different high level or low level viewpoints may be adopted. The expertise of the artist will be judged from the quality and variety of the *ts' un* brushstroke textures accomplished by the painter, while symbolism is a crucial aspect of the pictorial content and message. It includes the 'five pure things', the pine, plum blossom, bamboo, moon and water; the peach, a symbol of immortality; and the mandarin duck, a symbol of harmony. Contrast, too, is regarded as a crucial element in landscape painting, so that horizontal emphases will be contrasted with vertical ones, passages of detail with ones of simplicity, areas of darkness with those of light.

Symbolism is elusive and shifting, yet still a forceful component in our perception of places.

References

Barnes, T. and Duncan, J. (eds), *Writing Worlds: Discourse, Text and Metaphor in the Representation of Landscape* (London: Routledge, 1991).

Butlin, R. A. *Historical Geography* (London: Edward Arnold, 1993).

Cosgrove, D. *Social Formation and Symbolic Landscape* (London: Croom Helm, 1984).

Cosgrove, D. 'Geography is everywhere: culture and symbolism in human landscapes' in Gregory, D. and Walford, R. (eds), *Horizons in Human Geography* (London: Macmillan, 1989) pp. 118–135.

Cosgrove, D. 'Contested global visions: one-world, whole-earth, and the Apollo space photographs' *Annals of the Association of American Geographers* **84** (1994) pp. 270–94.

Cosgrove, D. and Daniels, S. (eds), *The Iconography of Landscape* (Cambridge: Cambridge University Press, 1988).

Cosgrove, D., Roscoe, B. and Rycroft, S. 'Landscape and identity at Ladybower Reservoir and Rutland Water' *Transactions of the Institute of British Geographers* NS **21** (1996) pp. 534–51.

242   *Approaches to Landscape*

Daniels, S. 'The political iconography of woodland in later Georgian England' in Cosgrove, D. and Daniels, S. (eds), *The Iconography of Landscape* (Cambridge: Cambridge University Press, 1988) pp. 43–82.

Daniels, S. 'The making of Constable country, 1880–1940' *Landscape Research* **12** (1991) pp. 9–17.

Daniels, S. *Fields of Vision: Landscape Imagery and National Identity in England and the United States* (Princeton, NJ: Princeton University Press, 1993).

Davies, D. 'The evocative symbolism of trees' in Cosgrove, D. and Daniels, S. (eds), *The Iconography of Landscape* (Cambridge: Cambridge University Press, 1988) pp. 32–42.

Duncan, J. S. 'Individual action and political power: a structuration perspective' in Johnston, R. J. (ed.), *The Future of Geography* (London: Edward Arnold, 1985) pp. 174–89.

Duncan, J. S. *The City as Text: The Politics of Landscape Interpretation in the Kandyan Kingdom* (Cambridge: Cambridge University Press, 1990).

Duncan, J. S. 'Landscapes of the self/landscapes of the other(s): cultural geography 1991–2' *Progress in Human Geography* **17** (1993) pp. 367–77.

Duncan, J. S. 'The politics of landscape and nature, 1992–3' *Progress in Human Geography* **18** (1994) pp. 361–70.

Duncan, J. 'Landscape geography, 1993–94' *Progress in Human Geography* **19** (1995) pp. 414–22.

Duncan, J. and Duncan, N. '(Re)reading the landscape' *Environment and Planning D: Society and Space* **6** (1988) pp. 117–26.

Gruffud, P. 'Reach for the sky: The air and English cultural nationalism' *Landscape Research* **16** (1992) pp. 19–24.

Hawkins, A. 'The discovery of rural England' in Colls, R. and Dodd, P. (eds), *Englishness: Politics and Culture, 1880–1920* (London: Croom Helm, 1986).

Hopkins, J. S. P. 'West Edmonton Mall: landscape of myth and elsewhereness' *The Canadian Geographer* **34** (1990) pp. 2–17.

Hoskins, W. G. *The Making of the English Landscape* (London: Hodder & Stoughton, 1955).

Hoskins, W. G. *English Landscapes* (London: BBC Publications, 1973).

Hoskins, W. G. *One Man's England* (London: BBC Publications, 1978).

Inglis, F. 'Landscape as popular culture' in Pugh, S. (ed.), *Reading Landscape: Country-City-Capital* (Manchester: Manchester University Press, 1990) pp. 197–213.

Jackle, J. A. 'The metropolis as an attraction' in *The Tourist: Travel in Twentieth-Century North America* (Lincoln: University of Nebraska Press, 1985) pp. 263–85.

Kenny, J. T. 'Climate, race, and Imperial Authority: the symbolic landscape of the British hill station in India' *Annals of the Association of American Geographers* **85** (1995) pp. 694–714.

Lai, T. C. *Chinese Painting* (Oxford: Oxford University Press, 1992).

Ley, D. 'Cultural/humanistic geography' *Progress in Human Geography* **5** (1981) pp. 249–57.

Lowenthal, D. 'Age and artefact' in Meinig, D. W. (ed.), *The Interpretation of Ordinary Landscapes* (New York: Oxford University Press, 1979) pp. 103–28

Meinig, D. W. 'Symbolic landscapes: some idealisations of American communities' in Meinig, D. W. (ed.), *The Interpretation of Ordinary Landscapes* (New York: Oxford University Press, 1979) pp. 164–92.

Nash, C. ' "Embodying the nation": the West of Ireland landscape and national identity' in Cronon, M. and O'Connor, R. (eds), *Tourism and Ireland: A Critical Analysis* (Cork: Cork University Press, 1993).

Penning-Rowsell, E. 'Themes, speculations and an agenda for landscape research' in Penning-Rowsell, C. C. and Lowenthal, D. (eds), *Landscape Meanings and Values* (London: Allen & Unwin, 1986) pp. 114–28.

Pentland, Lady *The Right Hon. John Sinclair, Lord Pentland G.C.S.I.: A Memoir* (London: Methuen, 1928).

Pringle, T. R. 'The polar landscape in English and American popular culture 1845–1990' *Landscape Research* **16** (1991) pp. 43–8.

Pulbrook, E. C. *The English Countryside* (London: Batsford, 1915).

Rose, G. 'Place and identity: a sense of place' in Massey, D. and Jess, P. *A Place in the World?* (Oxford: Oxford University Press, 1995) pp. 87–132.

Ryan, J. R. 'Imperial landscapes, photography, geography and British overseas exploration, 1858–1872' in Bell, M., Butlin, R. and Heffernan, M. *Geography and Imperialism 1820–1940* (Manchester: Manchester University Press, 1995) pp. 53–79.

Said, E. *Orientalism* (London: Routledge, 1978).

Samuels, M. S. 'The biography of landscape' in Meinig, D. W. (ed.), *The Interpretation of Ordinary Landscapes* (New York: Oxford University Press, 1979) pp. 51–88.

Short, J. R. *Imagined Country* (London: Routledge, 1991).

Sinha, A. 'Nature in Hindu art, architecture and landscape' *Landscape Research* **20** (1995) pp. 3–10.

Stone, L. 'History and post-modernism' *Past and Present* **131** (1991) pp. 217–18.

Taylor, J. 'The alphabetic universe: photography and the picturesque landscape' in Pugh, S. (ed.), *Reading Landscape: Country-City-Capital* (Manchester: Manchester University Press, 1990) pp. 177–96.

Taylor, P. J. 'The English and their Englishness: "a curiously elusive and little understood people" ' *Scottish Geographical Magazine* **107** (1991) pp. 146–61.

Tuan, Y.-F. 'Geography, phenomenology, and the study of human nature' *Canadian Geographer* **15** (1971) pp. 181–92.

Walbank, F. A. (ed.), *The English Scene* (London: Batsford, 1941)

Woolf, M. 'The Magic Kingdom: Europe in the American Mind' in Davies, P. J. (ed.), *Representing and Imagining America* (Keele: Keele University Press, 1996)

8

The Aesthetic Approach to Landscape

The aesthetic approach to landscape sets out to answer the questions 'What is it that we like about landscape, and why do we like it?' (Appleton, 1996 p. xv). Despite this simple formulation, several writers have remarked upon the need for a unified theory of landscape aesthetics to be developed. Bourassa wrote: 'A major obstacle in the way of development of a theory of landscape aesthetics is the fact that philosophers have given very little attention to landscape as an aesthetic object . . . As a consequence of their emphasis on art, landscape has been neglected in philosophers' writings on aesthetics' (1991 p. 10). 'Landscape', he added, 'is rarely, if ever, just a work of art. Even the most contrived garden is to some extent composed of natural phenomena beyond the control of the designer . . . Furthermore, the everyday landscape is typically a combination of art, artifact and nature, and the relationships among those categories are complex'.

The engagement of philosophers in the landscape debate may be one problem and the division between arts and science perspectives has been identified as another. Appleton commented:

> If we are to make real progress in furthering not only the co-existence but also the integration of the arts and the sciences in landscape research we should familiarise ourselves with the widest possible range of landscape experience . . . Our task is nothing less than to create a new field in which we must be prepared not, of course, to abandon our own special interests, but to make a real effort to see them in a new and broader perspective. (1986 pp. 42–3)

244

Several writers have stressed the importance of the human engagement with the landscape and the need to regard humans as participants in landscape rather than as detached observers of it: 'it is now commonly considered in geography that landscape is other than simply an object. Landscape carries meaning as well as minerals and agricultural wherewithal. That said, landscape does not therefore become seen as simply a matter of the subject' (Matless, 1992 p. 44).

Beauty and the Beast

The most influential of the earlier thinkers on landscape aesthetics was John Dewey (1859–1952). An established philosopher and educationalist, he turned to aesthetics and published *Experience and Nature* in 1929 and *Art as Experience* in 1934. Bourassa remarked that: 'Although Dewey's work did not address landscape as such in any detail, his assertion that art is implicit in all everyday experience clearly encompasses the aesthetics of the ordinary landscape' (1991 p. 15), while according to Appleton: 'Dewey's main message, for our purposes, is that beauty resides neither intrinsically in "beautiful" objects nor "in the eye of the beholder", but that it is to be discovered in the relationship between the individual and his environment, in short in what he calls "experience" ' (1996 p. 43). Three corollaries derive from this: that experience being a two-way contact between the viewer and that which he experiences, any distinction between perception and expression is meaningless, since they are both part of the one relationship; that since there is an infinite range of environmental conditions, so aesthetic experience can adopt innumerable forms, and that 'all experience presupposes certain mechanisms of a biological kind by which the relationship between man and his environment is maintained' (Appleton, 1996). Dewey (1934) argued that aesthetic experience is a more intense form of day-to-day experience and that aesthetic experience has both biological and cultural constituents. He considered that humans receive aesthetic pleasure from the satisfaction of basic drives which are shared with animals, and this assertion has greatly influenced the ideas on landscape aesthetics proposed by Appleton and described below.

An influential figure in the exploration of landscape aesthetics in Britain was Vaughan Cornish (1862–1948), a physical and political geographer who, in 1920, at the age of fifty-seven, devoted his study to the investigation of scenic beauty. Although he never held a university post, Cornish was one of the most prolific of geographical writers, producing over 90 papers and books in a career spanning just over six decades. 'C. O. Sauer, in his classic *Foreword to Historical Geography* (1941) selected Cornish as one of six geographical authors who would "in themselves provide a truly liberal geographic education, provided each is taken as a whole, and not skimmed eclectically in terms of pre-arranged views as to what is and is not geographic" (Goudie, 1972 p. 1).

Appleton contrasted the talents of Cornish and Dewey:

> It is interesting to compare [the] aesthetic excursions of Vaughan Cornish, full of rich, descriptive detail and emotional footnotes, with the more-or-less contemporary writing of John Dewey, full of theory but rarely touching on the details of landscape. Dewey writes about the difference between 'experience' and 'an experience'; Cornish about the difference between Grindelwald and Camberley. Neither can really get to grips with the language of the other, and when Dewey died in 1952, Vaughan Cornish having predeceased him by some four years, the gap between their disciplines may have narrowed but had certainly not been eliminated. (1996 p. 47)

In his Preface to *The Beauties of Scenery*, Cornish explained that: 'In the Presidential Address to the Royal Geographical Society in 1920, Sir Francis Younghusband declared that it was the duty of geographers to undertake the analytical study of beauty in scenery. I responded immediately to this appeal, and in works since published have recorded the advance in my investigation' (1943 p. 15). According to Matless: 'Younghusband was by 1920 already well known as a writer on mysticism, and used the occasion of his address to define the spiritual and mystical as within the purview of geography' (1991 p. 273). He urged his audience to adopt a broader and more profound view of their discipline and to accept the spiritual aspects of 'Mother-Earth'. Thereafter, 'Cornish, who hitherto had been as much concerned with measurement and quantity as almost any geographer of the age, turned to the study of quality in the environment, and he hoped that in addition to studying quantity – the preserve of every science – geographers would begin to study quality' (Goudie, 1972 p. 7).

Yet though Cornish attempted to provide an analytical study of beauty in scenery the results tended to be undisciplined, anecdotal and liberally interspersed with passages of florid and flowery prose. The style seems archaic even by the standards of its time, and the values sometimes unacceptable. His *Scenery and the Sense of Sight* begins:

> In the trinity of eternal values, Goodness, Truth and Beauty, the last is not accorded equality in the Churches, and indeed is suspect on account of the opinion that the aesthetic life often leads towards sybaritic luxury rather than spiritual exaltation. But the Pilgrim of Scenery is beset by no such snare, for a Spartan habit is needed for the enjoyment of Nature in her sterner moods. An illustration of this is provided by the noble sport of mountaineering where the supreme satisfaction of seeing the world spread out at one's feet is attained only by those who keep the body in fine discipline.
>
> In the cult of Scenery there are moreover other disciplines besides the athletic. Next in order comes the cultivation of the state of receptive contemplation, always difficult for the energetic Occidental to acquire, for it is not reached until busy thought is banished from the mind.
>
> The third and last discipline, the acquisition of the scientific faculty, is often the hardest of all for people of emotional temperament. (1935 p. xi)

Cornish made numerous attempts to explain the aesthetic attractions of particular scenes and types of scenery, of which the following is an example:

> It often happens . . . that the serrated outline of tree-tops on the crest of foothills in the foreground emphasises a pattern of bare, rocky mountain peaks standing up against the sky. An entirely different picture, but equally harmonious, is that of the broad-leaved forest of round-topped trees in the characteristically undulating landscape of the English Plain where the smaller mamillary pattern of the trees decorates the larger undulations of the land. (1935 p. 86)

He added that 'whereas the large curves with small curves superposed produce a patterned-pattern as restful to the eye as it is peaceful in its associations of rural quietude, there is no pictorial combination between the rounded tree-tops of the distant wood and the huge curves of the great cumulus above'. In the end, Cornish's work failed to provide a convincing theory of landscape aesthetics, and Appleton observed that: 'Any vocabulary which would have enabled Dewey to express his aesthetic philosophy in terms of particular components of landscape could equally have provided Vaughan Cornish with a framework for fitting together his landscape word pictures into something like a philosophical system' (1996 p. 232).

The searches for such a theory have led students of landscape aesthetics to consider the genetic inheritance of humanity: they are concerned with the relationship between humans and their setting and this poses questions about the biological or evolutionary bases of human behaviour and preferences. Noting that the occupation of territory is fundamental to human existence, Smith considered that:

> To survive even at the most 'primitive' level of social organization and technology requires access to natural resources of the land, sometimes supplemented by the sea but never wholly independent of *terra firma*. Whether perpetually on the move, as hunters and gatherers, or in fixed and permanent settlements, access to particular territory or to the product thereof is a necessary condition of life. (1990 p. 1)

Concerns such as these lead into the field of ethology and the work of Konrad Lorenz and his followers: 'Since ethology is the study of the biology of behavior, and has developed out of biology, it has introduced the methods and approach of biology into the study of behavior. Like all other behavior sciences, ethology looks for the causes of behavior' (Eibl-Eibesfeldt, 1979 p. 7).

Greenbie believed that:

> One of the most promising approaches currently being taken by a few – still too few – students of landscape aesthetics follows the discipline known as socio-biology . . . This is an essentially Darwinian science that seeks to explain at least some aspects of the behaviour of animals, including humans, in terms of evolutionary adaptation. Perhaps the most concrete attempt to apply this view to landscape aesthetics has been made by Appleton. (1992 p. 65)

Bourassa wrote that he was concerned about exploring the relationship between biological and cultural explanations of aesthetic experience and Appleton's (1996) habitat and prospect-refuge theories and Kaplan's (1987) information-processing theory were salient examples:

> Appleton . . . clearly reduces culture to its biological underpinnings by characterizing nonbiological manifestations of landscape aesthetics as simply variations in ways of responding to biological needs. On the other hand, some of Appleton's critics emphasize the cultural basis of aesthetic experience. There is a tendency on the part of the critics to assert that all biological needs are mediated by culture and, therefore, that there is no need to address directly a biological mode of aesthetic experience. (1990 p. 788)

Appleton's habitat theory and prospect-refuge theory were introduced briefly in Chapter 6, along with his belief that those landscapes that we find most attractive are those 'that once would have afforded us, as individuals involved in the struggle for survival, the opportunity to see without being seen, to eat without being eaten, to produce offspring that survive' (Greenbie, 1992 p. 65). Greenbie added that Appleton did not suggest that the human aesthetic response to the landscape involved a conscious perception of danger, but that those factors that once provided prospect and refuge now underscore our sensations of pleasure in the landscape. Habitat theory asserts human beings have an innate tendency to experience pleasure and satisfaction from their environment when it appears to be conducive to the fulfilment of their biological needs, while humans experience anxiety and dissatisfaction when it does not. This led Appleton to the proposition that: 'aesthetic satisfaction, experienced in the contemplation of landscape, stems from the spontaneous perception of landscape features which, in their shapes, colours, spatial arrangements and other visible attributes, act as sign-stimuli indicative of environmental conditions favourable to survival, whether they really *are* favourable or not' (1996 p. 62). He added that therefore habitat theory asserted that the relationship between the human observer and the physical environment was essentially similar to that of a creature to its habitat:

> It asserts further that the satisfaction which we derive from the contemplation of this environment, and which we call 'aesthetic'

arises from a spontaneous reaction to that environment as a habitat, that is to say as a place which affords the opportunity for achieving our simple biological needs . . . Habitat theory, in short, is about the ability of a place to satisfy *all* our biological needs. (1996 p. 63)

Prospect-refuge theory proposes that the ability to see without being seen is an intermediate step to the satisfaction of many biological needs so that aesthetic satisfaction is experienced in environments which can provide this capability (Figures 8.1, 8.2). Writing retrospectively, Appleton recalled that:

It seemed to me that the study of landscape had reached a kind of milestone, not unlike that which geomorphology had reached at the turn of the century, in that it needed some coordinating system that would enable its participants to see the significance of any one component of the landscape in terms of all the other components. (1992 p. 30)

He considered that the theory aimed at four objectives. First, it attempted to locate the aesthetics of landscape within the context of a biologically-based system. Second, the theory laid great emphasis on the need to obtain supporting evidence from the widest possible range of human experience. Third, the theory sought to reduce concepts which emerged from enquiry to a relatively simple form, perhaps even a formula, and fourth, having achieved this reduction the theory would be available as a potential explanatory model available to anyone interested in applying it to any particular area of investigation.

Prospect-refuge theory began, in Appleton's words:

by identifying environmental perception as the key to all adaptive behaviour. Without environmental information, so ran the argument, there can be no adaptation. It is reasonable, therefore, to suppose that individuals within each species of animal, including *Homo sapiens*, are motivated to perceive their surroundings in such a way that environmental information is acquired and stored in a form in which it can be efficiently and quickly retrieved when needed to ensure survival. Men and women, in short, perceive their environment in much the same way as other animals perceive their habitat, and to this idea I gave the name 'habitat theory'. (1992 p. 31)

Figure 8.1   Landscapes such as the one depicted in this view of Crummock Water in Cumbria seem to pose problems for prospect-refuge theory. Though generally regarded as highly attractive, this scene is virtually devoid of trees or other cover and therefore has little to offer by way of refuges. (Richard Muir)

252

Figure 8.2 This landscape in upper Nidderdale meets the demands of prospect-refuge theory. It provides a range of vantage points and also plenty of places where one can see without being seen. It is not parkland, but it has some distinct similarities. (Richard Muir)

Appleton considered that Nature ensures that we respond rapidly to information that concerns self-preservation by providing us with a powerful craving to satisfy our curiosity about the environment. Our chances of survival are improved if we keep open the channels by which we receive environmental information: seeing is crucial, as is the opportunity to seek concealment; hence the designation prospect-refuge theory. 'The prospect is light, openness, distance, panorama, opportunity but perhaps also danger. The refuge is dark, enclosed, close-by and represents safety and security' (Morgan, 1978 p. 528). In addition to *prospect* and *refuge*, Appleton introduced a third category, *hazard*, to encompass the various sources of danger which it might be necessary to avoid: 'The concept of hazard implies the proximity of something which threatens, menaces or disturbs our equilibrium; at another level, if we think of it in terms of our behavioural response, the symbolism of hazard prompts evasive action, like hiding, escaping or eliminating the source of danger' (Appleton, 1990 p. 26).

Prospect-refuge theory has been received with varying degrees of enthusiasm. One reviewer wrote:

Even if it is agreed that we as a species may inherit identical instinctive biological responses to landscape it is obvious that we as individuals evaluate, respond and react quite differently. It must be agreed that the cultural filters through which different societies and individuals have perceived the landscape are critically important and subject to such variation that one's instinct is to consider these cultural imprints to be vastly more significant and worthy of study than the biological ones, which presumably we all share in roughly equal measure. This is where the reviewer parts company with the author. It is no answer to take the view that each individual to a greater or lesser degree 'fine tunes' his perceptions of landscape according to his own disposition because that fatally damages the habitat theory by denying its universality. (Morgan, 1978 p. 528)

Cosgrove saw little place for biologically-based theories in landscape aesthetics. Short-lived excitement over landscape evaluation in the 1970s had, he claimed, 'led to various mechanistic theories of landscape aesthetics which, like Jay Appleton's ethologically-founded and influential "habitat theory" of landscape, had little in common with the humanism proclaimed in North American studies' (1985 p. 46)

Appleton was interested in the symbolic associations of landscape and wrote:

> If a symbol is an object which 'stands for, represents or denotes something else,' ought we not to be paying less attention to the objects which comprise a landscape and more attention to that 'something else'? The question is where to find it, and my suggestion is that we should look first to that system of natural symbolism which is central to the process by which creatures are enabled to establish favorable relationships with their natural habitats. (1990 p. 24)

Elsewhere he noted that:

> Symbolic meaning is often communicated by objects which are consistently associated with particular ideas over long periods of time. For instance, the association of evergreen trees and shrubs with eternal life goes back a long way before Spenser's 'cypress funeral'. Already, in classical literature, the cypress was sacred to Pluto, god of the underworld. There are many other symbolic associations of long standing which have important implications for landscape. (1986 p. 39)

He exemplified this by noting the association between elevated places and the venues for religious ceremonies, while:

> Water symbolism, which is of great antiquity, endows rivers, lakes and fountains with special religious values, while more dramatic expressions of the powers of nature, such as may be found in volcanic activity, have almost invariably invited some symbolic interpretation of an animistic kind, and much of this is recorded in the arts. (Appleton, 1986)

Greenbie employed a socio-biological approach to explore symbolism in landscape aesthetics and wrote:

> Higher animals communicate with one another through various signals, displays, and behaviors: They interpret their environments symbolically. The symbols that animals use are generally direct products of their bodies, including gestures, sounds, scents, and body markings of great variety and complexity. Humans have

learned to hide or disguise many of these symbols by clothing themselves and in other ways. In turn, clothing and other artifacts become social symbols with communicative value, although they may become exceedingly variable with culture. (1992 pp. 66–7)

Most important, however, in terms of this discussion was the human ability to extend all manner of symbolic representations: 'away from our bodies and into the landscape itself. Such symbols take on generalized abstract meaning, often representative of collective social orders rather than individuals. These landscape symbols may be modifications of the natural environment or constructions placed on it by humans' (Greenbie, 1992). He noted that the association of the female body with the earth is very old and perhaps universal in human imagery, and he concluded that: 'we are likely to find in the response to natural forms in the landscape, especially the controlled natural forms of the pastoral landscape, a symbolic association with the female body, with nurturance, with tranquility, an with absence of aggression' (p. 69). He considered that:

By contrast, we are most likely to find in the built environment symbols not only of man's attempt at dominance over nature, but also of man's dominance over man. The most assertive, phallic forms tend to be the work of humans: They are constructions on the landscape, rather than products of it. (Greenbie, 1992)

Greenbie contrasted the angular 'male' form of industrial architecture with the blending of male and female influences in pre-industrial buildings, and he added that in Appleton's terms:

we might say that the industrial landscape is largely a landscape of prospects without refuges, often exciting, dramatic, and dynamic, but physically overpowering. My own viewpoint stresses the competitive and aggressive symbols that stream from these male-dominated landscapes and that lack the moderation of more tranquil forms. (Greenbie, 1992)

Other researchers have explored the socio-biological background to landscape aesthetics, notably the environmental psychologists, S. and R. Kaplan, who are associated with long-standing research directed towards identifying and classifying the factors influencing human preferences for one kind of landscape over another. Green-

bie noted that: 'The Kaplans view the human being as an information seeking animal, reasoning that survival has depended to an
unusual degree on obtaining information from and about the
environment. Natural selection, they argue, would favor individuals
who develop a love of information for its own sake' (Greenbie, 1992
pp. 65–6). He added that:

> The most preferred landscapes, according to the Kaplans, are
> those that, among other things, have elements of 'mystery' and
> 'involvement' (Kaplan and Kaplan, 1978, 1982). In these land-
> scapes more information is promised than is actually revealed . . .
> The Kaplans' theory puts more stress on prospect than on refuge,
> but is wholly compatible with Appleton's. (Greenbie, 1992)

Bourassa observed that:

> The basic contention made by the Kaplans is that environments
> facilitating and stimulating the acquisition of knowledge will be
> preferred because such environments were essential to human
> survival and it is adaptive to prefer an environment conducive to
> survival. Information-processing theory is clearly a form of
> habitat theory, and it helps to round out Appleton's over-em-
> phasis on prospect and refuge. (1991 p. 83)

Zube described how the Kaplans proposed that the long-term
survival of the human species was dependent upon the development
of cognitive information processing skills. This led in turn to
preferences for landscapes that made sense to the observer. 'In other
words, landscapes were preferred that could be comprehended,
where information could be obtained relatively easily and in a
non-threatening manner that provided opportunity for involvement,
and that conveyed the prospect of additional information' (1984
p. 106). He considered that according to this framework the types of
landscapes that would be preferred were those that were coherent,
legible, complex, and mysterious. Stephen Kaplan argued that
animals need to like the type of environments in which they can
flourish, and ideally they should not need to have to learn such
inclinations for it would be wasteful for a creature to spend years
enduring unsatisfactory settings in order to recognise their unsuit-
ability: 'Hence, one can view preferences as an outcome of a
complex process that includes things and spaces and reacting to

them in terms of their potential usefulness and supportiveness. In this perspective, aesthetics must, at least to some degree, reflect the functional appropriateness of spaces and things' (1992 pp. 45–6). One potential weakness of this and similar theories concerns the assumption that *Homo habilis* and subsequent early humans existed as *hunters*, and a recent alternative interpretation, now quite popular, regards our forebears as *scavengers* from the kills of more credible and formidable predators.

Researchers such as Orians (1980, 1986) and Woodcock (1982) have noted that the evidence for primitive humans is associated with the African savannah and have speculated that it was evolutionarily adaptive for humans to prefer this form of habitat and that the species may have retained an innate preference for such settings. Orians considered that savannah habitats with isolated trees and small clusters of trees set in grassland should be the greatly preferred settings which should give rise to highly favourable emotions (1980). Efforts were made within civilised societies, subconsciously, to replicate the savannah environment and to include water, which had always been essential to human life: 'Parks and gardens in all cultures are neither closed forests nor open grasslands. In addition, great pains are taken in the creation of parks and gardens to create water or the illusion of water, or to enhance the quality and quantity of existing water resources' (Orians, 1986 p. 11).

Balling and Falk (1982) speculated that a preference for landscape of the savannah type could be embedded in the human genetic inheritance because such settings had furnished our distant ancestors with food supplies and relative security, and they hypothesised that this response might be most obvious in children. They investigated preferences for five different types of natural landscape (tropical rainforest, desert, savannah, temperate deciduous forest and coniferous forest) by showing four slides of each biome to subjects ranging in age from twelve to pensioners and requested that each slide be rated twice, once with regard to the attractiveness of the scene depicted as a place in which to live and once with regard to its appeal as a place to visit. The savannah and the deciduous and coniferous forests were preferred as places to live and visit, with their preference rating being strongest as places to visit. Woodcock's work compared the preferences for savannah and different forest types, and revealed a preference for savannah, with open forest being preferred to dense forest. These ideas have been summarised as follows:

for most of his existence man has been a hunter of large game in savannah or savannah-like environments, consisting of grass and isolated trees or groups of trees. Also, there has consistently been a need to remain fairly close to bodies of water because humans need a constant supply of fresh water. These facts seem to provide a plausible explanation for modern man's apparent desire to create parklike landscapes and to live in view of water when given the opportunity. (Bourassa, 1991 pp. 67–8)

However, it should be remembered that a potential weakness of habitat theory and related concepts concerns the priority given to biological over cultural factors as determinants of behaviour (Bourassa, 1990 pp. 787–8).

Figure 8.3   The parkland at Holkham, in Norfolk, landscaped by 'Capability' Brown in 1762. (Cambridge University collection: British Crown Copyright © MOD, reproduced with permission of the Controller of Her Britannic Majesty's Stationery Office)

Landscape and Painting

Prince wrote that: 'Geographers maintain fairly close relations with historians, they occasionally exchange views with scholars in English literature, but they are separated by a wide, largely uncharted interdisciplinary gulf from artists . . . Yet both geographers and artists share an interest in the study of landscapes' (1984 p. 3). He added a warning that:

> Pictures do not fully and faithfully record a section of environment. A pictorial view is limited by its frame. Sounds, smells and feel of a place may be alluded to but not reproduced, and three-dimensional objects moving through space are rendered into flat, still shapes on the surface of a canvas. A painter conjures a likeness of a scene out of a few carefully selected images. Imitating the visible world is not an objective that many painters rank as top priority . . . Artists depict not simply what they see, but what they know and understand, features to which they and their public attach significance. (p. 4)

Similarly, Appleton noted that one should never 'lose sight of the fact that aesthetic values spring initially from the direct observation of actual views. The definition of landscape as "a way of seeing" points in the right direction' (1994 p. 117).

The number of people who have their lives touched and habits formed by representations of landscape is far greater than the number of people who visit art galleries. Inglis observed that:

> A great communal act of public devotion . . . takes place on any sunny Sunday of a British summer, when the car-owning families of every city pile into the family automobile for a day in the country, at the seaside, at the wildlife park, going round the stately home, in the national park. Each member of those families, according to his or her lights, is joining in a messy, friendly, quite unritualised act of profane worship in the great church of Nature which the Romantic painters set up sometime after 1776. (1990 p. 197)

Various other examples could be invoked to demonstrate how the work of landscape painters can give rise to considerable changes in the nature and development of landscape, one concerning the way that Thomas Moran's depictions of the outlandish geysers and landforms of the Yellowstone area not only led to the growth of its tourist industry but also influenced its establishment of America's first national park. Indeed: 'When Congress in 1874 appropriated $10 000 for one of Moran's studies of the [Grand] Canyon to hang in the Senate lobby, wilderness received official endorsement as a mainspring of American nationalism' (Nash, 1975 p. 16).

At certain times the representation of landscape has exerted a powerful influence upon society, its tastes and values. Barrell recorded that the contemplation of landscape was not a passive activity but rather it involved reconstructing the landscape in the imagination, according to principles of composition that had to be learned,

> and were indeed learned so thoroughly that in the later eighteenth century it became impossible for anyone with an aesthetic interest in landscape to look at the countryside without applying them, whether he knew he was doing so or not. These principles were derived from the Roman landscape-painters of the seventeenth century, Nicolas and Gaspard Poussin, Salvator Rosa and Claude Lorrain. (1972 p. 6)

He also noted that:

> The Roman painters, of course, made no pretence that their work represented particular places: the painting of landscape was, for them, the creation of ideal landscapes, of models, as the critic Thomas Twining explained, 'of improved and selected nature'; and the rules of improvement and selection they established were found very hard to break by topographical painters who were hired on the guarantee of producing proper likenesses of the places they painted. (p. 12)

Landscape painters infuse their representations of landscape with cultural values, and in this way:

> The close connection of the Aborigine and the land permeates Aboriginal artworks, including works using primitive materials such as ochres on bark and contemporary paintings using materials such as synthetic paints and canvas. Aboriginal painting

almost always relates stories about the land, particularly stories about the creation of the Australian landscape by the primordial ancestors during the 'Dreamtime' . . . The ancestors, in creating the landscape and the people, animals and plants that inhabit it, traveled along Dreaming-tracks which are often the subjects of Aboriginal paintings. (Bourassa, 1991 p. 4)

Also, landscape painting can be seen to embody socio-political sentiments and tendencies, it can express a people's feelings about their landscapes and territory and can articulate and influence their sense of geographical identity and destiny, as the following examples drawn from nineteenth-century American landscape painting show.

Nash described how the history of American painting provides an excellent example of the way that the native landscape played a part in the development of American cultural nationalism. Before the 1820s, American artists were governed by European styles and subjects:

When they did attempt a landscape, it was usually in the English pastoral tradition with purling brooks, placid cows, and, perhaps, a rustic swain or two. No one ever thought of painting a landscape divorced from human significance. There was always some sign of man or his works in evidence. Nature was background and setting, never important for its own sake. (1975 pp. 14–15)

However, changes took place after 1823, when:

a young English immigrant, who had seen the beauty of the upper Ohio valley, resolved to abandon portrait painting and devote his considerable talents to depicting, as he put it . . . 'the wild and great features of nature: mountainous forests that know not man.' With this statement, Thomas Cole made a sort of declaration of independence for American painting . . . The result was a series of wilderness landscapes, such as his study of the Catskill Mountains, that won Cole artistic fame and launched the Hudson River School of American painting. . . The contrast of such paintings with the ordered, pastoral landscapes inspired by Europe was sharp. (Nash, 1975 p. 16)

Of the contrast between the European and American experiences, Novak noted that:

The opposition between Europe's antiquity and their own wilderness had given Americans an alternative past. They could not look back on a long tradition as could other cultures which, as some travelers in Arcadia pointed out, were often bloody and despotic. But they could relate to an antiquity still unspoiled by man – purer and by implication closer to God. Nascent American history was at that moment being bloodied by Indian conflicts, but this did not bother many of them. (1980 p. 145)

During the second and third quarter of the nineteenth century, the concept of nature was a vital influence on the youthful and expanding American nation, and it seemed to provide a confirmation of the national destiny. Novak considered that in the middle of the century this preoccupation with nature manifested itself in several distinct types of landscape paintings:

The large-scale, popular landscapes by such artists as Church, Bierstadt, and Moran seemed to satisfy the myth of a bigger, newer America. But a more modest kind of expression practised by some of the same artists, and by others who dealt more exclusively with this idiom, may have indicated some of the nineteenth century's profoundest feelings about nature . . . Both modes continued the late-eighteenth century notion of America as the 'Virgin Land,' a world unsullied by civilisation. In expressing this idea, the larger, more operatic paintings tended to impose older European conventions. The smaller paintings seem to have formulated their own conventions by a more original transformation of European models – tempered perhaps by paradigms of order established by the industrialism rapidly eradicating the primordial wilderness. (1980 pp. 18–19)

Leadership of the Hudson River School passed from Cole to his sole pupil, Frederic Edwin Church. Nash relates how the formative experience in Church's artistic development was a brief camping trip made into the Mount Katahdin region of northern Maine in 1856. Motivated by his experience, Church:

returned to his studio and painted a Maine lake and surrounding mountains at sunset. A crude road and a few sheep in the foreground are the only reminders of civilization. Four years later Church painted the little-known but magnificent *Twilight in the Wilderness*. Again the setting was northern Maine, but this time all traces of the pastoral had vanished. In the brilliant sunset and brooding Katahdin-like mountains there is a suggestion of the apocalyptic expectations of the virgin continent. (Nash, 1975 p. 16)

Church perfectly embodied and articulated the spirit of the American nation. Working during the middle years of the nineteenth century, when the notion of a 'Manifest Destiny' to settle and civilise the country westwards to the Pacific shore had captured the popular imagination, he produced images of pristine, spectacular wildernesses which seemed to be infused with spirituality and a divine will, and to be beckoning to the white settlers. Without contriving or compromising, Church provided the American audience with exactly the images of landscape that it then craved:

Church is the great exemplar of how the official concerns of the age found their way into landscape painting. His interests were broader, his involvement in natural science more intense, than those of any artist of his era. He is a paradigm of the artist who becomes the public voice of a culture, summarizing its beliefs, embodying its ideas, and confirming its assumptions. In his work, science, religion, and art all pursued the same goal, their harmonious co-existence embodying the ideal world-view of the nineteenth century before it was betrayed by the very instruments it used to advance its cause – observation, pragmatism, and science itself. (Novak, 1980 p. 67)

She added that: 'Church clearly understood the need to provide America with appropriate images and icons'.

Mills expressed the relationship which existed between the American patriotic enthusiasm for the colonisation of wilderness and the popular demand for paintings, with Western expansion being regarded as a focus of attention to which artists naturally responded:

Lithographs of western images were patriotic icons which, like the flag, could be hung publicly to proclaim loyalty to the republic. The general public came to see as spectacularly American those images which painters had already accustomed them to see thus. In a nation of newcomers – and in an expanding country, where even long-established residents were not familiar with newly acquired or distant locations – such a popularising of western images became very important. The vastness of the west had to be made intelligible. (1997 p. 65)

Church's contemporary, the German-American, Albert Bierstadt, painted panoramic landscapes on an even grander and more dramatic scale. Making his first trip to the Rockies with Colonel Frederick Lander's expedition in 1858, his work depicted the heroic colonisation of the American West, providing spectacular canvases for those profiting from or entranced by the westward advance of the frontier:

> Cole and Church painted wildernesses of the East; subsequent American landscape artists took their palettes and their national pride across the Mississippi. In the American West they found subjects ideal for both. Within a few years of his first visit to the Rocky Mountains in 1858, Albert Bierstadt was busy depicting their peaks, canyons, and lakes on gigantic canvases measuring up to 84 square feet . . . Bierstadt's exaggerated, dramatic style provoked criticism, but represented a sincere attempt to express his awe and delight in the American wilderness. (Nash, 1975 p. 16)

Though his paintings celebrated the landscapes of the western interior, in reality they provided a commemoration of essential yet doomed facets of the cultural and natural milieux: 'The Indians in Bierstadt's landscape represent nature, not culture. Like the forests, the Indian exists in a state of nature, before he is cut down. His tenancy as a natural citizen is premised on his inseparability from nature. When separated, he dies' (Novak, 1980 p. 189).

In the middle of the nineteenth century the belief in the unity of God and nature was firmly held, but in the decades that followed, interest in Darwinism, civil warfare and the rise of technology and industry undermined such simple values. By the closing years of the century American taste had deserted the vast, theatrical celebrations of the natural landscape by Bierstadt and Church, and a more poetic treatment was favoured. Nevertheless, during the decades which immediately preceded America's loss of innocence, painters such as Cole, Church and Bierstadt had been perfectly in tune with the sentiments and aspirations of their society and had expressed and preserved the prevailing feelings about the homeland and its frontiers on canvas: 'The truths of light and atmosphere that absorbed American artists quickly served a concept of nature as

God, turning landscape painting into proto-icons' (Novak, 1980 p. 273).

In England, too, landscape painting expressed the condition of the nation and the sentiments and aspirations of society. Rose described how, by the close of the nineteenth century, the economic centre of gravity of Britain was settling on London, the imperial capital, as the industrial north of the country was losing its position as the workshop of the world. It appeared, therefore, that the economic and political heart of the nation had migrated southwards:

> But London itself did not appear appropriate as a symbol of the nation, for many contemporary commentators could see only too clearly the deleterious effects of rapid urbanisation and indus-trialization on city life. Large cities seemed environmentally polluted, socially chaotic and morally degenerate; the slum was seen as a canker at the heart of the Empire. The search for a symbol of the nation thus turned to the countryside of the south of England. The soft hills, small villages around a green, winding lanes and church steeples of the English southern counties came to represent England and all the qualities the culturally dominant classes desired. (1995 p. 107)

According to Lowenthal (1991), this 'south country' landscape communicated three qualities: those of consensus, continuity and of the nation itself. Members of different ranks in the rural social hierarchy lived in conditions of stability and contentment in the harmonious world of the village, while in the surrounding country-side humans and nature co-existed in a long-established equilibrium. This image of a timeless, stable rural landscape was adopted as an icon representing England in its entirety, even though it embodied inaccuracies and omitted various crucial aspects of English life. 'Nevertheless, English men and women were asked to identify with this landscape and this sense of national identity, and seemed to a large extent to have done so. It was propagated in all sorts of media: in paintings, like Constable's, but also in novels and poems' (Rose, 1995 p. 107).

> England was more and more often being pictured in terms of a landscape still symbolically resonant today: a landscape of green rolling hills, shady nooks, copses, winding lanes and nestling thatched villages. This was the landscape Constable painted and

it was towards the end of the nineteenth century that his canvases became popular; it was at this time that *The Haywain* and Willy Lott's cottage came to symbolize all that was worthy and decent about England. (Rose, p. 106)

Daniels wrote that:

In the last two decades of the nineteenth century interest in Constable quickened on a variety of fronts. His children released hundreds of oil paintings, oil sketches, drawings and watercolours revealing a hitherto unknown range of subjects and styles, They had agreed 'the most important examples' of their father's work 'should eventually become national property. (1991 p. 9)

The Haywain, which had failed to attract an English buyer when exhibited in 1812, was repatriated from Paris in 1884, and by the turn of the century it was becoming a national icon. Constable's populist admirers knew what held his paintings together: 'their resemblance to the places they depicted and places like them, places which beckoned those in search of rural England . . . Constable's popular admirers were interested not so much in painting as in scenery' (p. 11). Towards the end of the nineteenth century a popular locational appreciation of the setting of Constable's work had become established, and by the 1890s, Thomas Cook and the Great Eastern Railway had organised coach tours of Constable Country. '*The Haywain* was sufficiently typical in 1916 to illustrate a piece in Country Life on the love that makes men die for 'England's Green and Pleasant Land' . . . Languid little England pastoral was a central ingredient of wartime patriotism' (p. 12). Daniels believed that Constable Country, in the form of *The Haywain*, developed a role as a crucial component of the metaphor of the 'south country' as the essential England which exerted such a compelling influence in the later nineteenth century.

Representations of landscape could be particularly expressive of the sentiments of a community, but it could also manipulate the subject matter in order to convey a socially acceptable message:

There are constraints too on what sort of image of the poor may be portrayed in the full light of day, and what in darkness. A basic rule of landscape composition in the eighteenth century – exemplified well enough by George Lambert's *Woody Landscape* of

1757 – is that the rich and their habitations must be illuminated, and the poor and theirs be left in the shadows of the 'dark side' of the landscape . . . This division has the advantage of marking the difference in status and fortune between rich and poor, while showing that the unity of the landscape and of the society it can be seen to represent is dependent on the existence of both, which combine in a harmonious whole. (Barrell, 1980 p. 22)

Habitat theory has been extended into the realm of landscape painting which: 'provides numerous examples that, like poetry and prose, may contribute to an understanding of the archetypal basis for a biological theory of aesthetics' (Bourassa, 1991 p. 78). Commenting on *Village Dancers* by David Teniers the Younger (1610–90), Appleton wrote that:

it embodies so many features which we have already encountered and portrays them in such an obvious way; I am not arguing that it is typical of Flemish paintings generally in the richness of its prospect and refuge symbolism. It is a special kind of 'edge of the wood' composition in which there is a general imbalance between a refuge-dominant right and a more open, prospect-dominant left, though it does illustrate the way in which numerous symbolisms of each kind can intrude into that part of the composition which is dominated by the other. (1996 p. 184)

He emphasised that he was:

not advocating the abandonment of established techniques of criticism, analysis or description and their replacement by an entirely new system. I merely propose that the accepted approach be supplemented by another which lays stress on the observation of a landscape as *environment*, using a terminology which allows us to relate that obseration to other experiences of environment as apprehended in other landscapes and through different media. (p. 185)

Bourassa noted that: 'Another means of elaborating habitat and prospect-refuge theory is to consider the writings of keen observers of landscape' (1991 p. 75).

Finally in this chapter, mention must be made of a form of art which has the landscape itself as its 'canvas'. During the 1970s, various practitioners explored the possibilities of land art. Perhaps the prehistoric creators of such imposing and enigmatic monuments as Silbury Hill, in Wiltshire, or causewayed enclosures, like Windmill Hill, nearby, were to some extent motivated by the aesthetic potentialities of their creations in landscape transformation. In 1970, Robert Smithson transported 10 000 tons of rock in order to create his *Spiral Jetty*, which curves out from the shore of the Great Salt Lake in Utah. This exposition in land art was conceived as a tribute to prehistoric works of earth art and is reminiscent of spiral symbols seen on some Irish megalithic monuments. Gradually, the rocks composing the spiral have sunk into the lake bed, but this process of decay is part of the concept. Meanwhile, James Tyrell has been engaged in modifying the outline of a volcanic crater in Arizona's Painted Desert to create tunnels, viewing chambers and pools to be used in association with viewing the light of the moon, sun and stars in a way that creates an interface between events of the geological and celestial types.

References

Appleton, J. 'The role of the arts in landscape research' in Penning-Rowsell, E. C. and Lowenthal, D. (eds), *Landscape Meanings and Values* (London: Allen & Unwin, 1986) pp. 26–47.

Appleton, J. *The Symbolism of Habitat* (Washington, DC: University of Washington Press, 1990).

Appleton, J. 'Prospects and refuges revisited' in Nasar, J. L. (ed.), *Environmental Aesthetics: Theory, Research and Applications* (Cambridge: Cambridge University Press, 1992).

Appleton, J. 'Running before we can walk: are we ready to map "beauty"?' *Landscape Research* **19** (1994) pp. 112–19.

Appleton, J. *The Experience of Landscape*, 2nd edn (Chichester: John Wiley, 1996).

Balling, J. D. and Falk, J. H. 'Development of visual preference for natural environments' *Environment and Behaviour* **14** (1982) pp. 5–28.

Barrell, J. *The Idea of Landscape and the Sense of Place 1730–1840* (Cambridge: Cambridge University Press, 1972).

Barrell, J. *The Dark Side of the Landscape: The Rural Poor in English Painting 1730–1840* (Cambridge: Cambridge University Press, 1980).

Bermingham, A. *Landscape and Ideology: The English Rustic Tradition 1740–1860* (London: Thames & Hudson, 1987).

Bourassa, S. C. 'A paradigm for landscape aesthetics' *Environment and Behavior* **22** (1990) pp. 787–812.

Bourassa, S. C. *Aesthetics of Landscape* (London: Belhaven Press, 1991).

Cornish, V. *Scenery and the Sense of Sight* (Cambridge: Cambridge University Press, 1935).

Cornish, V. *The Beauties of Scenery* (London: Frederick Muller, 1943).

Cosgrove, D. 'Prospect, perspective and the evolution of the landscape idea' *Transactions of the Institute of British Geographers* NS **10** (1985) pp. 45–62.

Daniels, S. 'The making of Constable Country, 1880–1940' *Landscape Research* **16** (1991) pp. 9–17.

Dewey, J. *Experience and Nature* (London: Allen & Unwin, 1929).

Dewey, J. *Art as Experience* (London: Allen & Unwin, 1934).

Eibl-Eibesfeldt, I. *The Biology of Peace and War* (London: Thames & Hudson, 1979).

Goudie, A. 'Vaughan Cornish: geographer' *Transactions of the Institute of British Geographers* **55** (1972) pp. 1–16.

Greenbie, B. B. 'The landscape of social symbols' in Nasar, J. L. (ed.), *Environmental Aesthetics: Theory, Research and Applications* (Cambridge: Cambridge University Press, 1992) pp. 64–73.

Inglis, F. 'Landscape as popular culture' in Pugh, S. (ed.), *Reading Landscape: County-City-Capital* (Manchester: Manchester University Press, 1990) pp. 197–213.

Kaplan, S. 'Perception and landscape: conceptions and misconceptions' in Nasar, J. L. (ed.), *Environmental Aesthetics: Theory, Research and Applications* (Cambridge: Cambridge University Press, 1992) pp. 45–55.

Kaplan, S. and Kaplan, R. *Cognition and Environment: Coping in an Uncertain World* (New York: Praeger, 1982).

Kaplan, S. and Kaplan, R. *Humanscape: Environments for People* (Belmont, Calif.: Duxbury, 1978).

Lowenthal, D. 'British national identity and the English landscape' *Rural History* **2** (1991) pp. 205–30.

Matless, D. 'Nature, the modern and the mystic: tales from early twentieth century geography' *Transactions of the Institute of British Geographers* NS**16** (1991) pp. 272–86.

Matless, D. 'An occasion for geography: landscape, representation, and Foucault's corpus' *Environment and Planning D: Society and Space* **10** (1992) pp. 41–56.

Mills, S. F. *The American Landscape* (Edinburgh: Keele University Press, 1997).

Morgan, M. 'Perspectives on landscape aesthetics' *Progress in Human Geography* **2** (1978) pp. 527–32.

Nash, R. 'Qualitative landscape values: the historical perspective' in Zube, E. H., Bush, R. O. and Fabos, J. G. (eds), *Landscape Assessment: Values, Perceptions and Resources* (Stroudburg, Pa: Halsted Press, 1975) pp. 10–17.

Novak, B. *Nature and Culture: American Landscape and Painting 1825–75* (London: Thames & Hudson, 1980).

Orians, G. H. 'Habitat selection: general theory and applications to human behaviour' in Lockard, J. (ed.), *Evolution of Human Social Behaviour* (New York: Elsevier, 1980) pp. 49–66.

Orians, G. H. 'An ecological and evolutionary approach to landscape aesthetics' in Penning-Rowsell, E. C. and Lowenthal, D. (eds), *Landscape Meaning and Values* (London: Allen & Unwin, 1986) pp. 3–25.

Prince, H. 'Landscape through painting' *Geography* **69** (1984) pp. 3–18.

Rose, G. 'Place and identity: a sense of place' in Massey, D. and Jess, P. (eds), *A Place in the World* (Cambridge: Cambridge University Press, 1995) pp. 87–132.

Smith, D. M. 'Introduction: the sharing and dividing of geographical space' in Chisholm, M. and Smith, D. M. *Shared Space, Divided Space* (London: Unwin Hyman, 1990).

Woodcock, D. M. 'A functionalist approach to environmental preference', Unpublished PhD dissertation, University of Michigan, Ann Arbor, 1982.

Zube, E. H. 'Themes in landscape assessment theory' *Landscape Journal* **3** (1984) pp. 104–9.

9

Landscape and Place

Within the humanities and social sciences there has been an upwelling of interest in both landscape and place. The escalation in interest has been most marked in the area of humanistic geography, which emerged during the 1970s and subsequently gathered strength: 'Humanistic geography is in large part a response to perceived inadequacies in the traditional geographical approach to understanding the cultural landscape. That approach, with its goal of objective scientific detachment, fails to grasp the fundamental matter of what it is to exist in or experience the landscape' (Bourassa, 1991 pp. 2–3). To some human geographers, the (re)discovery of place meant a return to relevance: 'If geography is to survive as a rational framework for teaching and research, it must identify a new integrative core. We argue that a return to our traditional disciplinary concern with a sense of place and landscape would allow geography to move forward again, as a unified and valued discipline' (Robinson and McCarroll, 1990 p. 1). As favour swung strongly away from positivism in the 1980s, interest in the sense of place existed as a strong strand – probably the strongest strand – of enquiry in the expanding humanistic geography. The developing approach had its critics, and disapproval was directed at the rather 'precious' nature of much of the discussion relating to the sense of place (Brookfield, 1989).

Before exploring the nature of place, it is necessary to establish the difference between place and landscape. Both embody connotations of being defined in part by the existence and values of insiders, landscape being regarded as the environment perceived and place consisting in part of social networks. According to Lowenthal (1978), localities are specific places whereas landscapes are generic types; no two landscapes are entirely alike, but their resemblances make it usual to classify landscapes into categories, such as mountains or deserts.

The distinction between landscapes and places is blurred at the local scale by similarity among places and specificity within landscape types. Landscapes in southern Britain, for example, are apt to be considered both generic and specific – Norfolk Broads, Weald, South Downs, all landscape *types*, but also particular locales. Nonetheless the distinction between the generic and the specific figures constantly in our awareness of environment. Our apprehension of the world is always divided between elements viewed as particulars and as types. (p. 378)

He added that:

Appreciation of localities differs from that of landscapes. We are fond of various *kinds* of city – medieval, cathedral, picturesque – in a fashion unlike our attachment to *particular* cities – York, Chester – even though the same elements may be prized in both instances . . . Attachment to a specific place is apt to reflect some intimate connection, like growing up in it; attachment to a landscape (or townscape) type is more apt to reflect scenic or recreational preferences. Particular experiences and images inspire attachment to York or Avebury or Box Hill; a shared consensual taste explains why we like cathedral cities, megalithic landscapes, or steep wooded escarpments. Preferences for localities are more dispersed, because more disparate, than for landscape types. Associations or aspirations that are uniquely their own attach most people to specific localities the world over, whereas tastes for landscape in general tend to converge on a few highly appreciated types. (Lowenthal, 1978)

Landscape and the Sense of Place

Landscape is likely to be an important factor in any discussion of place because it will normally be a crucial component of the sense of place:

All landscapes are more than an ensemble of physical and human components, and in turn, are more than aesthetic objects to be observed and appreciated. Respective cultures transcribe their endeavors into the land's record – what Relph has aptly termed the terra firma cenotaph. Landscapes have a deeper significance, identity and character, not easily quantified by traditional positivistic methods. This is because every landscape and artefact is associated with cherished attitudes, values and images, making them evocative, idiosyncratic and reflective of changing social values. (Park and Coppack, 1994 pp. 162–3)

The sense of place can be characterised in two different ways. First, places may be regarded as having their own intrinsic personalities, with some places being visually striking and possessed of powerful images: Mount Rushmore, Stonehenge or Lake Baikal are all associated with strongly developed senses of place. Second, the sense of place can be identified as the emotional attachments to localities developed by individuals and communities in the course of living and growing within the setting of home. Senses of place can be associated with a spectrum of different geographical levels, from the smallest of localities to the international region. They also 'relate to identity in different ways: they may invite identification with a place; they may establish identity by offering a contrast between the place that is "home" and the place that is "away"; or the meaning of a sense of place may be irrelevant to how people identify themselves' (Rose, 1995 p. 97).

Identity can also be exchanged between places and over time and Hopkins has described the adoption of icons ranging from a reproduction of the *Santa Maria* to rickshaws, pagodas and Ming vases by the creators of the West Edmonton Mall (WEM):

Icons are used by Triple Five as part of a spatial strategy to create a milieu of 'elsewhereness.' This is done, at least in part, in order to divert patron attention from the mall as a retailing money-making machine towards its spectacular design effects . . . the mall design constitutes a response to the sense of 'placelessness' that had saturated shopping centres by the early 1980s. (1990 p. 10)

Hopkins noted that Relph (1976) had coined the term 'placelessness' to describe those locations and physical structures that failed to reflect the unique, vernacular or local ways of the immediate surrounding of a place or landscape.

Shopping malls, with their redundant style and seemingly ubiqui-
tous set of chain stores, were deemed 'placeless'; they exhibited a
repetitive style and were directed primarily at outsiders. By
introducing special features, Triple Five has established at least
temporarily a distinct identity for WEM in a world of generic
malls, which lessens, but does *not* eradicate the sense of placelessness. (Hopkins, 1990)

Patrons at the WEM could choose from an array of 'consumable
environments' which were the contexts for social interactions based
upon mass participation through personal consumption of merchan-
dise 'experience'.

Places matter because they are the focus of personal sentiments,
with the feelings for place permeating day-to-day life and experience. Often, the significance of place and the meanings associated
with it lie at the core of a person's identity; even so, much
concerning the relationship between people and places remains
poorly understood. Relph remarked that: 'we live, act and orient
ourselves in a world that is richly and profoundly differentiated into
places, yet at the same time we seem to have a meagre understanding
of the constitution of places and the ways in which we experience
them' (1976 p. 6). Social scientists agree that places do not have
inherent meaning and possess only the meanings that humans give
to them, but they disagree in other respects. Some argue that the
need to belong to a particular place is a biologically-based survival
strategy closely related to territoriality. Others prefer a cultural
interpretation and suggest that the sense of place results from the
systems of meaning which people employ in order to make sense of
their world. Others still point out that there is not one human
culture but many, and believe that it is the awareness of these
differences which fosters the development of the sense of place:

They argue that different groups in a society may notice their
differences from other groups and want to mark that difference,
and that one of the ways in which they do that is by claiming that
they belong to a particular place to which other groups do not
belong. A sense of place can thus be a way of establishing a
difference between one group and another. (Rose, 1995 p. 99)

The notion that identity and character can derive from an
attachment to place has existed for quite some time; in 1919 the

English geographer, C. B. Fawcett, wrote that: 'the man or woman who has no love for and pride in his or her home region is not thereby qualified for wider views of life. Provincialism is in itself a good thing, and a necessary factor in the well being of humanity' (p. 151).

Yi-Fu Tuan described place as a centre of meaning constructed by experience, with experience being a cover-all term for the various modes through which a person knows his/her world:

Place is known not only through the eyes and mind but also through the more passive and direct modes of experience, which resist objectification. To know a place fully means both to understand it in an abstract way and to know it as one person knows another. At a high theoretical level, places are points in a spatial system. At the opposite extreme, they are strong visceral feelings. Places are seldom known at either extreme: the one is too remote from sensory experience to be real, and the other pre-supposes rootedness in a locality and an emotional commitment to it that are increasingly rare. To most people in the modern world, places lie somewhere in the middle range of experience. (1975 p. 152)

He continued by pointing out that:

Experience constructs places at different scales. The fireplace and the home are both places. Neighbourhood, town and city are places; a distinctive region is a place, and so is a nation. Common usage sanctions the application of the word 'place' to phenomena that differ greatly in size and in physical character. What do the fireplace, the corner drugstore, the city, and the nation-state have in common? They are all centers of meaning to individuals and to groups. (1975, p. 153)

Different people are likely to experience different senses of place, so that the long distance traveller looking down from the hill track can be expected to form a sense of the place that is different from the one associated with the farm workers from the nearby village who are toiling in the fields below, even though all are sensing the same valley. Rose wrote: 'The same location may become meaningful to different people through different senses of place. For example, it is very doubtful that Bedouins or Native Americans shared the same sense of place (of "the Orient", or the Midwest) as those who came from elsewhere to visit or settle' (1995, p. 97).

Places will be perceived differently according to differences in age, upbringing and class; differences in gender may also be significant. Commenting on recent studies of gender symbols and urban landscapes Bondi wrote that the built environment seemed immune from the activities and ideas of its inhabitants, though faithfully representing the ideas values and interests of its planners, designers and builders.

> This interpretation strips the built environment of the meaning it is given by the people who live in it and with the transformations, however modest, that they make. This radical opposition between makers and users, between doers and done to, can be construed as professional (planner or architect) versus ordinary person, but the emphasis on gender-based interests in feminist analyses results in a casting of the agents as professional men, the victims as women, with male inhabitants appearing as beneficiaries and perhaps, via patriarchal ideologies, as indirect agents. (1992 p. 162)

Gender relationships and landscape were discussed by Rose, who considered that with the development of mechanical theories of the world in the seventeenth century, women were regarded as the repositories of natural laws and 'being, like nature, tamed by men' could be studied by male science and rendered intelligible. She concluded: 'I have suggested that the feminine unknown is represented in cultural geography by visual pleasure, and that the geographers' gaze at landscape is structured by a distinction between nature (the feminine scene, to be interpreted) and science (the masculine look, the interpreter)' (1992 p. 17).

Some at least of the differences in the way that environmental awareness develops are culturally determined. Matthews (1995) studied a group of young Kenyan children and examined the relationship between environmental experience and environmental awareness. It emerged that children lacking in formal training and deprived of access to maps had an ability to draw relatively sophisticated representations of places and could vividly recall their local environment. Their representations of places were different from those of their counterparts in the UK, suggesting the effect of cultural influences on their styles of expression, if not on their cognitive ability. Matthews considered that conceptions of place and space were not universally even and that once they start to move, children enter a realm which is culturally construed and in which knowledge of places and environmental understanding become, in part, functions of socialisation:

> The children in this survey personalized their views on place to reflect cultural values. Accordingly, culture affords children different opportunities and provides meaning through its practices; culture organizes the context of activities and in so doing, conditions children's chances for developing environmental skills; and culture is the raw material out of which children fashion and shape their environmental meaning. (1995 p. 293)

Places can be characterised in different ways; the interpretation which currently enjoys most popularity amongst social scientists is one which regards places in a social sense as the location of particular sets of intersecting social relations so that every place is 'a unique mixture of the relations which configure social space' (Massey, 1995 p. 61). Thus:

> Each of us, as individuals, also has our own activity space . . . The basic shape is probably a set of fairly local paths and places as normal daily life is lived between home, school, work, church and club, with occasional trips further afield to a neighbouring town, or to a hospital maybe. This pattern may in turn be punctuated by forays much further afield – to friends or relatives for a visit, for weekend excursions, or to follow your team to an away match . . . The argument of the theorists . . . is that the present era (usually seen as beginning in the second half of this century) is witness to two major changes in the nature of activity spaces. *Firstly*, they are in general increasing in their spatial reach. *Secondly*, they are increasing also in their complexity and in the complexity of the linkages between them. (Massey, 1995 pp. 56–7)

We tend to associate a well-developed sense of place with societies which have experienced a long attachment to their settings. Relph, as noted, has described place and placelessness: 'An authentic sense of place is above all that of being inside and belonging to *your* place both as an individual and as a member of the community and to know this without reflecting upon it' (1976 p. 65), whilst an inauthentic attitude to place 'is essentially no sense of place, for it involves no awareness of the deep and symbolic significance of places and no appreciation of their identities' (p. 82). Precapitalist societies were largely characterised by 'authentic' attitudes to place and were associated with well-developed senses of place, whereas the condition of 'placelessness' has developed in many but not all capitalist societies. Massey wrote that:

> Very often, when we think of what we mean by a *place*, we picture a settled community, a locality with a distinct character – physical, economic and cultural. It is a vision which has entered the English language in phrases such as 'a sense of place', 'no place like home' and – perhaps most tellingly of all – the notion of things being on occasion 'out of place', meaning that they do not fit in with some pre-given coherence of character. (1995 p. 46)

However, she subsequently notes that various authors have proposed 'a questioning of the notion of places simply as settled, enclosed and internally coherent . . . and its replacement or supplementation by a concept of place as a meeting place, the location of the intersections of particular bundles of activity spaces, of connections and interrelations, of influences and movements' (pp. 58–9).

In general there is a sense of the weakening of ties between local communities and the places that they inhabit, with globalisation in its varied forms and time–space compression serving to undermine the sense of place. One may wonder, therefore, whether these and related tendencies have effected visible impacts upon the landscape as well as upon the associated senses of place? Park and Coppack have argued that the rustification impulses of city-dwellers have altered the surrounding countryside and imbued past sites with new social, cultural, economic and metaphorical meaning. They write that:

> Scenery has become commodified, marketed and sold to exurbanites by entrepreneurs in the form of rustic ambiance. The iconization of rural culture and values is exploited for contemporary consumption. Romantic historical images of local landmarks and structures are appropriated, developed and embedded within the popular consciousness of self-confident, highly educated and well-to-do consumers from nearby urban centers. (1994 p. 163)

These remarks call to mind Lowenthal's observation that:

For mobile modern man, nostalgia is not so much being uprooted as having to live in an alien present. If no longer fatal, it is an increasingly pervasive ailment. Once the solace of the few, nostalgia now attracts folks from all social levels. Antique buying has expanded to the middle class, while 'distressers' apply dirt, stones and hammers to new furniture, wear hobnailed boots on staircases, and use air rifles to make 'worm' holes. (1975 p. 3)

If globalisation is transforming the social and economic landscapes, could it also be changing the visible landscapes and homogenising the scenery with the extermination of local character? A century or so ago the countrysides of England had strongly developed regional identities. On the land and in the lanes one would have seen farm vehicles built by village craftsmen, many of them built in styles and painted in hues which identified their counties of origin. Today, as part of what is often regarded as capitalism's destruction of place, the land is worked by machines built by transnational corporations and shipped to markets all around the globe. With regard to the homogenisation of landscape, Blunden and Turner note that: 'The "timeless" appearance of the traditional countryside is now something we certainly cannot take for granted' (1985 p. 69). They add:

These changes have not affected all parts of the lowlands equally. The brunt of them has been borne largely in the traditional cereal-growing areas of East Anglia and the eastern and southern Midlands. Parts of Suffolk have received great attention with charges that their present-day appearance is more akin to the prairies of Canada than Olde England, and nowhere is this type of landscape more evident than in the Fens of Cambridgeshire and Lincolnshire. (Blunden and Turner, 1985)

In 1986, research produced by the Countryside Commission and Hunting Technical Services estimated that the absolute length of hedgerows in England and Wales was reduced by about 190 000 miles or 22 per cent during the survey period 1947–85. It revealed an acceleration in the rate of hedgerow loss from about 2600 miles per year during the early part of the survey period to about 4000 miles per year in the 1980s. Paralleling the destruction of hedgerows to create the large fields suited to mechanised farming has been the removal of ancient woodland, the draining of ponds and the replacement of traditionally-managed hay meadows. The effect of these and other recent changes has been to dilute the distinctive character of the English countrysides. Shoard considered that:

> The sudden public revulsion against modern agricultural methods that took place in the early 1980s has changed the atmosphere in which rural affairs are discussed. Between early 1981 and late 1982, it came to be accepted that the traditional English landscape was under threat from a group who had hitherto been seen as its protectors – our farmers. (1987 p. 550)

This erosion of the vernacular identity of the English countryside must have had considerable consequences for the English sense of place, which had been closely attached to English rural images. The harmonious and wholesome qualities of the countryside were contrasted with the pollution and congestion of the city, for: 'From its beginnings the industrial city has been regarded by its harshest critics as a pathological environment; chronically and irrevocably diseased by the very processes of industrial capitalism; "a pestiferous growth", as William Cobbett called London in 1821, on an otherwise harmonious landscape' (Bunce, 1994 p. 14). Rose described how, by the end of the nineteenth century, architecture and garden design were turning to vernacular rural traditions for inspiration while music like Elgar's, with its strong national associations, was praised and interest in English folksong revived. Also:

> The magazine *Country Life* started publication in 1897, and its accounts of leisured and harmonious English rural life made it very popular. Howkins (1986) points out that this sense of place became especially acute during the First World War; it was used to symbolize all the qualities for which the troops were fighting. And it also seems to have provided some kind of comfort to those trapped in the trenches; *Country Life* was avidly read there, a reminder of the better life that was somewhere possible. (1995 p. 107)

Changes to the character and contents of the local landscape will have impacted heavily on the indigenous societies since: 'Place is identity. Things out of place are not properly themselves, and move as living forces towards their natural home' (Turner, 1979 p. 6), while:

for people with a local identity their town or village is not *just* (or, for many, *even*) a space in which to work for a wage. It is a place where they have networks of friends, relatives and acquaintances, where they have learned about life and acquired a cultural frame of reference through which to interpret the social world around them; their place is where they are socialized as human beings rather than just reproduced as bearers of the commodity labour power. As a result, people have often become profoundly attached to particular places, which come to have socially endowed and shared meanings that touch on all aspects of their lives, helping shape *who* they are by virtue of *where* they are. (Beynon and Hudson, 1993 p. 182)

Though most frequently associated with rural landscapes and their inhabitants, the sense of place relates to townscapes as well. It is widely considered that – and particularly in the city – globalisation involves a destruction of places leading to homogenisation, but Berner and Korff (1995) argue that while the towns and cities of the world are becoming increasingly similar, each one of them is also becoming more complex and diverse. The stream of dynamic urban development finds a response in the development of urban localities as the foci of everyday life. Their basic hypothesis is that the present metropolises are characterised by conflicts between globalisation and localisation. For them, localisation is the quest for a local identity and for the creation of localities as foci of everyday life. Despite their apparently contradictory natures, localisation and globalisation are closely connected, with globalisation providing a process through which local diversity is created:

Instead of mere differentiation between world regions, centre and periphery today indicate a differentiation between global society and segmented localities, both spatially anchored in world cities. Centre and periphery face each other within the metropolis and form the background of intensifying urban conflicts in London, Paris and Los Angeles as well as in Bangkok, Manila, Rio de Janeiro and Mexico City. (pp. 211–12)

They concluded that:

Through globalization, urban traditions and symbols have been reduced to mere decor, and the economic production of urban space has given rise to uniform centres and dreary residential quarters. Instead of urbanity we find *Unwirtlichkeit* (inhospitability). The maintenance and defense of localities plays an important role in the preservation of diversity and heterogeneity that is a fundamental characteristic of urbanism. It is from the local context that steps towards an (at least partly) use-value oriented city can be taken in which the inhabitants are able to define the meaning of the places they live in. (1995 p. 220)

Harvey (1993) considered that the process of globalisation has led to the dissolution of place and the disintegration of identities, bringing a rise in xenophobia and of reactionary place-bound politics, with people responding to the changes wrought by globalisation by seeking to establish a stable, 'bounded' place identity and searching to restore old certainties. In this situation, interest in the local heritage rises as people seek to fix the meaning of places and to enclose and defend them. May studied the attitudes of the white residents who moved into historic Stoke Newington, an inner London neighbourhood, as part of a second wave of gentrification dating from the mid-1980s onwards, paying attention to how members of this new cultural class constructed their sense of place in relation to the social constructions of race and national identity. It was found that Stoke Newington's newer residents enjoyed a control over space which allowed them to construct the neighbourhood as a space in which 'one can have it all':

Whilst the neighbourhood's historical associations can support an image of place built around the iconography of a mythical village England, those same residents demonstrate a desire for difference that draws them towards a more obviously 'global sense of place'. Yet the way in which this latter place identity is constructed is anything but progressive, suggesting we may need to pay more attention to the way in which such connections are imaged, and by whom, before automatically assuming that a global sense of place describes a more progressive identity politics. (1996 p. 210)

In contrast, Western (1993) studied the place-related attitudes of twelve Barbadian families towards Notting Hill. This was, from the mid-1950s onwards, one of the first London districts to be settled by Afro-Caribbeans; it experienced a riot by young whites against black immigrants in 1958, housed a restaurant associated with members of the Black Power movement and has become famous for the annual Notting Hill street carnival. It might have been expected, therefore, that the district would have great symbollic significance in the black community. Instead, however, it was found that Barbadians in London did not feel strong attachments to Notting Hill or to any other purportedly 'black' locales. Even after 30 years of residence in London, the households interviewed regarded themselves only as sojourners in Britain and anticipated a return to Barbados, which attraced much stronger bonds of identification.

Biology, Literature, Culture and Heritage

As has been shown, human attitudes towards the aesthetic aspects of landscape have been related to our biological inheritance and evolutionary history, and so one might enquire whether the sense of place is also acquired from our distant ancestors? Walmsley and Lewis pointed out that: 'not all researchers would agree that the bonding of people to place is best studied through humanistic approaches and an emphasis on experience. An alternative view is to be found in the argument that an individual's relations with the environment are in some way innate' (1993 p. 120). They noted the association between studies of the biological bases of behaviour and territoriality and added that: 'To ethologists, the concept of territory is linked to the instinct of aggression. A territory is, in other words, a place to be defended on account of its role in providing food and a place for mateship' (1993). But is the sense of place experienced by humans capable of being equated with some innate drive which is territorial in nature? Walmsley and Lewis suggested that there is a strong link between territoriality and the sense of place, claiming that territoriality operates at the communal level to promote group identity and bonding, as reflected in the feelings of loyalty that citizens display towards their towns or suburbs or in the ways that teenage gangs associate with their gang territories (1993). Sack, who disregarded the question of whether or not territoriality is innate, considered that it means: 'the assertion by an organisation, or an individual in the name of the organisation, that an area of geographic space is under its influence or control' (1980 p. 167). He noted that the nature of the private ownership of land and the concept of the territorial state contrast with the views of space in current in 'primitive' societies for in the 'primitive' perspective land can be sliced up and sold as parcels:

> Land is not a piece of space within a larger spatial system. On the contrary, it is seen in terms of social relations. The people, as part of nature, are intimately linked to the land. To belong to a territory or place is a social concept which requires first and foremost belonging to a societal unit. The land itself is in the possession of the group as a whole. It is not privately partitioned and owned. Moreover, it is alive with the spirits and history of the people, and places on it are sacred. (1980 p. 22)

Such a response to place differs greatly from the attitudes current in industrialised societies, suggesting that if our receptiveness to the sense of places is innate it has been heavily conditioned by cultural factors.

Regarding the origins of the human association with specific places, the Australopithecines appear to have followed nomadic existences and the earliest evidence of a tie with places comes with the first human, *Homo habilis*. 'Living floors' associated with *Homo habilis* have been excavated in the Olduvai Gorge in northern Tanzania. They date back to 1.9 million years ago and one example studied covered an area of 300 square yards and contained more than 2400 tools and artefacts. The remains of animals were in two main piles, one consisting of bones which contained marrow, and the other of bones that did not. On another occupation site blocks of lava had been arranged in a rough circle, perhaps representing the remains of a hut built of slender branches, in which case it would be the first human dwelling or structure of any kind to be discovered. This, like several of the Olduvai living floors, was associated with a former body of water, and one reading of the evidence suggests that the favoured places for early human occupation were situated in landscapes where streams of drinkable fresh water flowed into alkaline lakes within settings which were rich in game, though authorities disagree on whether the humans were the hunters of game or scavengers from the kills of other hunters.

A concise explanation of the significance of place to an under- standing of the past has been provided by Binford: 'The archae- ologist "sees" the past segmentally from the perspective of fixed positions in space. The "fallout" from the events that "moved across" fixed places establishes the character of the archaeological

remains on sites. To understand the past we must understand places'
(1982 p. 6). Human societies develop different relationships with
places in the different parts of the landscape that they occupy:

> One of the more distinctive features of human systems is their
> spatial focus on a 'home base' or a residential camp. At any one
> time the way in which a group uses its habitat is directly condi-
> tioned by the pattern of moving out and then returning to a
> residential camp. This means that, aside from certain 'absolute'
> characteristics of the biogeography within the region, *there is
> always a 'cultural geography'* which is relative to the location of
> the residential camp. (pp. 6–7)

He used his experiences of the Nunamiut Eskimo to provide a
model of the economic zonation around settlement sites. In the
quickly overexploited zone around the camp is the *play radius* for
children and the campground for visitors, while beyond the play
radius is the *foraging radius*, which rarely extends more than six
miles from the camp. Beyond this is the *logistical radius*, the zone
exploited by task groups who stay away from the residential camp
for at least one night before returning, while beyond the logistical
radius is the *extended range*, an area which is regularly monitored
but which may not be experiencing exploitation at any particular
time.

With the adoption of places as settlement sites, relationships of
different kinds were established with the different places within the
territory occupied by a group. Other relationships of a more
spiritual nature would eventually be established:

> all monuments are in places, but it is given to very few places to
> become monuments. All too often prehistorians take those monu-
> ments for granted and construct their narratives around them.
> Once they concede the point that rituals must have accompanied
> the performance of everyday activities, they are under an obliga-
> tion to consider the role of natural places and the ways in which
> their uses changed through time. (Bradley, 1991 p. 136)

Bradley considered that hunter-gatherers recognise no conflict
between the natural and social worlds: nature rather than human
effort provides for them. To construct imposing monuments would
involve an intervention in that relationship which would require a

Figure 9.1

Figure 9.2

Figure 9.3

Figure 9.4

Completely different place associations are encountered with these contrasting human settings: the Northern industrial terrace (9.1); the picturesque old Southern village (9.2); the rugged upland setting (9.4); the flat, windswept Fenland countryside (9.4). (Richard Muir) reordering of the natural world. Thus people at the hunter-gatherer level of development attach special importance to places rather than to monuments; the places concerned may be the foci for rituals but they remain parts of the natural world. He adds that:

> Monuments that could be related to the commemoration of ancestors are far more characteristic of farmers and could reflect the fact that agriculture depends upon a sustained period of interference with the natural order: land needs to be cleared and prepared, and the food supply must be conserved if it is to provide sufficient resources for the future.

Mobile hunter-gatherers perceive time and place differently from cultivators, with each group being influenced by different attitudes to the natural world, while places command landscape and territories:

> agriculturalists tend to *enclose* resources, whilst hunter-gatherers control the *paths* running between places. Those places provide vantage points and define hunter-gatherer territories by commanding a view across them. It is worth underlining the significance of places in this scheme. Specific rituals might be performed in these locations, but they are not divorced from the economic activities happening there. (p. 136)

Monuments such as the Neolithic megalithic monuments of Western Europe are culturally constructed places, while a second group can be described as 'places as natural monuments' and involve a distinctive use of topography, like the prominent boulders and rock outcrops in the North of England which have been decorated with cup-and-ring symbols, or the sacred eminences. Natural and cultural features could also be combined in telling juxtapositions. In the British uplands, landscapes could have been used by hunter-gatherers long after the adoption of domesticates in the lowlands, and the use of places as monuments may belong to a transitional period when the expansion of agriculture threatened the traditional Mesolithic economy of the uplands. 'Conflicts between culture and nature might occur increasingly often, for if the dangerous character of such landscapes was to be brought under control, it would be important to incorporate these places into the 'domestic' world . . . The translation of places into monuments may be one way in which this was achieved' (Bradley, 1991 p. 139). Special places with striking topographical presences in their landscapes figure prominently in the spiritual life of various indigenous communities: Window Rock in Arizona is sacred to the Navajo; Ayers Rock features prominently in the iconography of the aboriginal people of central Australia; and the Black Hills of Dakota contain the sacred burial grounds of the Sioux. The incorporation of places into a landscape of ritual is evident in the North York Moors in northern England, where the tips of upland spurs and promontories were cut across by linear bank and ditch earthworks in the Bronze Age to detach small pieces of territory situated in commanding positions and which are assumed to have been used for ritual purposes (Vyner, 1994).

Culture serves to encourage the development of symbols, and one of the ways in which this can be achieved is through the medium of literature. It was, for example, through the popularity of the English nature novel that the senses of place associated with the industrial North of England or Hardy's Dorset were focused and developed. Pocock pointed out that: 'Medieval stories had traditionally recounted unchanged moral truths in timeless settings' (1981 p. 337). Place specificity took over a century to emerge, but in English literature the generalised worlds of Fielding or Richardson yielded to those of Scott and Austen, and 'During the second quarter of the nineteenth century the novelist's pen began more fully to depict particular localities, thereby giving rise to the genre of the English regional novel'. He quoted D. H. Lawrence, who considered that: 'Different places on the face of the earth have different vital effluence, different vibration, different chemical exhalation, different polarity with different stars: call it what you like. But spirit of place is a great reality' (1933 p. 12). Pocock considered that the novelist articulates the geographer's inarticulations, providing an insight into place so that imaginative literature offers a valuable storehouse within which the central theme of human-environment relationships can be explored. In particular, this literature 'is a source of wide interest to current humanistic approaches where experience has been conceptualized in terms of insideness-outsideness, lived reciprocity, or as a dialectic between rest and movement' (p. 345). Jay related the rise in interest in British regions and localities to the expansion of communication systems.

The art of describing areal differentiation within Britain during the last hundred years has been practised as much by novelists as by geographers. Drawing upon the great variety of landscapes and modes of living to be found within the confines of a comparatively small island, many British writers have chosen to emphasize the influence of real localities upon the life and action of their fictitious characters. The burgeoning of the regional novel was largely coincident with, and probably assisted by, dramatic improvements in communications across the surface of Britain by railways and roads. Towards the end of the nineteenth century many novelists preferred a rural setting for their stories, but since the first world war the tendency to select an urban and industrial background for a novel has become a marked feature of this genre. (1975 p. 57)

English literature is noted for its evocation of places. Birch wrote that:

One of the main supports of the great span of English literature is its richness in regional writing, a support which in turn rests on twin pillars. One of these is the relatively small number of major authors, like Scott, Bennett and Hardy whose names are closely associated with particular parts of Britain and with regional literature at its best. The other pillar is made up of a galaxy of less eminent, less fashionable or less prolific writers who also set their works within particular districts but who often gained little more distinction than being thought of as 'local' authors. (1981 p. 348)

Hardy revived the provincial term 'Wessex', and this imaginary land, which he described as being 'partly dream-country', incorporated real Wessex landscapes and places which were populated by his fictional characters. Like Pocock, Birch considered that the romantic novelist illuminated the human relationship with places and settings:

The selective use of the Wessex environment and the increased range and scale of settings later in his career reflects Hardy's primary interest in examining, by means of his fiction, the nature of the relationship between man, the community and the environment. It is probably in the examination of the development of this socio-ecological approach to fiction, which Hardy shared with several writers in the late nineteenth and early twentieth centuries that the geographer can most usefully contribute ideas about imaginative fiction. (pp. 352–3)

Birch concluded that:

Attempts to define the human predicament in fresh ways within imaginative literature might be seen to be essentially a process of fusing together people and places by means different from those used before, a fusion that seemed to owe something to the fiction-writer's enhanced awareness of the real region as well as a heightened concern for the region as it existed in the mind of the writer. Science and art were being drawn close together. (p. 358)

Novelists and commentators on literature may highlight and elaborate ideas about the sense of place in the same way that Barrell distinguishes between the sense of place possessed by Hardy's fictional villagers of Egdon and that of the outsider:

'Landscape' implies the detached experience of an observer who arrives from some place other than the landscape itself, and it implies a habit of pictorializing based on, among other things, the opportunity of comparing different places with an abstract, picturesque ideal. No less than 'Nature', then, 'landscape' is a concept produced by the comparison of the diverse, the accidental; whereas, for the 'heathfolk' of Egdon, where the local geography is represented as surviving less adulterated by intimations of a world outside than it does anywhere else in Hardy's Wessex, the heath is a place, as I have said, 'away from comparisons'. But we should be careful before deciding what such reflections can tell us about our relation to the heathfolk: for if words like 'nature' and 'landscape' put an unscalable wall between our language and theirs, our mode of knowing and theirs, they do so only within the context of the myth and of the novel – they do nothing to assert, as the novel asserts, that heathfolk *really did* have such and such a sense of place, or that we *really are* incapable of knowing, and Hardy of representing, what they knew. Nor, of course, do they tell us anything to the contrary. (1982 p. 350)

The associations between place and literature have been explored many times, but Tuan (1991) argues that speech as well as the written word should be considered integral to the construction of place:

> Language is important to students of place not only because a Thomas Hardy or Willa Cather has written evocatively on landscape, and has thus provided a literary standard that geographers should seek to emulate in their own writing; rather language is important – indeed central – because humans are language animals, and language is a force that all of us use everyday to build, sustain, and destroy. (p. 694)

He suggests that a warm conversation between friends can make the place in which the encounter took place itself feel warm, whereas malicious speech has the capacity to destroy the reputation of a place and thereby its visibility. Much earlier he wrote: 'Literature and painting induce an awareness of place by holding up mirrors to our own experience; what had been felt can now be seen, what was formless and vacillating is now framed and still' (1975 p. 161).

The sense of place is very frequently associated with landscapes defined and differentiated by distinctive cultural characteristics: in such a manner the sense of place of Kansas in pioneering times was heavily influenced by an opposition to slavery and an enthusiasm for prohibition. Describing the Mid-West in the early nineteenth century, Jackson wrote:

> we are dealing with a landscape largely settled and inhabited by men and women, whether Methodists or Baptists or Presbyterians or Mormons, who were participating in and promoting the Great Revival: the landscape of the Methodist circuit rider, the itinerant preacher and peddlar of religious literature, of the revival and camp meeting. (1979 p. 161)

He added:

> A traveller tells of a meeting out on the still vacant prairie with a man who announced that he was the prophet Elijah, and handed out a pamphlet warning of the end of the world . . . it was the landscape of the Millerites, of the latter Day Saints, of innumer-

able small millenial sects, all acutely aware of the approaching end of historical time. (Jackson, 1979)

Culture and place are strongly linked and Entrikin (1994 p. 227) has described a 'shift away from understanding places in themselves, and towards an appreciation of place as a social and cultural category'. Cuba and Hummon wrote:

Like other forms of identity, place identity answers the question – Who am I? – by countering – Where am I? or Where do I belong? From a social psychological perspective, place identities are thought to arise because places, as bounded locales imbued with personal, social and cultural meanings, provide a significant framework in which identity is constructed, maintained and transformed. (1993 p. 112)

The sense of place is rooted in time as well as in space and the historical associations of places make important contributions to their personality. Where a sense of place is associated with notable historical landmarks the potential may exist for the development and marketing of 'heritage':

This geography of place fluctuated with demographic, social, cultural, economic and political changes and these, in turn, shape not only people's perception of but also their behavioural actions towards rural places. Land becomes landscape/landscape becomes sacred space as the physical resource is reinterpreted through the lens of rural sentiment and human perception. (Park and Coppack, 1994 p. 162)

For Lowenthal, 'People used to express selective nostalgia about particular times and places in the more or less remote past. Today, nostalgia threatens to engulf all of past time and much of the present landscape' (1975 p. 3). Much of this can be explained by the alienating effects of an unwelcoming present, while Lowenthal considered that the past may operate as a guiding factor conditioning the way in which people establish a relationship with the land and affecting their relationship with amenity landscapes:

The historical past is a key frame of reference and provides the contrast that becomes post-modern society's key structural device. Yesterday's artifact becomes today's art, seen any summer weekend as well-heeled YUPPIES scour flea and antique markets, searching for country decor with city decorum. This conservation of rural characteristics captures the spirit of place and sense of connectedness with the past. (1975 p. 169)

Michael Bunce echoed William Cowper's words of more than two centuries ago: 'God made the country, and man made the town', and he observed that:

At its most profound level, the affection for the countryside may reflect fundamental human values and psychological needs which can be traced to a basic human desire for harmony with land and nature, for a sense of community and place and for simplicity of lifestyle. With the rise of urban-industrial society these needs have been magnified and projected on to a countryside redefined as the symbolic antithesis of the city; a place for reconnecting to natural processes and ancestral roots. Yet the idealisation of the country-side is intricately bound up in the development of modern urban civilisation. It is the product of three centuries or so of changes which have accentuated the cleavage between country and city through the transformation of their respective landscapes and the redefinition of human relationships with land, nature and com-munity. (1994 p. 2)

Landscape and place are intimately connected but not identical. Static interpretations of places as bounded spaces are falling from favour and Massey has described places as being meeting places located at the intersections of particular bundles of human activity spaces, the locations of connections and interrelations, influences and movements (1995 p. 59). Such an interpretation casts places in cultural terms, while it is generally accepted that places have no meanings other than those that humans give them. Landscapes are, to greater or lesser extents, the creations of humans, but if humans had never arrived and modified them the landscapes would be very different yet they would *still* exist as landscapes. When regarded as passages of scenery, landscapes would continue to exist if humanity became extinct. Landscape makes a forceful contribution to the spirit of place but it can never be the sole contribution. It does, however, determine so many of the qualities of that spirit: the lie of the land, the character of the scenery, the resources of water, soil and minerals and so much more besides.

References

Barrell, J. 'Geographies of Hardy's Wessex' *Journal of Historical Geography* **8** (1982) pp. 347–81.

Berner, E. and Korff, R. 'Globalization and local resistance: the creation of localities in Manila and Bangkok' *International Journal of Urban and Regional Research* **19** (1995) pp. 208–22.

Beynon, H. and Hudson, R. 'Place and space in contemporary Europe: some lessons and reflections' *Antipode* **25** (1993) pp. 177–90.

Binford, L. R. 'The archaeology of place' *Journal of Anthropological Archaeology* **1** (1982) pp. 5–31.

Birch, B. P. 'Wessex, Hardy and the nature novelists' *Transactions of the Institute of British Geographers* NS **6** (1981) pp. 348–58.

Blunden, J. and Turner, G. *Critical Countryside* (London: BBC Publications, 1985).

Bondi, L. 'Gender symbols and urban landscapes' *Progress in Human Geography* **16** (1992) pp. 157–70.

Bourassa, S. C. *The Aesthetics of Landscape* (London: Belhaven Press, 1991).

Bradley, R. 'Monuments and places' in Garwood, P., Jennings, D., Skeates, R. and Toms, J. (eds), *Sacred and Profane*, Oxford University Committee for Archaeology Monograph No. 32, 1991, pp. 135–40.

Brookfield, H. C. 'The behavioural environment: how, what for, and whose?' in Boal, F. W. and Livingstone, D. N. (eds), *The Behavioural Environment* (London: Routledge, 1989) pp. 311–28.

Bunce, M. *The Countryside Ideal* (London: Routledge, 1994).

Countryside Commission and Hunting Technical Services *Monitoring Landscape Change* (Cheltenham, 1986).

Cuba, L. and Hummon, D. 'A place to call home: identification with dwelling, community, and region' *Sociological Quarterly* **34** (1993) pp. 111–31.

Entrikin, N. J. 'Place and region' *Progress in Human Geography* **18** (1994) pp. 227–33.

Fawcett, C. B. *The Provinces of England* (London, 1919).

Harvey, D. 'From space to place and back again: reflections on the condition of postmodernity' in Bird, J., Curtis, B., Putnam, T., Robertson, G. and Tickner, L. (eds), *Mapping the Futures: Local Cultures, Global Change* (London: Routledge, 1993) pp. 3–29.

Hopkins, J. S. P. 'West Edmonton Mall: Landscape of myths and elsewhereness' *The Canadian Geographer* **34** (1990) 2–17.

Howkins, A. 'The discovery of rural England' in Colls, R. and Dodd, P. (eds), *Englishness: Politics and Culture 1880–1920* (London: Croom Helm, 1986).

Jackson, J. B. 'The order of a landscape: reason and religion in Newtonian America' in Meinig, D. W. (ed.) *The Interpretation of Ordinary Landscapes* (New York: Oxford University Press, 1979) pp. 153–63.

Jay, L. J. 'The Black Country of Francis Brett Young' *Transactions of the Institute of British Geographers* **66** (1975) pp. 57–72.

Lawrence, D. H. *Studies in Classic American Literature* (London, 1933).

Lowenthal, D. 'Past time, present place: landscape and memory' *Geographical Review* **65** (1975) pp. 1–36.

Lowenthal, D. 'Finding valued landscapes' *Progress in Human Geography* **2** (1978) pp. 373–418.

Massey, D. 'The conceptualization of place' in Massey, D. and Jess, P. *A Place in the World* (Oxford: Oxford University Press, 1995) pp. 45–86.

May, J. 'Globalization and the politics of place: place and identity in an inner London neighbourhood' *Transactions of the Institute of British Geographers* NS **21** (1996) pp. 194–215.

Park, D. C. and Coppack, P. M. 'The role of rural settlement and vernacular landscapes in contriving sense of place in the city's countryside' *Geografiska Annaler* **76B** (1994) pp. 161–72.

Pocock, D. C. D. 'Place and the novelist' *Transactions of the Institute of British Geographers* NS **6** (1981) pp. 337–47.

Relph, E. *Place and Placelessness* (London: Pion, 1976).

Robinson, V. and McCarroll, D. *The Isle of Man: Celebrating a Sense of Place* (Liverpool: Liverpool University Press, 1990).

Rose, G. 'Geography as a science of observation: the landscape, the gaze and masculinity' in Driver, F. and Rose, G. (eds), *Nature and Science: Essays in the History of Geographical Knowledge* Institute of British Geographers Research Series No. 28 (1992) pp. 8–18.

Rose, G. 'Place and identity: a sense of place' in Massey, D. and Jess, P. *A Place in the World* (Oxford: Oxford University Press, 1995) pp. 87–174.

Sack, R. D. *Conceptions of Space in Social Thought* (London: Macmillan, 1980).

Shoard, M. *This Land is Our Land* (London: Paladin, 1987).

Tuan, Y.-F. 'Place: an experiential perspective' *Geographical Review* **65** (1975) pp. 151–165.

Tuan, Y.-F. 'Language and the making of place: a narrative-descriptive approach' *Annals of the Association of American Geographers* **81** (1991) pp. 684–96.

Turner, J. *The Politics of Landscape* (Oxford: Blackwell, 1979).

Vyner, B. E. 'The territory of ritual: cross-ridge boundaries and the prehistoric landscape of the Cleveland Hills, Northeast England' *Antiquity* **68** (1994) pp. 27–38.

Walmsley, D. J. and Lewis, G. J. *People and Environment* (Harlow: Longman, 1993).

Western, J. 'Ambivalent attachments to place in London: twelve Barbadian families' *Environment and Planning D: Society and Space* **11** (1993) pp. 147–70.

Postscript

In writing this text I have attempted to deal with each perspective on landscape in as objective and as even-handed a manner as possible. Even so, it would be dishonest for me to claim an equal level of interest in all the approaches discussed. My background is in landscape history and landscape archaeology, and there can be little doubt that had I developed a career in, say, cultural studies or art history a different book would have resulted. Landscape provides a source of fascination for enthusiasts from many different disciplinary and social backgrounds. Here we have been concerned with the *intellectual exploration* of landscape rather than with *applied* work such as that associated with planning, landscape gardening or landscape design. It has been demonstrated that a spectrum of different approaches has been adopted by writers and researchers engaged in this intellectual exploration, each one reflecting a different perspective on the subject matter of landscape.

Several of these approaches are complimentary, and their adoption can provide or suggest new insights. In this way, for example, the landscape historian considering the topic of castles could benefit from the ideas embodied in a perspective which regarded landscapes as incorporating the effects of status and power. It is being realised that medieval castles often stood in settings which were carefully and expensively manipulated with the creation of artificial bodies of water, earthworks and plantings which were designed to impress the visitor and guest. Thus, the interpretation of landscape as an expression of status and influence will facilitate the recognition and explanation of such landscapes. The relevance of a geology-and-scenery approach to landscape history is quite obvious, though that of a psychological approach may be less so. A part of the complimentary value of this approach is that it provides a reminder of the quirky and unpredictable nature of human decision-making. There are reasons for everything that we encounter in the cultural landscapes, but these reasons may not reflect the choices of a rational 'economic man'. The Dorset village of Milton Abbas is not the outcome of logical decision-making, but results from the fact that the landowner, Joseph Damer, MP, an 'imperious and un-mannerly lord', built it as a replacement for the town of Milton, which he systematically destroyed, partly because he believed that his neighbours, the townspeople, were mocking him. If paranoia was the *raison d'être* of Milton Abbas (Figure P. 1), the pattern of colonisation of the American West was to some degree conditioned by misconceptions concerning the nature of the environments of the interior.

Not all the approaches to landscape history have proved to be complimentary, and in some cases the contradictions are having unfortunate consequences. For some students of landscape and its evolution these tensions are of scant concern. Physical scientists such as geologists, hydrologists and geomorphologists investigating the lithology, drainage or landforms of landscapes have no cause to worry about whether landscape is really 'a way of seeing', and neither does the palynologist or palaeo-botanist taking samples from a peat bog to elucidate the post-glacial succession of vegeta-tion. Instead, it is in the field of the humanities, notably in human geography and history, that one becomes aware of differences in approach which extend far beyond perspective and into the realms of personality type. Strong cases could be made for arguing both

Figure P.1   The replacement village at Milton Abbas, Dorset. (Richard Muir)

that the study of the evolution of cultural landscapes, as represented by landscape history and landscape archaeology, has its natural home in geography, and that within geography, such studies of landscape lie at the very core of the discipline. However, while geographers who are landscape historians have a lively record of publication, they tend to publish in non-geographical publications. A glance at recent and rather less recent issues of British establishment geography journals, will reveal a surprising disregard for landscape history.

Perhaps no other subject is more prone to faddism, and on seeing a bandwagon approaching, many geographers cannot resist the urge to hurl themselves aboard. The result has been a disciplinary progress characterised by huge lurches from one direction of enquiry to another, with vast reserves of energy being wasted on areas which have proved largely or entirely fatuous and sterile. As has been described, the current enthusiasm for landscape derived from a reaction against geography's fruitless infatuation with quantification, but some of the more recent work seems to have led back into the realm of inaccessibility and obscurity. Meanwhile, forms of landscape research which involve empirical evolutionary studies of real cultural landscapes employing proven specialist techniques have been marginalised and excluded. The landscape historian looking back on a career in geography may review the development of the discipline and claim, as some have, that twice in his or her working life the subject has gone off the rails, to the great disadvantage of historical landscape study. History escaped the excesses of the 'quantitative revolution', but one can readily detect similar feelings of unease about contemporary tendencies within the subject.

Whatever the approach or perspective employed, interpretations of landscape should be expressed in an accessible, comprehensible manner and be guided by the duty to inform. Landscape is not about subatomic physics or the mathematical modelling of black holes; it is about the settings of human existence and development. Not surprisingly, interest in landscape and the processes which have created it are subjects of great fascination to large number of amateur enthusiasts and hosts of country-lovers. Most of the leaders in landscape history can pack a village hall as well as fill a university lecture theatre. Professionals working in the field have an obligation to recognise this audience and supply it with information and interpretations in forms which encourage rather than alienate involvement.

Allowing for the need to refer to specialist techniques in some cases, the level of accessibility is good in most areas of landscape study, like landscape history, the aesthetic, political and psychological approaches and studies of place. In some other areas which involve no field research, the situation leads me to recall a quantitative geographer that I knew early in my career. He would recount how, as a schoolboy, he and his friend would write complicated equations on the steamed-up windows of their Manchester bus in order to impress and mystify fellow passengers. Much, one suspects, concerns the furthering of careers by impressing small numbers of like-minded peers, while bemusing the rest of the audience.

It has often been pointed out that it is hard for the researcher to stand apart from the landscape under scrutiny; as well as being targets for investigations, landscapes also contain our homes and milieus and we are parts of the landscapes that we study. This is not to say, however, that all work on landscapes is bound to be subjective. It is claimed that Hoskins did not describe the English landscape objectively, but rather provided a subjective account of Hoskins's England. Admittedly, he had strong (indeed passionate) views on the English landscape and its imminent fate, and he made no secret of them. At the same time, he had the benefit of a long schooling in an important and genuine discipline, history, in the course of which he had acquired valuable professional skills. Hoskins's work in history and landscape history rested on a basis of objective facts and conclusions based upon them. If his interpretation of historical documents, like charters, manorial rolls or terriers was wrong it could be shown to be so. Where he did make significant mistakes was in his interpretations of the prehistoric contributions to English landscape development, largely because the evidence from specialist techniques, like aerial photography, field walking and rescue excavations had not accrued at the time when he was working. Early in my own career in landscape history I wrote of a dilapidated gibbet on a Cambridgeshire roadside, not appreciating that it was a fairly modern recreation rather than the original. I was easily shown to be wrong and felt greatly embarrassed, but this demonstrates that work in the field is susceptible to testing, with the subject progressing as claim and counter-claim are evaluated. Much of what is published under the banner of post-modernism is incapable of being tested, and when one is told by authors that even the terminology employed is unstable one may begin to despair. Much of what is published under a landscape studies heading seems rightly to belong to the realm of the history of art, yet in this realm research and theory must surely be guided by factual accuracy and a quest for truth as they are in any other valid field of enquiry.

To argue for a more realistic treatment for empirical landscape research focusing on the real landscapes which are 'out there' is not to argue against the validity of subjective enquiries which are concerned with the human reaction to landscape. Much of the work accomplished not only informs the understanding of how real landscapes may have developed but stands in its own right as work of substance, like the various perceptions of England and its subdivisions that have been described. It is pointless to claim and impossible to demonstrate that one approach to landscape is 'better' or 'more relevant' than another although within the various approaches it will be possible to identify work that is deficient in quality, comprehensibility or relevance. It is much more realistic to argue that no valid perspective on landscape should be excluded from its proper disciplinary homeland by another. Though the techniques employed by their practitioners are very different, the objective and subjective approaches could be regarded as different sides of the same coin, with each approach gaining from an awareness of the other.

The tensions and contradictions will surely be resolved with the passage of time, with those aspects of enquiry which are soundly based and relevant to our understanding of landscape and its origins surviving and re-emerging strongly on the basis of their inherent merits. The frustrations experienced by one generation of landscape students will be forgotten as a new generation arises. What is unfortunate about the current confusion in the field is the fact that with each week that passes whole countrysides are having their historic characters extinguished, sites and monuments which contain the evidence of landscape evolution are being destroyed, and the country people who remember the names of fields, the abandoned routeways and the sites of former dwellings are passing away. The tendency to obliterate greatly exceeds the capacity to record and appraise. The rates of destruction and change have never been so great and the potential for landscape-related research is immense.

It is often implied that conversational perspectives express a new management with landscape. The truth is rather different: the landscape gardens of the eighteenth century recreated the scenic qualities of the medieval deer park and Palladianism involved a rediscovery of the work of Palladio. But: 'Although Palladianism was born from a return of the inexhaustible well of classical architecture, interest in medieval architecture never really died out in England, and a renewed enthusiasm can be detected in the same circles as those in which Palladianism was first nurtured' (Reed, 1997 p. 248). The ideas about landscape which permeate society derive partly from (sometimes whimsical) recreations of past scenery and party from fashion. Sometimes the two currents converged, and at other times they were in opposition:

> The treatment of landscape in English literature indicates roughly the changing temper of each cultural era. The medieval mind sees in the face of nature chiefly wonders, outward signs of an inscrutable creation. With the renascence there begins cultivation of the pastoral scene, often a plagiarism of Italian climes and conventions: sylvan England becomes peopled with naiads, oreads and dryads of classical descent. Then, as science finds foothold and man aspires to control his environment, ordered gardens and regimented shrubberies supplant less amenable aspects of the wild countryside. (Walbank, 1941 p. 101)

Green perspectives can point towards saner and safer ways of living but one may doubt whether, in the long term, they can securely conserve landscapes. Each landscape is the creation of a most intricate interplay of social and ecological forces. As these controlling influences evolve, so landscape must be made to evolve with them. Wolves were introduced to the Yellowstone National Park in an attempt to reverse an ecological imbalance reflected in a rise in the herbivore population occurring since the extinction of wolves which had been killed for the bounties offered by the region's cattle ranchers. But the wolves quit the confines of the park and began to kill cattle, resulting in a court ruling that the re-introduction of wolves had been illegal. Even in a long-established and high profile national park the process of landscape evolution cannot be reversed. Similarly, the cherished upland countrysides of England were the creations of poverty, back-breaking toil and overbearing local cultural traditions. These have gone. The countrysides which they created must surely follow.

The need for 'traditional' landscape and those values that it symbolised remains. We in the West pursue rootless and footloose existences and endure levels of occupational stress never previously encountered. The insecurities associated with flexible production and globalisation form part of larger identity crises linked to the rise of placelessness in Western culture. As people seek to establish roots and recreate identities, an awareness of landscape, its origins and cultural characteristics can provide a rock or a peg around which new perceptions of self can be constructed. Whatever the direction of human progress, we will always inhabit landscapes, while these landscape will have their histories, will be affected and changed be our occupation of them, and will exert strong influences upon ourselves and our visions of ourselves.

References

Reed, M. *The Landscape of Britain* (London: Routledge, 1997).
Walbank, F. A. *The English Scene* (London: Batsford, 1941).

Index